The Concierge's Guide™ to New York

Other Books in This Series

The Concierge's Guide™ to New York

McDowell Bryson
Adele Ziminski

John Wiley & Sons, Inc.

New York • Chichester • Brisbane • Toronto • Singapore

Copyright © 1991 by John Wiley & Sons, Inc.

All rights reserved. Published simultaneously in Canada.

Reproduction or translation of any part of this work beyond that permitted by Section 107 or 108 of the 1976 United States Copyright Act without the permission of the copyright owner is unlawful. Requests for permission or further information should be addressed to the Permissions Department, John Wiley & Sons, Inc.

The Concierge's Guide™ is a trademark of John Wiley & Sons, Inc.

Library of Congress Cataloging-in-Publication Data

Bryson, McDowell. 1938-
    The concierge's guide to New York / McDowell Bryson. Adele Ziminski.
    p.   cm.
    ISBN 0-471-52649-5
    1. New York (N.Y.)—Directories.   2. New York (N.Y.)-—
Description—1981- —Guide books.   I. Ziminski, Adele.   II.
Title.
    F128.18.B78 1990
    974.7'1'025—dc20   90-35526
                                                          CIP

Printed in the United States of America

91 92 10 9 8 7 6 5 4 3 2 1

Contents

Contents

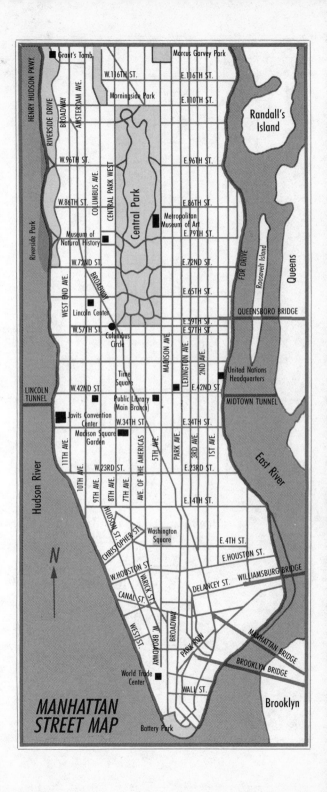

MANHATTAN STREET MAP

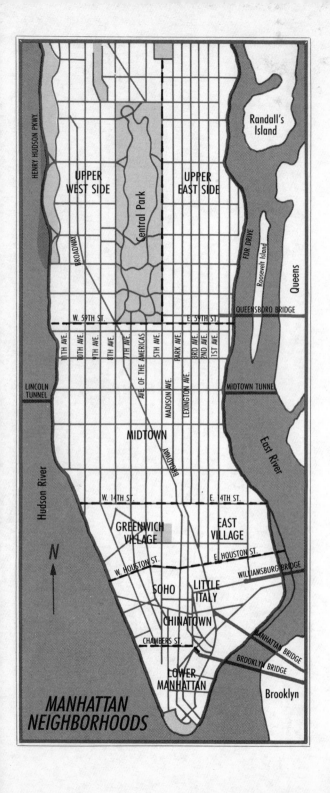

MANHATTAN
NEIGHBORHOODS

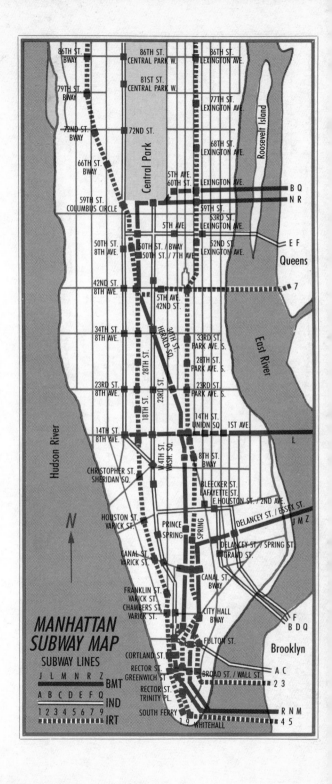

MANHATTAN
SUBWAY MAP

SUBWAY LINES

J L M N R Z   BMT
A B C D E F Q   IND
1 2 3 4 5 6 7 9   IRT

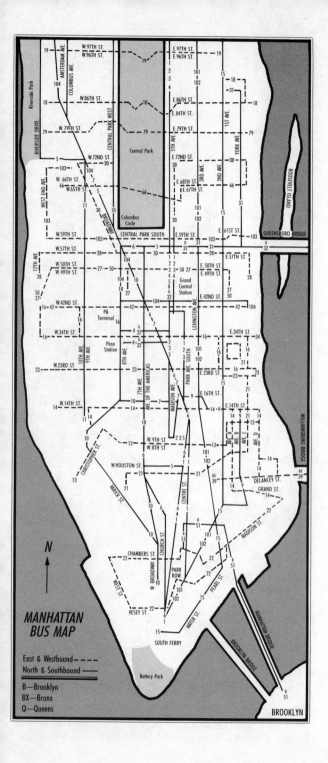

MANHATTAN BUS MAP

East & Westbound - - - -
North & Southbound ———

B—Brooklyn
BX—Bronx
Q—Queens

N

Riverside Park
AMSTERDAM AVE.
COLUMBUS AVE.
CENTRAL PARK WEST
RIVERSIDE DRIVE
Central Park
Columbus Circle
5TH AVE.
1ST AVE.
YORK AVE.
3RD AVE.
2ND AVE.
Roosevelt Island
Queensboro Bridge
WEST END AVE.
BROADWAY
12TH AVE.
10TH AVE.
9TH AVE.
8TH AVE.
7TH AVE.
AVE. OF THE AMERICAS
MADISON AVE.
PARK AVE. SOUTH
LEXINGTON AVE.
Grand Central Station
PA Terminal
Penn Station
AVE. A
AVE. B
AVE. C
AVE. D
Williamsburg Bridge
CHRISTOPHER ST.
WEST ST.
CHURCH ST.
W. BROADWAY
VARICK ST.
CENTRE ST.
Park Row
PEARL ST.
MADISON ST.
GRAND ST.
DELANCEY ST.
Chambers St.
Vesey St.
South Ferry
Battery Park
Manhattan Bridge
Brooklyn Bridge
BROOKLYN

W. 97TH ST.
W. 96TH ST.
E. 97TH ST.
E. 96TH ST.
W. 86TH ST.
E. 86TH ST.
E. 84TH ST.
W. 79TH ST.
E. 79TH ST.
W. 72ND ST.
E. 72ND ST.
W. 66TH ST.
W. 65TH ST.
E. 68TH ST.
E. 67TH ST.
E. 61ST ST.
W. 59TH ST.
CENTRAL PARK SOUTH
E. 59TH ST.
W. 57TH ST.
E. 57TH ST.
W. 50TH ST.
W. 49TH ST.
E. 50TH ST.
E. 49TH ST.
W. 42ND ST.
E. 42ND ST.
W. 34TH ST.
E. 34TH ST.
W. 23RD ST.
E. 23RD ST.
W. 14TH ST.
E. 16TH ST.
E. 14TH ST.
W. 9TH ST.
W. 8TH ST.
W. HOUSTON ST.
CHAMBERS ST.
VESEY ST.

INTRODUCTION

This book was written for the millions of people who visit New York every year, as well as for the millions who live here year-round. It contains answers to the questions that we, as concierges in the major hotels, have been asked over and over again. In fact, it is an expanded version of our own "Little Black Book," organized in the concise and immediately accessible manner that brings the major tool of concierges—information—to your fingertips.

Because of our unique position as arbiters and dispensers of service to so many guests, we know you have no time to be inundated with excess information, so we have deliberately excluded out-of-the-way places and obscure "finds." Our experience has shown that most visitors, be they savvy cosmopolites, busy executives, or harried parents with small children in tow, have limited time and want to visit the places famous around the world as representing New York. On the other hand, since New York is famous around the world for the diversity of its offerings, we've included a variety of listings to reflect this quality as well. Thus, you'll find here not only expansive (and somewhat opinionated) listings of the city's major hotels, restaurants, museums, department stores, night clubs, and comedy clubs, as you'd well expect, but also a number of surprises, such as:

- Horse-drawn carriages and helicopter rides
- Yacht charters and the Yonkers Racetrack
- Flea markets, furriers, and a fount of free activities
- Singles bars, piano bars, sports bars, and gay bars
- Tennis courts, television tickets, tobacconists, and tipping advice

To provide you with the same easy, fingertip accessibility that we as concierges have come to depend upon, we've organized the book alphabetically. Most entries appear at least twice: on their own and under a broader category. For example, if you are a bibliophile, you might have heard of the historic Gotham Book Mart ("Wise Men Fish Here") and, therefore, need only its address and phone number, you'll find this listing under "Gotham." But if you want to find the bookstore nearest to where you're staying, or want to read about each of the many bookstores New York has to

1

offer, you can look under "BOOKSTORES," where you'll find not only "Gotham," but an annotated listing of the many notable bookstores which cater to a wide variety of tastes and budgets.

Unless otherwise noted, all telephone area codes are 212; and to make getting around easier, we've noted cross streets, whenever possible, in parentheses after the address. Prices and times are the most current available, but, of course, are always liable to change. We suggest that you always call and double-check before making your plans.

We've found our book easy to use and think you will too. Enjoy our city and don't forget to make use of the concierges at your hotel—they're there to help you.

A

A & B Bicycle World 663 Amsterdam Avenue	866-7600
A & S (Abraham & Straus) 33rd Street and Avenue of the Americas	594-8500
A La Vieille Russie 781 Fifth Avenue (59th St.)	752-1727
A-Fax International 990 Sixth Avenue (36th St.)	489-7307
A-Z Luggage 425 Fifth Avenue	686-6905
A. Sulka 301 Park Avenue	980-5226
AAA Road Service	757-3356
AAA-U-Rent 861 Eagle Avenue, Bronx	923-0300 665-6633
Abbey Bus Service	1-718-784-5130
Abbey Transport	1-201-961-2535
Abercrombie & Fitch Trump Tower, 725 Fifth Avenue (56th/57th Sts.)	832-1001
Academy Tours	964-6600
Acker Merrall & Condit 160 West 72nd Street (Broadway/Columbus Ave.)	787-1700
Actors Playhouse 100 Seventh Avenue South	691-6226
Aer Lingus	557-1110

AEROBICS CLASSES

Staying fit on the road is a constant battle. Or perhaps you'd just like to trim down without the expense of joining a health club. It's possible either to sign up for a series of classes or just take individual classes at:

Body Design by Gilda

139 East 57th Street	**759-7966**
187 East 79th Street	**737-8440**
65 West 70th Street	**799-8540**

Monday–Friday 7:00 A.M.–7:00 P.M.
Saturday & Sunday 9:00 A.M.–5:00 P.M.

Founded by Gilda Marx, these stores offer not only exercise wear but a full range of classes, from low impact aerobics to strenuous workouts. Each location has a suspended wooden floor, as well as a boutique. Lockers, showers, and towels are available on the premises. Call for class schedule.

Aeroflot	**1-800-535-9877**
Aerolineas Argentinas	**698-2050**
Aeromexico	**1-800-237-6639**
Aeroperu	**1-800-255-7378**
Air Canada	**869-1900**
Air France	**247-0100**
Air France Concorde	**265-5460**
Air India	**751-6200**
Air Jamaica	**1-800-523-5585**
Airline Delivery Services 60 East 42nd Street	**687-5145**

AIRLINE SHUTTLES

La Guardia

Pan Am **1-718-803-6600**
Departures to Boston and Washington, DC, every hour on the half hour
Monday–Friday 6:30 A.M.–9:30 P.M.
Saturday 7:30 A.M.–8:30 P.M.
Sunday 8:30 A.M.–9:30 P.M.

Pan Am Water Shuttle **1-800-54-FERRY**
The Pan Am Shuttle boat from Wall Street to La Guardia operates Monday through Friday. It makes one stop at 34th Street and the East River. One-way fare is $20.00 and round trip is $38.00.

From Pier 11 (Wall St.)	From 34th Street
8:30 A.M.	8:45 A.M.
9:30 A.M.	9:45 A.M.
10:30 A.M.	2:45 P.M.
3:30 P.M.	3:45 P.M.
4:30 P.M.	4:45 P.M.
5:30 P.M.	5:45 P.M.

Trump Shuttle, The   **1-800-247-8786**
Departures to Boston and Washington, DC, every hour
on the hour
> Monday–Friday 7:00 A.M.–9:00 P.M.
> Saturday 8:00 A.M.–9:00 P.M.
> Sunday 9:00 A.M.–9:00 P.M.

Newark

Continental Airlines
Unlike Pan Am and Trump, Continental has a complex
schedule. It's best to call for current information.
> **Departures to Boston:** 7:00 A.M., 7:30 A.M., 8:00 A.M.,
> 8:30 A.M., 9:30 A.M., 10:30 A.M., 11:30 A.M., 12:30 P.M.,
> 1:30 P.M., 2:30 P.M., 3:00 P.M., 3:30 P.M., 4:00 P.M., 4:30 P.M.,
> 5:30 P.M., 6:00 P.M., 6:30 P.M., 7:30 P.M., 8:30 P.M.,
> 10:40 P.M.
> **Departures to National Airport in Washington, DC:**
> 7:00 A.M., 8:00 A.M., 9:00 A.M., 11:00 A.M., 1:00 P.M., 3:00
> P.M., 4:00 P.M., 5:00 P.M., 6:00 P.M., 7:00 P.M., 8:00 P.M.

AIRLINES

Aer Lingus	**557-1110**
Aeroflot	**1-800-535-9877**
Aerolineas Argentinas	**698-2050**
Aeromexico	**1-800-237-6639**
Aeroperu	**1-800-255-7378**
Air Canada	**869-1900**
Air France	**247-0100**
Air France Concorde	**265-5460**
Air India	**751-6200**

Air Jamaica	1-800-523-5585
Alaska Air	1-800-426-0333
ALIA	949-0050
Alitalia	582-8900
American Airlines	431-1132
Austrian Airlines	265-6350
Avianca	246-5241
British Airways	1-800-247-9297
Continental Airlines	1-718-565-1100
Delta Airlines	239-0700
Eastern Airlines	986-5000
East Hampton Air	1-516-537-0560
Egypt Air	581-5600
El Al	768-9200
Iberia Airlines	1-800-772-4642
Japan Airlines	838-4400
KLM	759-3600
Korean Airlines	371-4820
LAN Chile	1-800-735-5526
Lufthansa	1-718-895-1277
MGM Grand Air	1-800-933-2646
Midway Airlines	1-800-621-5700
Midwest Express Airlines	1-800-452-2022
Northwest Airlines	736-1220
Olympic Airways	838-3600
Ozark Airlines	1-201-433-6967
Pan American	687-2600
Pan American Shuttle	1-718-803-6600
Qantas	1-800-227-4500

Regent Air	**1-800-538-7587**
Sabena	**1-800-955-2000**
SAS–Scandinavian Airlines	**1-718-657-7700**
Swissair	**1-718-995-8400**
Tower Airlines	**1-718-917-4368**
Trump Shuttle	**1-800-247-8786**
TWA	**290-2121**
United Airlines	**1-800-241-6522**
US AIR	**1-800-428-4322**
Varig Airlines	**682-3100**
Viasa Airlines	**486-4360**
Virgin Atlantic Airlines	**1-800-862-8621**

AIRPLANE CHARTER SERVICES

Jet Air International   **233-2282**
                                     1-516-752-8985
                                     1-800-622-2205
Jet Air has a complete range of jets and turbo props which serve all of the airports in the New York vicinity. They operate 24 hours a day, 7 days a week and have world-wide operating authority.

La Guardia Aircraft Charter Service   **1-718-476-5366**
(Division of East Coast Airways)   **1-800-732-9001**
Corporate and personal charters. Service 24 hours a day, every day. Single and multi engine turboprop and jets departing from all area airports. They also have aircraft available on a nationwide basis.

United Air Fleet   **262-2200**
823 Eleventh Avenue   **1-800-262-2209**
Worldwide air charters. Service from all area airports. Equipment consists of Learjets, Gulfstreams, Westwinds, Falconjets, Hawkers, and turboprops.

AIRPORTS

New York is served by three major airports: John F. Kennedy International (JFK), La Guardia, and Newark. Of the three, La Guardia is the most easily accessible. *See* AIR-PORTS, TRANSPORTATION TO (below) for complete information.

JFK International	**1-718-495-5400**
JFK International Arrivals	**1-718-656-4520**
La Guardia (Ground information)	**1-800-AIR-RIDE**
La Guardia (Port Authority)	**1-718-476-5000**
Newark	**1-201-961-2000**

AIRPORTS, TRANSPORTATION TO

JFK International

Carey Buses   1-718-632-0500
Departure Points:
125 Park Avenue (near Grand Central Station)
Port Authority Bus Terminal (Eighth Ave. & 42nd St.)
   5:00 A.M.–1:00 A.M. Every 30 minutes
Marriott Marquis (Broadway & 45th St.)
New York Hilton (Sixth Ave. & 53rd St.)
Sheraton City Squire (Seventh Ave. & 51st St.)
   5:45 A.M.–10:00 P.M. Every 20 minutes
   Fare: $8.00 one-way; $13.00 round trip

Mini-Van
Stops at most major midtown hotels. Reservations are required. The trip takes approximately 45 minutes. See your hotel concierge.

Limousine
The trip takes approximately 45 minutes. Fare: $35.00 to $50.00 from midtown depending upon company. Not including tips and tolls.

Taxi
The trip takes approximately 45 minutes to an hour. Fare: $20.00 to $25.00 depending upon time. Does not include tips and tolls.

New York Helicopter   1-800-645-3494
A 10-minute ride to JFK with a breathtaking view of Manhattan. Departs from 34th Street and the East River every half hour: 2:00 P.M.–7:30 P.M. Fare: $58.00 one-way. Helicopter service may be included free or at a discount if you are flying first or business class. Check with your airline. They will make reservations for you if appropriate.

La Guardia

Carey Bus Lines   1-718-632-0500
Departure Points:
125 Park Avenue (near Grand Central Station)
Port Authority Bus Terminal (Eighth Ave. & 42nd St.)
  5:45 A.M.–10:00 P.M. Every 20 minutes
Marriott Marquis (Broadway & 45th St.)
New York Hilton (Sixth Ave. & 53rd Street)
Sheraton City Squire (Seventh Avenue & 51st St.)
  5:45 A.M.–10:00 P.M. Every 20 minutes
  Fare: $6.00 one-way; $10.00 round trip

Mini-Van
Stops at most major midtown hotels. Reservations are required. The trip takes approximately 30 minutes.See your hotel concierge.

Limousine
Fare: $30.00 to $45.00 from midtown. Does not include tips and tolls. The trip takes approximately 30 minutes.

Taxi
Fare: $15.00 to $20.00 depending upon time. Does not include tips and tolls. The trip takes approximately 30 to 40 minutes.

Pan Am Water Shuttle   1-800-54-FERRY
The Pan Am Shuttle Boat from Wall Street to La Guardia, operates Monday through Friday. It makes one stop at 34th Street and the East River.

From Pier 11 (Wall St.)	From East 34th Street
8:30 A.M.	8:45 A.M.
9:30 A.M.	9:45 A.M.
10:30 A.M.	2:45 P.M.
3:30 P.M.	3:45 P.M.
4:30 P.M.	4:45 P.M.
5:30 P.M.	5:45 P.M.

Newark

Abbey Transport   1-201-961-2535
Bus service from the major hotels. Call for the exact schedule.

Mini-Van
Stops at most major midtown hotels. Reservations are required. See your hotel concierge. The trip takes approximately 45 minutes.

New Jersey Transit   **1-201-460-8555**
Bus #300 departs from the Port Authority Bus Terminal (Eighth Ave. & 42st St.) 24 hours a day, approximately every 15 minutes.
    Fare: $7.00 one-way

Limousine
Fare: $35.00 to $50.00 from midtown, depending upon company. Does not include tips and tolls. The trip takes approximately one hour.

Taxi
Fare: $45.00 to $50.00 from midtown, depending upon time. Does not include tips and tolls. The trip takes approximately 30 minutes to one hour.

Between Airports

Carey Bus Lines
Carey buses leave every half-hour from La Guardia to JFK and every hour from JFK to La Guardia.
    Fare: $7.00 one-way; $10.00 round trip

Akbar   838-1717
475 Park Avenue (57th/58th Sts.)

Al Lieber's World of Golf   242-2895
147 East 47th Street (Lexington/Third Aves.)

Alaska Air   1-800-426-0333

Alexander's   593-0880
731 Lexington Avenue (59th St.)

Alfred Dunhill   489-5580
620 Fifth Avenue

Algonquin Hotel   840-6800
59 West 44th Street

ALIA   949-0050

Alice Tully Hall   877-2011
Lincoln Center, Broadway (64th/66th Sts.)

Alice Zotta   840-7657
2 West 45th Street, Rm. 1504

Alitalia   582-8900

All Service Computer Rentals, Inc.   524-0003
600 West 58th Street, Suite 9119

Altman   254-7275
135 Orchard Street

AMACOM (American Management Association)	**586-8100**

135 West 50th Street (7th Floor) (Sixth/Seventh Aves.)

Ambassador Theater	**239-6200**

215 West 49th Street

Ambulance	**911**

American Airlines	**431-1132**

American Craft Museum	**956-6047**

40 West 53rd Street

American Cruise Lines	**1-203-345-8501**
1 Marine Park	**1-800-243-6755**

AMERICAN EXPRESS

If you have had the foresight to obtain a PIN (Personal Identification Number), you can get cash advances on your American Express Card at the locations listed below. The understanding folks at American Express will issue you a PIN on 24-hours notice if you call them up and whine. There are American Express offices at:

65 Broadway (Exchange Pl.)
199 Water Street (Seaport Plaza)
150 East 42nd Street (Lexington/Third Aves.)
822 Lexington Avenue (63rd St.)
Bloomingdale's, Lexington Avenue at 59th Street
Macy's, Seventh Avenue at 34th Street

In addition, the cash machines at all branches of Republic National Bank and Crossland Savings honor the American Express Card. Some convenient locations are:

452 Fifth Avenue (40th St.)
3 West 57th Street (off Fifth Ave.)
515 Madison Avenue (53rd St.)
1166 Avenue of the Americas (46th St.)
101 West 14th Street (Avenue of the Americas)

Many branches of D'Agostino contain cash machines as well. If you need more help, dial 1-800-227-4669, and the operator will locate the closest machine to you.

American Festival Cafe	**246-6699**

20 West 50th Street (north of Rockefeller Skating Rink)

American International Executive Business Center	**308-0049**

14 East 60th Street, Suite 307

American Museum of Natural History   **769-5000**
Central Park West (79th St.)

**American Sightseeing
    International/Short Line Tours**   **354-4740**
166 West 46th Street

**American Society of Interior
    Designers**   **685-3480**

Amoco
153 Seventh Avenue (20th St.)   **255-9611**
1855 First Avenue (96th St.)   **289-8832**

AMTRAK   **582-6875**
Pennsylvania Station (Seventh Ave. & 32nd St.)
    Baggage   **560-7636**
    Lost and Found   **560-7388**
    Metroliner Service   **736-3967**
    Package Express   **560-7385**

An American Place   **684-2122**
2 Park Avenue (32nd St.)

Andrew Pallack   **242-4412**
85 Fifth Avenue

Angelo's of Mulberry Street   **966-1277**
146 Mulberry Street (Grand/Hester Sts.)

Angry Squire   **242-9066**
216 Seventh Avenue (23rd St.)

Animal Emergency Clinic   **988-1000**
240 East 80th Street (Second/Third Aves.)

Animal Medical Clinic   **988-1000**
240 East 80th St. (Second/Third Aves.)

Animal Outfits for People   **840-6219**
252 West 46th Street

Ann Taylor   **832-2010**
3 East 57th Street

Annex Antiques and Flea Market   **1-718-965-1076**
Avenue of the Americas (26th St.)

ANNUAL EVENTS

Dates for these events vary from year to year. To obtain exact dates call the New York Convention and Visitors Bureau. The phone number for their Information Center is 397-8222.

January

National Boat Show (mid-January)
Javits Convention Center   **216-2000**

Winter Antiques Show
Seventh Regiment Armory   **665-5250**
Park Avenue (66th/67th Streets)

Greater New York International
    Auto Show

February

Chinese New Year (early February)   397-8222
The big event of the year for Chinatown. Don't miss the
Lion Dance and the dragons. Be prepared for lots of noise
and firecrackers. If you're planning to eat in the neighborhood, be sure to make reservations.

Manhattan Antiques and
    Collectibles Expo   1-201-768-2773
Piers 88, 90, and 92, The Hudson River (48th/55th Sts.)
Occupying three huge piers, this is obviously the largest
show of antiques and things to be seen in New York. As
typical apartment dwellers, we're constantly amazed at
what people find room to collect.

Westminster Kennel Club Dog Show
    (Mid-February)
Madison Square Garden   **564-4400**
If you are a dog lover this is for you. Over 2,500 dogs of
141 breeds compete.

Virginia Slims Women's Tennis
    Championships(late February)

March

Greek Independence Day Parade
    (Third Sunday in March)
Fifth Avenue from 62nd to 79th Streets.

St. Patrick's Day Parade (March 17th)
Held every year since 1762, this is the world's oldest and
largest St. Patrick's Day Parade. Starting at 11:00 A.M., thousands march up Fifth Avenue (whose center line is painted
green for the occasion) from 44th to 86th Street.

April

Baseball Season Begins (early April)

13

International Auto Show
Javits Convention Center   **216-2000**

Macy's Annual Flower Show

Cherry Blossom Festival, Brooklyn
        Botanic Gardens (late April)

May

Martin Luther King Day Parade

Memorial Day Parade (May 30th)

Ninth Avenue International Food
        Festival (mid-May)

Salute to Israel Parade

Washington Square Art
        Show(Memorial Day Weekend)

June

Belmont Stakes (mid-June)

Feast of St. Anthony (first two weeks)

Irving Place Festival

Lesbian/Gay Pride Day Parade
Exact date varies. Parade route is from 61st Street and
Central Park West down Fifth Avenue to Washington
Square, then West on Waverly Place and Christopher Street
in Greenwich Village.

Lexington Avenue Festival

Museum Mile Festival (mid-June)
Fifth Avenue (86th/106th Sts.)

Pier 11 International Food Festival

Puerto Rican Day Parade

Washington Square Art Show
        (first two weekends)

July

American Crafts Festival
        (first two weekends)

July 4th Street and Harbor Festival
A special fair at Battery Park capped by fireworks at the Statue of Liberty.

August

Autumn Crafts Festival
Lincoln Center   **877-2011**

Avenue of the Americas Festival

Greenwich Village Jazz Festival

Third Avenue Summerfest

Washington Square Art Show

U.S. Open Tennis Championships
    (late August–mid- September)

September

African-American Day Parade

Brazilian National Independence
    Day Street Festival

Columbus Avenue Festival

Feast of San Gennaro
    (mid-September)
The patron saint of Naples in honored in Little Italy.

Football Season Opens

Labor Day Parade

New York is Book Country
    (mid-September)
Fifth Avenue becomes a readers' paradise between 48th and 57th Streets. All major publishers set up booths, and personalities as notable as Isaac Asimov and Edward Gorey autograph books for adoring fans.

One World Festival
St. Vartan's Cathedral
East 35th Street and Second Avenue

Steuben Day Parade
New Yorkers honor their German heritage by marching up Fifth Avenue from 61st Street to 86th Street, then East on 86th Street to Yorkville.

Washington Square Art Show

October

Aqueduct Racetrack Opens

Basketball Season Opens

Columbus Day Parade (October 12th)
Starting at 11:30 A.M., marchers honor the discoverer of America.

Greenwich Village Halloween
Parade (October 31st)
One of the nation's top Halloween events. The parade begins at 7:00 P.M. at the intersection of West Houston and West Streets, proceeds up Sixth Avenue to 14th Street and turns east to Union Square.

Harvest Festival

Hispanic American Day Parade
(October 12th)
Parade route is from 44th Street to 72nd Street on Fifth Avenue, then east on 72nd Street to Third Avenue.

Hockey Season Opens

Ice Skating Season begins at
Rockefeller Center

New York City Marathon
(last Sunday)
The whole town joins in to cheer the runners and demonstrate that New Yorkers are not cold and unfriendly. The race starts at the Verazzano Bridge on Staten Island and proceeds through all five boroughs. We concierges are kept busy booking masseurs for the participants.

Pulaski Day Parade
Adele's parents march up Fifth Avenue from 26th to 52nd Streets and then east to Third Avenue in honor of the Revolutionary War hero, Casimir Pulaski.

November

Macy's Thanksgiving Day Parade
(last Thursday in November)
Starts at 9:30 A.M. at Central Park West and 77th Street, down to Columbus Circle, then continues down Broadway to Macy's at Herald Square, where it turns right and disbands on 34th Street. If you are in New York on Thanksgiving Day you will see or be affected by the parade because the whole city is concentrated upon it.

Virginia Slims Championship
    Tennis   (Tickets) 563-8954
Madison Square Garden, 4 Penn Plaza
The richest tournament in women's tennis! Takes place in mid-November. Call early for tickets because it's very popular.

Veteran's Day Parade

December

Giant Christmas Tree Lighting at
    Rockefeller Center
The lighting of the huge tree heralds the beginning of the Christmas season in New York. The 1989 guest of honor was a 70 foot Norway Spruce lit by 20,000 lights! A crowd estimated at over 50,000 people braved bitterly cold weather to witness the ceremony, which included ice-skating performances, music, and the Rockettes.

Living Christmas Tree, South Street
    Seaport

Radio City Music Hall Christmas
    Spectacular   247-4777
Avenue of the Americas (50th St.)
Featuring the Rockettes.
    Tickets: Ticketmaster   **307-7171 or 1-800-877-1414**

Tuba Christmas Carols
    (Rockefeller Center)
400 (count 'em) tuba players converge to serenade harried shoppers at this marvelous event.

Antiquarian Booksellers Center   246-2564
50 Rockefeller Plaza

ANTIQUES

A La Vieille Russie   752-1727
781 Fifth Avenue
Faberge, antique jewels, Russian icons, and *objets d'art*. You can even buy a tiara here. Don't pass up the opportunity to browse through these treasures of the past. Lovely salespeople add to the experience.

Arthur Ackermann & Son, Inc.   753-5292
50 East 57th Street
The undisputed leader for 18th century English furniture.

Charlotte Moss   772-3320
131 East 70th Street
English country-look accessories to go with the fine collection of four poster beds and Victorian furniture.

Chinese Porcelain Co., The   628-4101
25 East 77th Street
Specialists in the fine Chinese porcelain we all love. They also have hardwood and lacquer furniture and *objets d'art.*

Florian Papp   288-6770
962 Madison Avenue
A must for the serious collector of English and European furniture —18th and 19th century.

Israel Sack, Inc.   753-6562
15 East 57th Street
Specializing in 18th century American furniture, Israel Sack is a famous (and reputable) name in the antique trade.

James Robinson   752-6166
15 East 57th Street
Internationally known for its outstanding quality, James Robinson specializes in jewelry, silver, and porcelain. Also notable are their handmade silver flatware and coffee sets in classic patterns. For additional information see our entry under STORES.

James II   355-7040
15 East 57th Street
19th century English decorations, accessories, and antique furniture. One of their main interests is in Victoriana.

Kentshire Galleries   673-6644
37 East 12th Street
One of the important galleries dealing in furniture from William and Mary to William IV. What caught Adele's fancy, however, was the antique jewelry in the Collector's Gallery on the 8th floor.

Laura Fisher   838-2596
1050 Second Avenue
An authority on Americana, Laura Fisher has assembled tables, baskets, needlework, hooked rugs, coverlets, and quilts.

Manhattan Art and Antiques Center   355-4400
1050 Second Avenue
A mecca for antique lovers—contains 104 galleries with everything you can think of.

Newell Art Galleries   **758-1970**
425 East 53rd Street
Claims to have the world's largest collection of antiques.
They're certainly worth a visit regardless of the period of
your interest.

Pierre Deux   **243-7740**
369 Bleecker Street
French provincial style in a lovely Greenwich Village
shop. Furniture that will make your mouth water . . . prices
to make it go dry.

Place des Antiquaires   **758-2900**
125 East 57th Street
Like its Parisian cousin, Le Louvre des Antiquaires, Place
des Antiquaires displays a comprehensive assortment of
museum-quality antiques. An informal cafe and brasserie-
style restaurant allow shoppers to fortify themselves for
more spending. Lectures, seminars, tours, and exhibitions
are offered free of charge.

Stair and Company   **517-4400**
942 Madison Avenue
Another fine collection of 18th and 19th century furniture from one of the most prestigious companies.

Thomas Schwenke, Inc.   **772-7222**
956 Madison Avenue
American Federal furniture for the serious collector.

Whitehead & Mangan   **242-7815**
375 Bleecker Street
Decorative, topographical, and historical prints from the
17th, 18th, and 19th centuries.

Aquavit   **307-7311**
13 West 54th Street

Aqueduct Racetrack   **1-718-641-4700**
Rockaway Boulevard at 106th Street, Queens

Arcadia   **223-2900**
21 East 62nd Street (Fifth/Madison Aves.)

**Archdiocesan Cathedral of the Holy
    Trinity (Greek Orthodox)**   **288-3215**
319 East 79th Street

Argentina (Consulate of)   **397-1400**
12 West 56th Street

Arizona 206   **838-0440**
206 East 60th Street (Second/Third Aves.)

Armory Tennis Corp.   **663-6900**
68 Lexington Avenue (25th/26th Sts.)

ART GALLERIES

TriBeCa

The Clocktower   **233-1096**
108 Leonard Street, 13th floor
   Thursday–Sunday Noon–6:00 P.M.

Franklin Furnace Archive   **925-4671**
112 Franklin Street
   Tuesday–Saturday Noon–6:00 P.M.

Printed Matter   **925-0325**
7 Lispenard Street
   Tuesday–Saturday 10:00 A.M.–6:00 P.M.

SoHo

SoHo is full of galleries. If you are not knowledgeable about the "art scene" you may find it easier to think of this area in terms of buildings rather than individual galleries. Try the following which have numerous galleries:

379 West Broadway	130 Prince Street
415 West Broadway	142 Greene Street
420 West Broadway	164 Mercer Street

Galleries of particular merit are:

Brooke Alexander   **925-4338**
59 Wooster Street
   Tuesday–Saturday 10:00 A.M.–6:00 P.M.

Mary Boone   **431-1818**
417 West Broadway
   Tuesday–Saturday 10:00 A.M.–6:00 P.M.

Leo Castelli   **431-5160**
420 West Broadway
   Tuesday–Saturday 10:00 A.M.–6:00 P.M.

Paula Cooper   **674-0766**
155 Wooster Street
   Tuesday–Saturday 10:00 A.M.–6:00 P.M.

Paula Cooper is one of the most noteworthy dealers in town. Her attention and fairness to her artists has made her gallery one of the most desirable to show in and she handles some of the best and most thought-provoking work. Don't miss this one even if you are on a tight schedule.

O.K. Harris   **431-3600**
383 West Broadway

Tuesday–Saturday 10:00 A.M.–6:00 P.M.

Ivan Karp's gallery is such a legend that there is little more that can be said about it. If you want to see the oldest gallery in SoHo and the one that has caused the most controversy over the years, this is it.

Broadway

The newest, and one of the buiest gallery areas, is Broadway. The following buildings have the bulk of the dealers.

558 Broadway	560 Broadway
568 Broadway	580 Broadway
584 Broadway	588 Broadway
591 Broadway	596 Broadway

57th Street

This is an area of such high real estate prices that only galleries that really sell can afford to remain. Some of the plushest galleries in the world have their homes here. Again, start by going from building to building. Take the elevator to the top and work your way down.

20 West 57th Street	40 West 57th Street
24 West 57th Street	50 West 57th Street
41 West 57th Street	41 East 57th Street

You should also go around the corner on Fifth Avenue to 724 Fifth Avenue.

Galleries of particular interest are:

Pace Gallery   **421-3292**
32 East 57th Street

One of the very bluest of the blue chips. Arnold and Millie Glimpsher have become famous for their nurturing of artists like Louise Nevelson.

Sidney Janis Gallery   **586-0110**
110 West 57th Street

Mr. Janis shares with Leo Castelli the honor of being the oldest of the blue chip dealers. It is a toss-up as to which of them has discovered and aided more of the biggest names in the contemporary art world. Don't leave New York without going to this gallery.

Art Consultant

Carlo Lamagna   **873-0238**
140 Riverside Drive

After years in the Soho and 57th Street gallery scenes, Carlo has become a private dealer in order to concentrate his efforts on consulting and curatorial services. His speciality is contemporary and twentieth-century art although his expertise extends far beyond these areas. Many of the important collections of today are the result of Carlo's thoughful nurturing of young collectors.

Arthur Ackermann and Son, Inc. 50 East 57th Street	**753-5292**
Asia Society Galleries 725 Park Avenue (70th St.)	**288-6400**
Astor Place Theater 434 Lafayette Street	**254-3760**
AT & T Infoquest Center 550 Madison Avenue	**605-5555**
Athlete's Foot 16 West 57th Street (Fifth/Sixth Ave.)	**586-1936**
Atlantic City Bus and Subway Information	**1-718-330-1234**
Atlantic City Central Reservations	**1-800-833-7070**

ATLANTIC CITY HOTELS

Atlantic City attracts an average of 30 million tourists a year—an astonishing 25% of all Americans live within 300 miles of Atlantic City. As the only American city on the sea which allows gambling, it has also become a mecca for tourists. The following hotels will give visitors a taste of the casino life.

Atlantis Florida Avenue & the Boardwalk	**1-609-344-4000**
Bally's Park Place Park Place & the Boardwalk	**1-609-340-2000**
Caesar's Arkansas Avenue & the Boardwalk	**1-609-348-4411**
Claridge Indiana Avenue & the Boardwalk	**1-609-340-3400**
Golden Nugget Boston & Pacific Avenues at the Boardwalk	**1-609-347-7111**
Harrah's Marina 1725 Brigantine Boulevard	**1-609-441-5000**
Resorts International North Carolina Avenue & the Boardwalk	**1-609-344-6000**
Sands Indiana Avenue at Brighton Park	**1-609-441-4000**
Taj Mahal 1000 Boardwalk at Virginia Avenue	**1-609-449-1000**

Tropicana	**1-609-340-4000**
Iowa Avenue at the Boardwalk	
Trump Castle	**1-609-441-2000**
Brighton Boulevard & Huron Avenue	
Trump Plaza	**1-609-441-6000**
Mississippi Avenue at the Boardwalk	

You can also make arrangements through the central booking bureau:

Atlantic City Room Reservations   **1-800-327-6000**

ATLANTIC CITY, TRANSPORTATION TO

Helicopter

Trump Air   **972-4444**
900 Lincoln Harbor Airport,
Weehawken, NJ   **1-800-448-4000**
West 30th Street Heliport (Hudson River)
    One-way fare $99.00

24 passenger helicopter airline departs from 30th Street Heliport in Manhattan, to either Bader Field or Steeplechase Pier, Atlantic City. Complimentary transportation from the 30th Street Heliport to midtown Manhattan. This is a wonderful way to travel. Flight time is 45 minutes with a beautiful view of New York.

Bus

Academy Tours	**964-6600**
Domenico Bus Service	**1-718-442-8666**
Fugazy	**1-718-507-7000**
New Jersey Transit	**1-609-344-8181**
Vanguard Tours, Inc.	**931-9250**

Atlantis Casino Hotel   **1-609-344-4000**
Florida Avenue & the Boardwalk (Atlantic City, NJ)

Atlas Garage   **865-3311**
303 West 96th Street

Au Bar   **308-9455**
41 East 58th Street

Au Chat Botte   **772-7402**
903 Madison Avenue (72nd/73rd Sts.)

Au Tunnel   **582-2166**
250 West 47th Street (Broadway/Eighth Ave.)

AUCTIONS

If you read any newspapers or magazines, you will become aware of the enormous amount of activity in the auction world today. Prices for everything have soared to heights undreamed of a few years ago. The auction houses vie with Wall Street as the place where the moneyed giants meet to do battle. With the influx of international money into the arena, the pace of bidding and the excitement have outdone fiction. Millions of dollars for antiques, jewelry, and paintings are commonplace. This is where the action is . . . and the New York auction houses are the hub of it. Try to go to at least one of the places listed below on a day when important collections are being auctioned. *The New York Times* lists when and what so you can make your plans. Note that there are "viewing days" prior to the actual auctions so that you can go and get a close-up view of the items to be sold.

Christie's East Auction Gallery   606-0400
219 East 67th Street (Second/Third Aves.)
    Monday–Saturday 9:30 A.M.–5:00 P.M.
    Call for Sunday hours
    Closed Saturday and Sunday during the summer
Fine art, glass, china, furniture, and paintings that are less expensive than those offered by the parent company.

Christie's Fine Art Auctioneers   546-1000
502 Park Avenue (59th St.)
    Monday–Saturday 9:00 A.M.–5:00 P.M.
    Sunday 9:30 A.M.–5:00 P.M.
    Closed Saturday and Sunday during the summer
    Fine art auctions several times a week

Phillips Fine Art Auctioneers   570-4830
406 East 79 Street
    Monday–Friday 9:00 A.M.–5:00 P.M.

Sotheby's   606-7000
1334 York Avenue (72nd St.)
    Monday–Saturday 9:00 A.M.–5:00 P.M.
    Call for Sunday hours

Swann Galleries   254-4710
104 East 25 Street
    Monday–Saturday 9:00 A.M.–5:00 P.M.
    Call for Sunday hours

William Doyle Galleries   427-2730
175 East 87 Street
    Monday–Saturday 9:00 A.M.–5:00 P.M.
    Call for Sunday hours

AUDIO VISUAL EQUIPMENT RENTALS
See RENTALS, AUDIO VISUAL

Aureole	319-1660
34 East 61st Street (Madison/Park Aves.)	

Aurora	692-9292
60 East 49th Street (Madison/Park Aves.)	

Australia (Consulate of)	245-4000
636 Fifth Avenue	

Austria (Consulate of)	737-6400
31 East 69th Street	

Austrian Airlines	265-6350

Authorized Repair Service	586-0947
30 West 57th Street	

Automat, Horn & Hardart	599-1665
200 East 42nd Street (corner of Third Ave.)	

It's still possible to put money into a slot in the wall and get food in the original (and last remaining) automatic cafeteria. McDowell still remembers the thrill of his first years in New York, when he would go to the automat and put nickels in the slots. What an awesome experience to open the door and find food! He says that he felt like a rat in a training program. It is a not-to-be-missed event. Do take the kids. You'll eat far more than you want just to be able to keep going back to shovel in more coins. We can't imagine why these places died out.

Automatic Teller Machines. *See*
   MONEY MACHINES

AUTOMOBILE RENTALS
See RENTALS, AUTOMOBILE

Avalon Registry	245-0250
116 Central Park South	

Avery Fisher Hall	874-2424
Lincoln Center, Broadway (65th St.)	

Avianca	246-5241

Avis	1-800-331-1212

B

B. Smith's   **247-2222**
771 Eighth Avenue (47th St.)

Babysitter's Guild   **682-0227**
60 East 42nd Street

BABYSITTERS

We have found these agencies to be the most reliable. Both are bonded and work for all of New York's major hotels.

Avalon Registry   **245-0250**
116 Central Park South
Avalon provides not only sitters, but housekeepers, nurses, nannies, and hospital equipment.

Babysitters Guild   **682-0227**
60 East 42nd Street, Suite 912
    Open daily 9:00 A.M.–9:00 P.M.
    $7.50 per hour for first child
    $.25 for each additional child
Babysitters Guild prides itself on matching the sitter to the needs of the child. Infants are cared for by motherly types, while active youngsters are watched over by vigorous, energetic young women. There is a four hour minimum. In addition, the sitter receives $4.00 taxi fare before Midnight, and $5.50 after midnight. Their sitters are available on extremely short notice.

Baccarat   **826-4100**
625 Madison Avenue (58th/59th Sts.)

Backstage on Broadway   **575-8065**
228 West 47th Street

Baja, The   **724-8890**
246A Columbus Avenue (71st/72nd Sts.)

Balducci's   **673-2600**
424 Avenue of the Americas (9th St.)

BALLOONS

Eastern Onion   **741-0006**
39 West 14th Street
Have your balloons delivered by either a gentleman in a tuxedo or a gorilla.

Inflatably Yours   **580-2776**
318 West 77th Street
Beautiful three foot balloons with attached flowers, champagne, and teddy bears.

Rialto Florists   **688-3234**
707 Lexington Avenue (57th/58th Sts.)
  Open 24 hours a day, 7 days a week

BALLROOM DANCING

See **DANCING for detailed descriptions**
When asked "Where can we go dancing?" the concierge must ascertain as tactfully as possible whether the guest is interested in disco or "old fashioned" dancing. Fortunately, dancing cheek to cheek is experiencing a rebirth in Manhattan. Perhaps the reopening of the Rainbow Room will bring about a revival of this delightful pastime.

City Lights Bar and Hors d'Oeuvrerie   **938-1111**
One World Trade Center (107th Floor)

Maxim's   **751-5111**
680 Madison Avenue (61st St.)

Rainbow Room   **632-5000**
30 Rockefeller Plaza

Red Blazer, Too   **262-3112**
349 West 46th Street (Eighth/Ninth Aves.)

Roma di Notte   **832-1128**
137 East 55th Street

Roseland Ballroom   **247-0200**
239 West 52nd Street

Ballroom, The   **244-3005**
253 West 28th Street (Eighth Ave.)

Bally   **751-2163**
681 Madison Avenue (62nd St.)

Bally's Park Place Hotel/Casino   **1-609-340-2000**
Park Place and the Boardwalk (Atlantic City, NJ)

BANK MACHINES. *See* **MONEY
    MACHINES**

Barbetta   **436-9171**
321 West 46th Street (Eighth/Ninth Aves.)

Barclay Terrace, The   **755-5900**
The Hotel Inter-Continental, 111 East 48th Street

Barnes & Noble   **807-0099**
105 Fifth Avenue (18th St.)
600 Fifth Avenue (48th St.)

Barney's   **929-9000**
106 Seventh Avenue (17th St.)

Barrymore Theater   239-6200
243 West 47th Street

BARS

See also **DANCING, NIGHTCLUBS, JAZZ, SINGLES BARS, GAY BARS, PIANO BARS, and SPORTS BARS**

Amsterdam's on Amsterdam   874-1377
428 Amsterdam Avenue (80th/81st Sts.)
A typical singles bar. Lots of noise, smoke, and pretty decent basic food.

Arizona 206   838-0440
206 East 60th Street (Second/Third Aves.)
Not only a singles bar but a haven for those in search of delicious southwestern food.

Bemelman's Bar   744-1600
The Carlyle Hotel (Madison Avenue/76th St.)
A piano bar of distinction. Barbara Carroll and Michael Devine share the keyboards.

Cafe Carlyle   744-1600
The Carlyle Hotel, 35 East 76th Street (Madison Ave.)
Made famous and kept that way by Bobby Short. Don't miss him if you can get in.

Chez Josephine   594-1925
414 West 42nd Street (Ninth/Tenth Aves.)
One of our favorite places. Hosted by owner Jean Claude Baker, one of Josephine Bakers's "rainbow tribe" of adopted children, two impressive pianists treat you to the show tunes that made the theater district famous. An elegant but comfortable place which draws not only the typical theater and business crowd but also the international set.

City Lights Bar   938-1111
One World Trade Center (107th Floor)
The highest place in the world to get high.

Fortune Garden Pavilion   753-0101
209 East 49th Street
An unbeatable combination: great Chinese food and jazz pianists.

Grand Sea Palace   265-8133
346 West 46th Street
Who would believe a Thai restaurant with a great pianist? Try this one. Danny Appolinar is a real treat.

Jim McMullen's   861-4700
1341 Third Avenue (76th St.)
A trendy watering hole for young professionals.

Mickey Mantle's   688-7777
42 Central Park South

TV screens all over the place showing different live sporting events. It also has a comprehensive sports tape library. The food isn't bad if you stick to simple things like hamburgers, chicken pot pie, and the pasta.

Notes   247-8000
The Omni Hotel, Seventh Avenue (55th St.)
    Tuesday–Thursday from 8:30 P.M. to 12:30 A.M.
Listen to the music of Buck Buchholz.

One if by Land, Two if by Sea   255-8649
17 Barrow Street (Seventh Ave.)

A romantic Greenwich Village bar complete with two fireplaces.

Peacock Alley   355-3000
The Waldorf Astoria Hotel, Park Avenue (49th St.)

No list of greats would be complete without Peacock Alley. Jimmy Lyon and Penny Brook play on Cole Porter's piano to entertain one of the city's most cosmopolitan crowds.

P.J. Clarke's   759-1650
915 Third Avenue (55th St.)

One of the best-known singles bars in the city. A great bar and an equally great jukebox. If you are a tourist with limited time, try this place.

T.G.I. Friday's   832-8512
1152 First Avenue (63rd St.)

A great singles bar on the Upper East Side.

The View   704-8900
Marriott Marquis Hotel, 1535 Broadway (45th St.)

New York's only revolving bar! A marvelous view of midtown with live entertainment and dancing. A choice of the View Lounge, for drinks in a darkened, romantic atmosphere, or the View Restaurant, which features three cuisines: French, Italian, or American. Reservations are recommended, particularly for before or after theater.

BASEBALL

New York's two home teams, the "Amazin' Mets" and the "Bronx Bombers" delight millions of fans each year from April to September.
    For tickets:

Shea Stadium (Mets)   672-3000
126th Street and Roosevelt Avenue, Queens

Yankee Stadium (Yankees)   293-6000
River Avenue and West 161st Street, The Bronx

Telecharge	239-6200
Ticketron	246-0102

BATHROOMS

Nothing is as important and as difficult to find as a public bathroom in New York. In an effort to aid the weary traveler, we list a few of the ones which have been important to us over the years. Keep in mind that most department stores and all hotels have bathrooms.

Avery Fisher Hall
Lincoln Center, 65th Street and Broadway
    Open daily 10:00 A.M.–6:00 P.M.
    Performance nights 10:00 A.M.–11:00 P.M.
These are the only easily accessible public toilets on the Upper West Side. They're open the same hours as the building, and nobody bothers you.

Barney's
Seventh Avenue at 17th Street

Grand Central Station
42nd Street (Park Ave.)
We feel obliged to list these, but be warned, they are highly undesirable. The owners have taken steps to clean up the waiting rooms; maybe they will be able to do the same for the bathrooms.

Grand Hyatt Hotel
42nd Street and Lexington Avenue
    Open 24 hours
In the back of the lobby, near the shops are the sparkling rest rooms.

Macy's
Seventh Avenue (34th St.)

The New York Public Library
Fifth Avenue (42nd St.)

Saks Fifth Avenue
Fifth Avenue (50th St.)

Trump Tower
725 Fifth Avenue (56th/57th Sts.)
The basement rest rooms are awash with pink marble.

Waldorf Astoria, The
50th Street and Park Avenue
    Open 24 hours
Just off the main lobby, the elegant ladies' room has petite built-in marble sinks.

B. Dalton Bookseller
396 Avenue of the Americas (8th St.)   **674-8780**
666 Fifth Avenue (53rd/54th Sts.)   **247-1740**

BEAUTY SALONS

From among the thousands of salons all over Manhattan, we have selected the most outstanding and frequently asked for.

Elizabeth Arden   **407-1000**
691 Fifth Avenue (54th St.)
    Monday–Saturday 9:00 A.M.–5:30 P.M.
    Thursday 9:00 A.M.–8:00 P.M.

We've had nothing but good luck in dealing with these people. Whether you want a manicure or to spend a day getting the works, they treat you well. We recommend that you call in advance because they are very popular. And do ask about the various services they offer . . . many guests have gone to have their hair done and ended up in a seaweed wrap.

Georgette Klinger
501 Madison Avenue (52nd St.)   **838-3200**
978 Madison Avenue (76th St.)   **744-6900**
    Monday–Saturday 9:00 A.M.–6:00 P.M.
    Thursday 9:00 A.M.–8:00 P.M.

Kenneth   **752-1800**
19 East 54th Street (Fifth/Madison Aves.)

Larry Matthews 24 Hour Beauty
    Salon   **246-6100**
536 Madison Avenue
    Monday–Saturday 7:00 A.M.–10:00 P.M.
    Sunday 9:00 A.M.–5:00 P.M.

Vidal Sassoon   **535-9200**
767 Madison Avenue (58th St.)
    Monday–Saturday 8:30 A.M.–5:00 P.M.
    Thursday 8:30 A.M.–7:00 P.M.
Excellent for haircuts on short notice.

Suga   **421-4400**
115 East 57th Street
    Monday–Saturday 9:00 A.M.–6:00 P.M.
    Wednesday 9:00 A.M.–8:00 P.M.

When Dorothy Hamill skated into our hearts in the 1976 Olympics, the judges watched her ankles and women all over wondered, "Who does her hair?" It was Suga.

Bedford Hotel   697-4800
118 East 40th Street (Lexington/Park Aves.)

Beekman Downtown Hospital   233-5300
170 William Street

Beekman Tower Hotel   355-7300
First Avenue (49th St.)

Belasco Theater   239-6200
111 West 44th Street

Belgium (Consulate of)   586-5110
50 Rockefeller Plaza

Bellevue Hospital   561-4141
First Avenue and 27th Street

Bellini   265-7770
777 Seventh Avenue (50th/51st Sts.)

Belmont Park   1-718-641-4700
Hempstead Turnpike at Plainfield Avenue, Queens

Bemelman's Bar   744-1600
The Carlyle, Madison Avenue (76th St.)

Ben Benson's   581-8888
123 West 52nd Street (Sixth/Seventh Aves.)

Benihana of Tokyo   581-0930
47 West 56th Street (Fifth/Sixth Aves.)

Benjamin Book Store   432-1103
408 World Trade Center

Beny's Authorized Sales and Service   226-8437
86 Canal Street

Bergdorf Goodman   753-7300
754 Fifth Avenue (57th St.)

Bermuda Star Lines   1-800-237-5361

Beth Israel Hospital   420-2000
Stuyvesant Square and 17th Street

Beverly Hotel   753-5300
125 East 50th Street

BFO   254-0059
149 Fifth Avenue

Bice   688-1999
7 East 54th Street (Madison/Fifth Aves.)

BICYCLE RENTALS
See **RENTALS, BICYCLE**

Big Apple Circus	**391-0767**
Trump Tent, Damrosch Park, Lincoln Center	
Bikes in the Park	**861-4137**
Loeb Boathouse, Park Drive North (72nd St.)	
Biltmore Theater	**582-5340**
261 West 47th Street	
Biography Book Shop	**807-8655**
400 Bleecker Street (11th St.)	
Bloomingdale's	**355-5900**
1000 Third Avenue (59th St.)	
Blue Note	**475-8592**
131 West 3rd Street (Sixth Ave.)	
Body Design by Gilda	**759-7966**
139 East 57th Street	
Bolivia (Consulate of)	**687-0530**
211 East 43rd Street	
Bolton's	
225 East 57th Street	**755-2527**
53 West 23rd Street	**924-6860**
Books of Wonder	
464 Hudson Street	**645-8006**
132 Seventh Avenue (18th St.)	**989-3270**

BOOKSTORES

AMACOM (American Management
Association)   586-8100
135 West 50th Street (7th Floor)(Sixth/Seventh Aves.)
    Monday–Friday 8:30 A.M.–5:30 P.M.

The AMA Bookstore has all of the important books concerning life in the business world. Topics range from sales techniques and positive thinking to books telling you how to deal with stress, job hunting, or mergers and acquisitions.

Antiquarian Booksellers Center
50 Rockefeller Plaza   246-2564
    Monday–Friday 10:00 A.M.–5:30 P.M.
    Closed in August

Browsers are welcome in this impressive showroom, which also acts as a referral center for rare-book dealers nationwide.

Barnes & Noble

105 Fifth Avenue (18th St.)	**807-0099**
128 Fifth Avenue (18th St.)	**807-0099**
600 Fifth Avenue (Rockefeller Ctr./48th St.)	**765-0590**

Penn Plaza (Seventh Ave./33rd St.)
City Hall (38 Park Row)
86th Street (Lexington Ave.)
45th Street (Broadway)
The Ansonia (73rd St./Broadway)
Third Avenue (47th St.)
Seventh Avenue (57th St.)
The Bromley (83rd St./Broadway)
36th Street (Fifth Ave.)
> Monday–Friday 9:30 A.M.–7:45 P.M.
> Saturday 9:30 A.M.–6:15 P.M.
> Sunday 11:00 A.M.–5:45 P.M.

When you think of books, you think of Barnes & Noble. And for good reason: they are the world's largest bookstore. For years, we knew them as the leading supplier of textbooks to New York college students. Now, however, an enormous assortment of all types of books is available at considerable discounts, with special discounts on those that have made *The New York Times* bestseller list. The two main stores (across the street from each other on lower Fifth Avenue and 18th Street) are huge and offer an unbelievable selection of books, tapes, records, magazines, and even school supplies. We have been shopping at these locations for many years and have always been pleased with both the selections and the quality of service provided.

B. Dalton Bookseller

396 Avenue of the Americas (8th St.)	**674-8780**

> Monday–Saturday 10:00 A.M.–11:30 P.M.
> Sunday Noon–7:00 P.M.

The largest of the B. Daltons in town and one of the most complete bookstores in Greenwich Village carries, we are happy to say, a wide selection of travel books. It also has comprehensive mystery and science fiction sections, children's books, and a complete range of nonfiction.

666 Fifth Avenue (53rd/54th Sts.)	**247-1740**

> Monday–Friday 8:30 A.M.–7:00 P.M.
> Saturday 9:30 A.M.–6:30 P.M.
> Sunday 11:30 A.M.–5:00 P.M.

This choice location in the heart of Fifth Avenue shopping always entices customers with fabulous display windows. Inside, a well-informed staff assists you in choosing just the right book or computer software.

Benjamin Book Store 432-1103
408 World Trade Center
    Monday–Friday 7:00 A.M.–6:45 P.M.
    Saturday 10:00 A.M.–4:45 P.M.
    Closed Sunday

You'll find branches of Benjamin Books in many major airports, including La Guardia, Dulles, and O'Hare. Their branch in the World Trade Center features a broad selection of general books, a large travel section, and irresistible bestsellers.

Biography Book Shop 807-8655
400 Bleecker Street (11th St.)
    Tuesday–Friday 1:00 P.M.–9:00 P.M.
    Saturday Noon–10:00 P.M.
    Sunday Noon–5:30 P.M.
    Closed Monday

As the name implies, this shop specializes in biographies. Some travel and art books have infiltrated.

Books of Wonder 645-8006
464 Hudson Street
    Monday–Saturday 11:00 A.M.–7:00 P.M.
    Sunday Noon–6:00 P.M.

One of the most attractive and well cared for children's bookstores in the city. It's obvious that the staff enjoys what they're doing. Story readings for children every Sunday morning at 11:30 A.M. introduce young audiences to the joy of books. They carry a nice assortment of beautiful hard-covers which will be passed from generation to generation.

132 Seventh Ave (18th St.) **989-3270**

This location, in Chelsea, is slightly larger than the shop in Greenwich Village and handles antique editions as well as current books. Instead of having a story hour, they have special events such as your favorite authors signing their books.

Brentano's 826-2450
597 Fifth Avenue (48th St.)
    Monday–Friday 8:00 A.M.–7:00 P.M.
    Saturday 9:00 A.M.–6:00 P.M.
    Sunday 11:00 A.M.–6:00 P.M.

There was a public outcry when the beloved Scribner Booksellers were forced from this beautiful store. But the new resident, Brentano's, seems eager to please with an extremely high staff- to-customer ratio and courteous service. Its early opening is a boon to those who wish to shop en route to the office. We're certainly glad to see the old Scribner's store in such good hands.

Classic Bookshop & Sale Annex   **221-2252**
1212 Avenue of the Americas
    Monday–Friday 8:00 A.M.–7:00 P.M.
    Saturday 10:00 A.M.–6:00 P.M.
    Sunday Noon–6:00 P.M.

This large, well-stocked location does a booming business with discounted bestsellers, a large science fiction selection, and a complete range of computer manuals.

Classic Bookshop   **466-0668**
133 World Trade Center Concourse
    Monday–Friday 7:30 A.M.–7:00 P.M.
    Saturday 10:00 A.M.–4:45 P.M.
    Sunday Noon–5:45 P.M.

Book lovers will delight in this wonderful location on the main concourse of the World Trade Center—bestsellers, books on tape, business and finance, health, sports, New Age, and juvenile books can be found here. The long hours accommodate everyone.

Coliseum Books, Inc.   **757-8381**
1771 Broadway (57th St.)
    Monday 8:00 A.M.–10:00 P.M.
    Tuesday–Thursday 8:00 A.M.–11:00 P.M.
    Friday 8:00 A.M.–11:30 P.M.
    Saturday 10:00 A.M.–11:30 P.M.
    Sunday Noon–8:00 P.M.

This is a dangerous locale—it's almost impossible to walk in and not buy something. They've got classics, bestsellers, cookbooks, New Age, self-help, magazines, mysteries, children's books, romance—the works. The travel book section is large and well organized. We have both worked within walking distance and have spent many lunch hours and probably thousands of dollars here.

Commuter Book Center, Inc.   **599-1056**
89 East 42nd Street (in Grand Central Station)
    Monday–Friday 7:30 A.M.–7:45 P.M.
    Saturday 9:30 A.M.–5:45 P.M.
    Closed Sunday

If you are a New Yorker, you must have shopped here. The glass walled shop, on the main level of the terminal, supplies the needs of thousands of commuters and travelers who are using the trains. They have a complete selection of current bestsellers and an extensive selection of travel guides. Be sure to stop here before leaving town. It will make your trip much more pleasant.

Complete Traveller Bookstore, The   **679-4339**
199 Madison Avenue (35th St.)

Monday–Friday 9:00 A.M.–6:30 P.M.
Saturday 10:00 A.M.–6:00 P.M.
Sunday Noon–5:00 P.M.

A tiny store dedicated exclusively to books about travel. No matter what you're looking for, they probably have it here. If not, the friendly owners will order it.

Doubleday
724 Fifth Avenue (57th St.)   **397-0550**
Monday–Saturday 9:00 A.M.–Midnight
Sunday Noon–5:00 P.M.

With its premier location (just across the street from Tiffany's and Trump Tower) and carefully chosen selection, Doubleday is crowded from the moment the doors open. They seem to have almost everything. Adele found it convenient to dash over here from The Pierre when additional reference books were needed at the Concierge desk.

777 Third Avenue (49th St.)   **888-5590**
Monday–Friday 8:30 A.M.–7:00 P.M.
Saturday 11:00 A.M.–6:00 P.M.
Sunday closed

Not as large as its 57th Street counterpart, it still has a fairly comprehensive selection, with everything from children's books to bestsellers.

Citicorp Center (Third Ave./53rd St.)   **223-3301**
Monday–Friday 8:00 A.M.–9:00 P.M.
Saturday Noon–8:00 P.M.
Sunday Noon–7:00 P.M.

It's certainly good to know that there is a major bookstore in this area. All of the Doubleday service and selection right in the Citicorp Center. Please note that they are open late and on Sunday. Everything you could want in a good location.

Drama Book Shop, Inc.   **944-0595**
723 Seventh Avenue (2nd Floor, between 48th/49th Sts.)
Monday–Friday 9:30 A.M.–7:00 P.M.
Saturday 10:30 A.M.–5:30 P.M.
Sunday Noon–5:00 P.M.

Don't be put off by the neighborhood or the grubby building. On the second floor is a clean, well lit, little shop that must be a mecca for people in the performing arts.To put it simply, they have everything relating to their area and haven't cluttered the shop with extraneous books. We saw books on face painting, mime, and scores to musicals we'd never heard of. Every play you might be interested in is here. If your interest is in the performing arts, you must pay a visit to this resource.

Forbidden Planet
821 Broadway (11th/12th St.)   **473-1576**

Monday–Saturday 10:00 A.M.–7:00 P.M.
Sunday 11:00 A.M.–6:00 P.M.

We try to keep it quiet, but McDowell is a science fiction nut. This is his first stop when he is on the prowl for new books to add to his ever-growing collection. The store is no beauty. It's your basic bare walls with rows of racks for books. But the aisles are wide enough to maneuver in and it's a comfortable place to shop. It may also be the largest science fiction store in town. In addition to the books, there is an assortment of masks, games, and comic books to delight the hearts of the young.

227 East 59th Street   751-4386

Monday–Saturday 10:00 A.M.–9:00 P.M.
Sunday Noon–9:00 P.M.

This second store is also a gold mine for science fiction fans. It carries much of the same assortment of books, comic books, bookends, calendars, games, movie posters, toys, and Chewbacca face masks as the downtown store and is definitely worth a visit.

**Foul Play Books of Mystery &
   Suspense**   675-5115
10 Eighth Avenue (12th St.)
Monday–Friday 11:00 A.M.–9:45 P.M.
Saturday 11:00 A.M.–10:00 P.M.
Sunday 11:00 A.M.–7:00 P.M.

A shop dedicated to the art of the mystery—one of our favorite escapes. How can anyone resist a good suspense story? And Foul Play has all of them. The main advantage, of course, is that it's in our neighborhood.

Gotham Book Mart   719-4448
41 West 47th Street
Monday–Friday 9:30 A.M.–6:30 P.M.
Saturday 9:30 A.M.–6:00 P.M.

Their motto is "Wise Men Fish Here." And the knowledgeable staff will cheerfully assist you in your fishing. Finding your wish among the half-million titles takes no time at all with their help. Edward Gorey fans will delight in finding a complete selection of his works and may even run into Gorey himself autographing copies.

Hacker Art Books   688-7600
45 West 57th Street
Monday–Saturday 9:00 A.M.–6:00 P.M.

If you can't find it anyplace else, it's probably here. Their main drawback is that they only take cash. It's saved McDowell a fortune because art books are expensive and only a fool would carry several hundred dollars in cash in this city. The Strand is much cheaper if you are just browsing or if you are buying gifts.

J.N. Bartfield   245-8890
30 West 57th Street
> Monday–Friday 10:00 A.M.–5:00 P.M.
> Saturday 10:00 A.M.–2:30 P.M.

For serious collectors, Bartfield's has sold first editions and rare books for nearly 60 years. The company also offers cataloging and appraisal services at $30.00 an hour, plus travel expenses.

Kitchen Arts & Letters, Inc.   876-5550
1435 Lexington Avenue (93rd St.)
> Monday 1:00 P.M.–6:00 P.M.
> Tuesday, Wednesday, Friday 10:00 A.M.–6:30 P.M.
> Thursday 10:00 A.M.–8:00 P.M.
> Saturday 11:00 A.M.–6:00 P.M.
> Closed Saturday during the summer and all of August.

Nachum Waxman's stock of books and materials about cooking is one of the best in the country. He not only has all of the most recent publications, but searches for the out-of-print and esoteric books of yesterday. If you don't find what you want, he'll be delighted to obtain it for you. This store is a must for cookbook collectors.

Literary Bookshop, Inc.   633-1151
15 Christopher Street
> Tuesday–Thursday Noon–9:00 P.M.
> Friday & Saturday Noon–10:00 P.M.
> Sunday Noon–9:00 P.M.

L.K. Evans, the personable owner, having devoted 20 years of her life to publishing books, is now happily selling them. Through the wrought iron gate and down the stairs into an attractive and surprisingly spacious basement bookstore, she stocks all the items her Greenwich Village clientele request. Be sure to ask about her custom-made "Baskets of Books," a great gift for friends in the hospital. Small leather goods, handmade stationery, and a variety of hard-bound blank journals complete the selection.

Logos   697-4888
342 Madison Avenue (43rd/44th Sts.)
> Monday–Thursday 9:00 A.M.–6:30 P.M.
> Friday 9:00 A.M.–6:00 P.M.
> Saturday 10:00 A.M.–6:00 P.M.

Logos specializes in books on spirituality, with a selection of Bibles and extensive writings on Church History, Ethics, and the Christian Experience. Thomas Merton and C.S. Lewis are well represented here.

McGraw-Hill   512-4100
1221 Avenue of the Americas (48th/49th Sts.)
Monday–Saturday 10:00 A.M.–5:45 P.M.

McGraw-Hill has one of the best business, scientific, and technical book collections around, and their selection of computer books and software is great. They also have the staff to support it—most of their people seem to be technically oriented. Their travel selection is small but includes most of the core books and a nice assortment of maps.

Morton, The Interior Design
Bookshop   421-9025
983 Third Avenue (59th St.)
Monday–Saturday 11:00 A.M.–8:00 P.M.
Friday 11:00 A.M.–6:00 P.M.
Closed Sunday

A small shop dedicated to architecture, interior design, gardening, and the fashionable things that support these topics.

Murder, Ink.   362-8905
271 West 87th Street
Friday–Wednesday 11:00 A.M.–7:00 P.M.
Thursday 11:00 A.M.–10:00 P.M.

Fans of detective fiction, mysteries, out-of-print, new and true crime head for this tiny but comprehensive shop. They claim to stock every mystery in print, so you're sure to find something entertaining.

Mysterious Book Shop, The   765-0900
129 West 56th Street
Monday–Saturday 11:00 A.M.–7:00 P.M.

This is where we add to our collection of E. Phillips Oppenheim. While they seem to have everything, our interest is in the fabulous collection of hard-to-find oldies on the second floor. Highly recommended as a friendly resource for the serious collector of mysteries.

New York Bound Bookshop   245-8530
50 Rockefeller Plaza (50th/51st Sts.)
Monday–Friday 10:00 A.M.–6:00 P.M.
Saturday Noon–4:00 P.M.

If it has to do with New York, Barbara Cohen and Judith Stonehill probably have it. Now in their greatly expanded ground floor location in the heart of the city, service is better than ever. While much of their stock is aimed at the historical aspects of the city, they have not neglected the new. Books, guidebooks, maps, and all kinds of unusual "finds" make this a wonderful place for getting in touch with the Big Apple.

Rizzoli   **223-0100**
31 West 57th Street
> Monday–Friday 9:30 A.M.–10:00 P.M.
> Saturday 9:30 A.M.–7:30 P.M.

As elegant as a private library, Rizzoli concentrates on art, ballet, literature, music, and photography, with a superb selection of foreign-language books and newspapers.

250 Vesey Street (Battery Park City)   **385-1400**
> Monday–Saturday 10:00 A.M.–7:00 P.M.
> Sunday Noon–7:00 P.M

Location and content vie for your attention here. Just off the Winter Garden of the World Financial Center, Rizzoli emphasizes coffee-table books with beautiful pictures of gardens, chateaux, and lavish estates. Travel books—including the entire Michelin series—are well represented. Foreign language magazines, tapes, and compact discs round out the excellent selection.

St. Marks Bookshop   **260-7853**
13 St. Marks Place (Second/Third Aves.)
> Daily 11:00 A.M.–11:00 P.M.

An old standby in East Greenwich Village, St. Marks Bookshop has something for everyone. Whether it's the most recent novel or something from a small press, it's probably in stock. One of the best general bookstores in the area.

Shakespeare & Co.
2259 Broadway (81st St.)   **580-7800**
716 Broadway (Waverly Place)   **529-1330**
> Sunday–Thursday 10:00 A.M.–11:30 P.M.
> Friday & Saturday 10:00 A.M.–12:30 A.M.

Extremely popular with the young professionals who have chosen to live on the Upper West Side and East Greenwich Village, these large stores' well-displayed items range from classics to cookbooks. Theirs are among the largest and best-organized selections of travel books we have encountered. Signs urge, "If you don't see it, ask us to check the stockroom," and they really will.

**South Street Seaport Museum Book
    and Chart Store**   **669-9455**
209 Water Street
> Monday–Saturday 10:00 A.M.–7:00 P.M.
> Sunday 11:00 A.M.–7:00 P.M.

This cozy and inviting locale specializes in maritime books—sailing, navigation, boat building, and novels of the sea from *20,000 Leagues Under the Sea* and the Hornblower series, to *Hunt for Red October*. Gifts range from sea shell soaps to do-it-yourself models of the Titanic.

Manager Michael Flynn assists buyers in finding the perfect purchase.

Storyland   517-6951
1369 Third Avenue (78th St.)
> Monday–Saturday 10:00 A.M.–6:00 P.M.
> Sunday 11:00 A.M.–6:00 P.M.

Children will like the tiny shop full of tapes, games, and books, of course. On Sunday they have special events. Call for more information.

Strand Bookstore   473-1452
828 Broadway (12th St.)
> Monday–Friday 9:30 A.M.–9:30 P.M.
> Saturday 9:30 A.M.–6:25 P.M.
> Sunday 11:00 A.M.–5:00 P.M.

Has success spoiled the Strand? Once a charming place to buy used books, the Strand has been discovered by the masses. There are still bargains to be found here, if you know your author and don't mind being stepped over.

Three Lives & Company, Ltd.   741-2069
154 West 10th Street (Waverly Place)
> Monday & Wednesday–Saturday 1:00 P.M.–9:00 P.M.
> Tuesday 1:00 P.M.–8:00 P.M.
> Sunday 1:00 P.M.–7:00 P.M.

Just what you'd think a Greenwich Village bookstore should look like—brick walls, shiny wooden tables, restful green lamps, and discreet classical music. The book-filled windows are designed to seductively draw you inside, where the three owners concentrate on personal service. On the other hand, they leave you alone to browse if you want. McDowell has been going here since the day they opened their doors. They are known for their support of writers through readings and personal appearances.

Traveller's Bookstore, The   664-0995
22 West 52nd Street (75 Rockefeller Plaza)
> Monday–Friday 9:00 A.M.–6:00 P.M.
> Saturday 11:00 A.M.–5:00 P.M.

Whether you're planning a safari, a honeymoon, or a trip to a dude ranch, you'll find the information you need right here. Just reading through their catalog makes you want to get out your suitcases. Travel-related items such as money belts, inflatable pillows, and flashlights complete the selection.

Urban Center Books   935-3592
457 Madison Avenue (51st St.)
> Monday–Saturday 10:00 A.M.–6:00 P.M.

Located in the north wing of the Villard Houses, this beautiful shop is the bookstore of the Municiple Art Society. It specializes in books on city architecture, urban planning, and historic preservation.

Waldenbooks

57 Broadway (Rector/Exchange Sts.)	**269-1139**

Monday–Friday 8:00 A.M.–6:00 P.M.
Closed Saturday & Sunday

931 Lexington Avenue	**249-1327**

Monday–Friday 9:00 A.M.–6:45 P.M.
Saturday 9:00 A.M.–5:00 P.M.
Sunday Noon–5:00 P.M.

270 Park Avenue (48th St.)	**370-3758**

Monday–Friday 8:30 A.M.–5:30 P.M.
Closed Saturday & Sunday

One of the largest bookstore chains in the country can't fail to have the book you're looking for. In fact, that's what they specialize in—everything. We could go on for pages talking about the various departments and special areas they have, but the basic thing to know is—if anybody has it, it's Waldenbooks.

Wittenborn Art Books	**288-1558**

1018 Madison Avenue
Monday–Saturday 10:00 A.M.–5:00 P.M.
Closed Saturday during the summer

For many years, Wittenborn has been one of the very best purveyors of fine art books. Their stock is up to date and includes all aspects of the visual arts. They also maintain a collection of old and rare publications and have a knowledgeable and caring staff that can support the entire spectrum of materials they provide.

Booth Theater	**239-6200**

222 West 45th Street

Bottega Veneta	**371-5511**

635 Madison Avenue (60th St.)

Bouley	**608-3852**

165 Duane Street (Hudson/Greenwich Sts.)

BOW TIES

HOW TO TIE THEM

Besides being able to read a map upside down, a concierge must possess the ability to tie a bow tie. Inevitably, on days when there is a big wedding in the hotel, the concierge will receive a frantic call in the late afternoon,

"Does anybody down there know how to tie a bow tie?"

The Art of Bow Tying

by

Ferrell Reed

Shown as you see it when you are looking at yourself in a mirror!

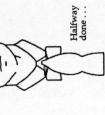

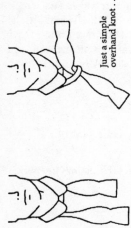

1.
Start with end in left hand extending 1" longer than end in right hand.

2.
Cross longer end (left) over shorter end (right) and pass it up through the loop at your neck so it is tied loosely at the throat.

Just a simple overhand knot . . .

3.
Fold lower hanging end up and to the right to form what will be the front of your bow tie, making sure the folded side is to your right.

Make the front bow . . .

Halfway done . . .

4.
Hold this folded bow with your left hand and bring the other end down and over the bow.

44

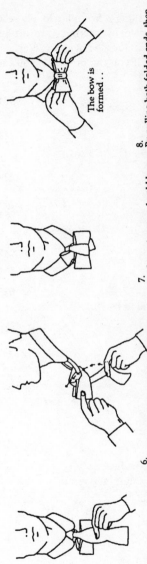

The bow is formed . . .

5.
Place your right thumb and forefinger on the hanging end where it will be folded to form the back loop of your bow.

6.
Now, with your left thumb and forefinger, fold the front bow ends together, around the hanging end. By pulling the folded bow forward you will make a small passage behind which you can push the looped end of the back bow using your right forefinger.

7.
At this point, you should have a bow tie that is uneven and needs to be tightened.

8.
By pulling both folded ends, then both flat ends on each side, you can smooth out the bow and tighten the knot (like your shoelaces).

To untie, simply pull the flat ends . . .

45

"Come down to the desk and we'll take care of you."

Seating the guest in a low chair while wondering what sort of insurance the hotel carries against accidental strangulation, we strive to put the guest at ease with something like,

"The most important thing is to remain totally relaxed."

We have seen our Director of Catering whip through this in 45 seconds, but it is best for the novice to allow at least a half hour's time. Relax. If you can tie a bow, you can tie a bow tie.

Bowery Service Station   674-2827
326 Bowery

Box Tree, The   758-8320
250 East 49th Street (Second/Third Aves.)

Bradley's   228-6440
70 University Place (11th St.)

Brasserie   751-4840
100 East 53rd Street (Lexington/Park Aves.)

Brazil (Consulate of)   757-3080
630 Fifth Avenue

Break, The   627-0072
232 Eighth Avenue (22nd St.)

Brentano's   826-2450
597 Fifth Avenue (48th St.)

BRIDGES

Brooklyn Bridge
Park Row at Broadway

George Washington Bridge
178th Street at Ft. Washington Avenue

Manhattan Bridge
Canal Street at Bowery

Queensboro Bridge
59th Street at Second Avenue

Throgs Neck Bridge
Throgs Neck Expressway, Bronx

Triboro Bridge
125th Street at Second Avenue

Verrazano Narrows Bridge
Connects the Brooklyn–Queens Expressway and the
Staten Island Expressway

Whitestone Bridge
Hutchinson River Parkway, Bronx

Williamsburg Bridge
Delancey at Clinton Street

British Airways   1-800-247-9297

Broadhurst Theater   239-6200
235 West 44th Street

Broadway Hal's Big Hit Oldies   475-9516
170 Bleecker at Sullivan Street

Broadway Theater   239-6200
1681 Broadway (53rd St.)

Bronx Zoo   220-5100
Bronx Park, Fordham Road and Bronx River Parkway,
The Bronx

Brooke Alexander   925-4338
59 Wooster Street

Brooklyn Academy of Music   1-718-636-4100
30 Lafayette Avenue, Brooklyn

Brooklyn Battery Tunnel
Battery Park at West Street

Brooklyn Botanic Garden   1-718-622-4433
1000 Washington Avenue

Brooklyn Bridge
Park Row at Broadway

Brooklyn Museum   1-718-638-5000
300 Eastern Parkway, Brooklyn

Brooks Atkinson Theater   719-4099
256 West 47th Street

Brooks Brothers   682-8800
346 Madison Avenue (44th St.)

Buccellatti   308-5533
Trump Tower, 725 Fifth Avenue (56th/57th Sts.)

Budget Rent-a-Car   807-8700

Bukhara   838-1811
148 East 48th Street (Lexington/Third Aves.)

Bulgari   315-9000
730 Fifth Avenue (57th St.)

Bullit Courier
42 Broadway (Wall St.)   952-4343
Chrysler Building, 405 Lexington Avenue
(42nd St.)   983-7400

Burberry   371-5010
9 East 57th Street

Bus and Subway Information   1-718-330-1234

BUS LINES

The main bus terminal in New York is the Port Authority
Bus Terminal at Eighth Avenue between 40th and 42nd
Streets. It is located in midtown and is convenient to all hotels. A word of warning: It is unfortunately one of the least
desirable places in town. Do not stray away from the heavy
traffic areas and do not let strangers help you with your
luggage. Go straight to the legitimate waiting areas if you
are waiting for a bus or straight to the front door (Eighth
Ave.) if you are looking for a taxi. Hold up your hand to get
your own taxi and do not be intimidated by teenagers who
may try to take advantage of you. If you have a choice, arrive by plane.

There are approximately 4,000 diesel-powered city
buses which create most of the foul air you will breathe
while you are here. The fare is $1.15. You may use either
exact change or a subway token—no paper currency and
the driver will not make change for you. If you are switch-
ing to another bus that intersects your route, ask the driver
for a free transfer when boarding the bus.

Abbey Bus Service	1-718-784-5130
Carey Bus Lines	1-718-632-0500
Greyhound	636-0800
Package Express Information	971-6405
Hampton Jitney	267-1392
Mini Bus (Airports)	355-1992
New Jersey Transit	1-201-762-5100
	1-800-772-2222
Olympia Bus Service	964-6233
Port Authority Bus Terminal	564-8484
Short Line	436-4700
Trailways	730-7460
Package Express	563-9674

C

C.J. Blanda   206-7880
209 Seventh Avenue (22nd St.)

Cabrini-Columbia Hospital   725-6000
227 East 19th Street

Caesar's Hotel/Casino   1-609-348-4411
Arkansas Avenue and the Boardwalk (Atlantic City, NJ)

Cafe Carlyle, The   744-1600
The Carlyle, 35 East 76th Street (Madison Ave.)

Cafe Des Artistes   877-3500
1 West 67th Street (Central Park West)

Cafe Luxembourg   873-7411
200 West 70th Street (Amsterdam/West End Aves.)

Cafe Pierre   940-8185
The Pierre Hotel, Fifth Avenue (61st St.)

Cafe Un Deux Trois   354-4148
123 West 44th Street (Sixth Avenue/Broadway)

Calendar of Events. *See* **ANNUAL
        EVENTS**

Cameo's   874-2280
169 Columbus Avenue (68th St.)

CAMERAS

47th Street Photo   398-1410
67 West 47th Street (Sixth & Seventh Aves.)
    Monday–Thursday 9:00 A.M.–6:00 P.M.
    Friday 9:00 A.M.–2:00 P.M.
    Sunday 10:00 A.M.–4:00 P.M.
If you know exactly what you want, you can find excellent prices on cameras, computers, typewriters, and electronic equipment. However, don't expect much in the way of service or advice.

Hirsch Photo   557-1150
699 Third Avenue (44th St.)   1-800-223-7957
    Monday–Friday 8:30 A.M.–5:45 P.M.
    Saturday 10:00 A.M.–4:00 P.M.
From your initial purchase through developing and repairs, Hirsch's capable staff assists you in all aspects of pho-

tography. Use their toll-free number for ordering from out
of town.

Willoughby's Camera Store   564-1600
110 West 32nd Street (Sixth/Seventh Aves.)
   Monday–Wednesday, Friday 9:00 A.M.–7:00 P.M.
   Thursday 9:00 A.M.–8:00 P.M.
   Saturday 9:00 A.M.–6:30 P.M.
   Sunday 10:30 A.M.–5:30 P.M.
New York's largest camera shop, Willoughby's sells, ser-
vices, and rents all kinds of cameras.

Campus Coach Lines   682-1050
545 Fifth Avenue

Canada (Consulate of)   757-4917
1251 Sixth Avenue

Canal Street Flea Market   226-7541
Canal Street (Greene St.)

Candle Bar   874-9155
309 Amsterdam Avenue (74th/75th Sts.)

Canton   226-4441
45 Division Street (Bowery/East Broadway)

Capitol Service Stations
1124 First Avenue (62nd St.)   759-9334
640 First Avenue (36th St.)   679-7585

Captain of the Port of New York   668-7936

Captain's Table, The   697-9538
860 Second Avenue (46th St.)

Carey Bus Lines   1-718-632-0500

Carey Limo   517-7010

Carlo Lamagna Gallery   245-6006
50 West 57th Street

Carlyle Hotel, The   744-1600
35 East 76th Street

Carlyle Restaurant, The   744-1600
The Carlyle Hotel, 35 East 76th Street

Carnegie Charge   247-7800

Carnegie Deli   757-2245
854 Seventh Avenue (54th/55th Sts.)

Carnegie Hall   247-7800
154 West 57th Street (Seventh Ave.)

Carnegie Recital Hall   **247-7800**
Carnegie Hall, 57th Street (Seventh Ave.)

Caroline's at the Seaport   **233-4900**
89 South Street, Pier 17

CAR RENTAL
See **RENTALS, AUTOMOBILE**

CARRIAGES, HORSE DRAWN

What could be more romantic than a carriage ride through Central Park? The horse-drawn carriages can be picked up at Grand Army Square (Fifth Ave. at 59th St.).
　　　Hours: 8:00 A.M.–9:00 P.M.
　　　Rates: $34.00 first half hour
　　　$10.00 each additional 15 minutes

Chateau Stables   **828-4636**
608 West 48th Street   **828-4496**
Chateau Stables also offers gift certificates. For $40.00 you can treat up to four people to a carriage tour of Central Park, lasting just shy of one-half hour.
　　　For Groups: Contact Gloria McGill   **246-0520**
　　　　　　　　　　　　　　　　　　　　　　　　 246-0521

Cartier   **753-0111**
653 Fifth Avenue (52nd St.)

Cash Machines. *See* **MONEY
　　MACHINES**

Catch A Rising Star   **794-1906**
1487 First Avenue (77th/78th Sts.)

**Cathedral Church of St. John the
　　Divine (Episcopal)**   **678-6888**
Amsterdam Avenue (112th St.)

CAVIAR
　　Caviarteria   **759-7410**
　　29 East 60th Street
　　　　Monday–Friday 9:00 A.M.–6:00 P.M.
　　　　Saturday 9:00 A.M.–5:30 P.M.
All varieties of caviar, from pressed to luscious Beluga, plus serving pieces and caviar spoons.

　　Petrossian   **245-2214**
　　182 West 58th Street (Seventh Ave.)
　　　　Monday–Saturday 11:00 A.M.–8:00 P.M.

Adjoining their elegant restaurant, the New York branch of the famous Parisian specialty shop offers exquisite caviar, foie gras, and smoked salmon.

Caviarteria	759-7410
29 East 60th Street	

Cellar In The Sky	938-1111
One World Trade Center (107th Floor)	

Cent'anni	989-9494
50 Carmine Street (Bleecker/Bedford Sts.)	

Central Park	360-1333
59th–110th Streets between Fifth Avenue and Central Park West	

Central Park Zoo	439-6500

Century Club	944-0090
7 West 43rd Street	

Century Paramount Hotel	764-5500
235 West 46th Street (Broadway/Eighth Ave.)	

Cerutti	737-7540
807 Madison Avenue (67th/68th Sts.)	

Chalet Suisse	355-0855
6 East 48th Street (Fifth/Madison Aves.)	

Chandris Fantasy Cruises	223-3003
900 Third Avenue	1-800-621-3446

Chanel	355-5050
5 East 57th Street	

Chanterelle	966-6960
2 Harrison Street (Hudson St.)	

Charivari	333-4040
18 West 57th Street	

Charles Jourdan	644-3830
Trump Tower, 725 Fifth Avenue (56th/57th Sts.)	

Charlotte Moss	772-3320
131 East 70th Street	

Chateau Stables	828-4636
608 West 48th Street	

CHELSEA

With two notable exceptions, Chelsea offers little to attract visitors. Named for the estate of Captain Thomas Clarke that once covered most of the area, Chelsea stretches roughly from 14th to 30th Streets between Sixth Avenue and the Hudson River. Captain Clark's grandson, Clement Clarke Moore, author of *The Compendious Lexicon of the Hebrew Language*, is certainly better known for his less scholarly Christmas poem, "A Visit from St. Nicholas."

It's worth venturing down here to shop at Barney's (Seventh Ave. at 17th St.) for the latest in men's and women's clothing, or to attend a performance at the Joyce Theater (175 Eighth Ave. at 19th St.) by any of the innovative dance companies that make this their New York home.

Chelsea once attracted artists and writers—Mark Twain, O Henry, Tennessee Williams, Bob Dylan, Janis Joplin, and Sid Vicious are but a few of the many who lived at the landmark Chelsea Hotel (222 West 23rd St.). Now, alas, soaring real estate prices have driven all but the young professionals away.

Chelsea Hotel   243-3700
222 West 23rd Street (Seventh/Eighth Aves.)

Chequepoint USA   980-6443
551 Madison Avenue (55th St.)

Cherry Lane Theater   989-2020
38 Commerce Street

Chez Josephine   594-1925
414 West 42nd Street (Ninth/Tenth Aves.)

Chicago City Limits   772-8707
351 East 74th Street (First/Second Aves.)

Childcraft   753-3196
150 East 58th Street (Lexington/Third Aves.)

CHILDREN'S ACTIVITIES

Big Apple Circus   391-0767
Trump Tent, Damrosch Park
Lincoln Center (Broadway & 66th St.)
The holiday engagement (late October–early January) of this one-ring wonder features equestrian arts, acrobatics, legendary aerialists, and hilarious clowns.

Children's Museum of Manhattan   721-1234
The Tische Building
212 West 83rd Street (Broadway/Amsterdam Ave.)
Tuesday–Sunday 10:00 A.M.–5:00 P.M.
Thursday 3:00 P.M.–5:00 P.M
Admission:
Children & Adults $4.00
Free to students

Not really a museum, CMOM could be called a learning center. Built around a theme of "self-discovery" for children, exhibits and workshops contribute to a creative approach that draws 150,000 kids a year. Just reopened in new and larger quarters, the museum has four floors of exhibits in which children can actually participate. The most prominent of the permanent exhibits is The Brainatarium. This is a multimedia amphitheater in which visitors are introduced to the brain and how it works in conjunction with the five senses. There is a Media Center where children make their own video programs, an art studio, and a fascinating series of exhibits about patterns and how they affect us and our world.

While the name may be misleading, CMOM is an organization we'll be hearing a lot more about. Its concepts are exciting because they work. We would like to see enough funding made available from private sources so that they could lower their admission charges—$4.00 is too high for children.

Hayden Planetarium (American Museum of Natural History)   769-5919
Central Park West (81st St.)

The Wonderful Sky is a special program which uses the Sesame Street Muppets to explore all of the wonderful features of the sky. There is also a program for children ages 6 to 9. Called *The Secret of the Cardboard Rocket*, it is the story of a space voyage taken by two children in a rocket they make from cardboard. Both of these programs require advance reservations. Plan ahead and call for detailed information and prices.

Little People's Theater Company, The   765-9540
39 Grove Street

The repertory includes such classics as *Hansel and Gretel*, *Cinderella*, *Sleeping Beauty*, and *Goldilocks*. They also host birthday parties.

Museum of Broadcasting   752-7684
23 West 52nd Street
Admission:
Adults $4.00
Students $3.00
Senior citizens and Children (under 13) $2.00

On Saturday mornings from January through March, the museum offers a variety of workshops for children in which they participate in creating radio programs. Tickets are available on a first-come, first-served basis and cost $5.00 for both adults and children.

Special screenings of favorite children's books are held during the school year on Saturday afternoons. Kids love these great films. Be sure to phone for exact times.

Saturday October 14th–April 21st 12:30 P.M.–3:30 P.M.

Puppet Company, The   **741-1646**
31 Union Square West, Loft 2-B

South Street Seaport Children's
    Center   **669-9400**
165 John Street
    Open daily: 10:00 A.M.–5:00 P.M.
    Adults $5.00
    Children $2.00

Focuses on the use of an archaeological dig to explain to children the way artifacts from Manhattan's past are discovered and recovered.

Children's Museum of Manhattan   **721-1234**
212 West 83rd Street (Broadway/Amsterdam Ave.)

Chin Chin   **888-4555**
216 East 49th Street

China Grill   **333-7788**
60 West 53rd Street (Sixth Ave.)

CHINATOWN

The enormous influx of immigrants from Taiwan, mainland China, and Hong Kong have pushed the boundaries of Chinatown beyond its former borders of Baxter, Canal, the Bowery, and Worth Streets, into areas once considered parts of "Little Italy" and the Lower East Side. Wandering along Mott Street will give you a wonderful look at exotic groceries and clothing stores, and a chance to indulge in some of the city's most authentic (and cheapest!) Chinese food. During Chinese New Year celebrations (the first full moon after January 19th), fireworks displays, and dancing dragons abound.

Chinese Porcelain Co., The   **628-4101**
25 East 77th Street

Chippendale's   **935-6060**
1110 First Avenue (61st St.)
    Wednesday–Thursday 6:30 P.M.–4:00 A.M.
    Friday–Saturday 6:00 P.M.–4:00 A.M.
    Cover charge Wednesday through Friday is $25.00 and on Saturday $30.00; tickets are also available through Ticketron

The famous male strip joint where the women get a chance to act like animals. After 10:00 P.M. it becomes one of the most popular clubs on the East Side.

CHOCOLATE

Foucher Paris Chocolatier   **759-0027**
789 Lexington Avenue (61st St.)

Godiva
701 Fifth Avenue (55th St.)   **593-2845**
560 Lexington Avenue (50th St.)   **980-9810**
85 Broad Street   **514-6240**
The first and probably best known of European Chocolates, Godiva has suffered a decline in quality in recent years. Most of their candies are now made in the United States.

Hewyler Chocolates   **308-1311**
510 Madison Avenue (53rd St.)

Perugina Chocolate   **688-2490**
636 Lexington Avenue (54th St.)
Started by Signor Buitoni (yes, the spaghetti Buitoni), Perugina is best known for its Baci (Italian for "kisses"). The individual wrappings unfold to reveal secret messages of love.

Teuscher Chocolate
620 Fifth Avenue (49th/50th Sts.)   **246-4416**
25 East 61st Street   **751-8482**
Conveniently located just around the corner from The Pierre, Teuscher is the home of the best truffles in town, luscious bonbons flown in directly from Zurich. A label inside the box reminds the buyer that these fragile creme fraiche fillings have a shelf life of only 10 days. Fortunately, most chocaholics have no problem meeting this deadline.

Christ Cella   **697-2479**
160 East 46th Street (Lexington/Third Aves.)

Christ Church United Methodist   **838-3036**
520 Park Avenue

Christie's East Auction Gallery   **606-0400**
219 East 67th Street (Second/Third Aves.)

Christie's Fine Art Auctioneers   **546-1000**
502 Park Avenue (59th St.)

Church of All Souls   **535-5530**
Lexington Avenue (80th St.)

**Church of Jesus Christ of the
    Latter-Day Saints**   **595-1825**
2 Lincoln Center

Church's English Shoes   **755-4313**
428 Madison Avenue (49th St.)

CHURCHES

Assemblies of God

Glad Tidings Tabernacle   **563-4437**
325 West 33rd Street
    Sunday 3:30 P.M. & 6:30 P.M.
    Sunday School 2:15 P.M.

Baptist

Madison Avenue Baptist Church   **685-1377**
Madison Avenue at 31st Street
    Sunday 10:00 A.M.
    Church School 11:00 A.M. Worship Service

Catholic

St. Malachy's (The Actor's Chapel)   **489-1340**
239 West 49th Street
    Weekdays 7:00 A.M., 8:00 A.M., 12:10 P.M.
    Sunday 9:00 A.M., 11:00 A.M., 12:30 P.M., 5:00 P.M.
    Saturday 5:00 P.M.

St. Patrick's Cathedral   **753-2261**
Fifth Avenue at 50th Street
    Weekdays 7:00 A.M., 7:30 A.M., 8:00 A.M., 8:30 A.M.
    Noon, 12:30 P.M., 1:00 P.M., 5:30 P.M.
    Saturday 5:30 P.M.
    Sunday 7:00 A.M., 8:00 A.M., 9:00 A.M., 10:15 A.M., Noon,
    1:00 P.M., 4:00 P.M., 5:30 P.M.

Christian Science

Second Church of Christ, Scientist   **877-6100**
Central Park West at 68th Street
    Sunday Service 11:00 A.M.
    Sunday School 11:00 A.M.

Episcopal

**Cathedral Church of St. John the
    Divine**   **678-6888**
Amsterdam Avenue at 112th Street
    Sunday: H.C. 8:00 A.M. & 9:00 A.M.
    Sermon and H.C. 11:00 A.M.
    Choral Vespers 7:00 P.M.

St. Bartholomew's 751-1616
109 East 50th Street
Holy Eucharist, Sermon, Choir, 9:00 A.M., 11:00 A.M.

St. Thomas Church 757-7013
1 West 53rd Street (Fifth Ave.)
Sunday 8:00 A.M., 9:00 A.M., 11:00 A.M., 4:00 P.M. (October–May)

Trinity Church 602-0872
Broadway and Wall Street
Monday–Friday 7:45 A.M.
8:00 A.M., Noon, Holy Eucharist
5:15 P.M., Prayer
Saturday 8:45 A.M.
9:00 A.M., Holy Eucharist
Sunday 9:00 A.M., 11:15 A.M., Holy Eucharist

Greek Orthodox

Archdiocesan Cathedral of the Holy Trinity 288-3215
319 East 79th Street
Sunday Divine Liturgy 10:30 A.M.
Fellowship Hour: Noon

Inter-Denominational

The Riverside Church 222-5900
Riverside Drive at West 122nd Street
Sunday 10:45 A.M.

Jewish

East 55th Street Conservative Synagogue 752-1200
308 East 55th Street
Monday–Friday 9:00 A.M., Noon
Saturday Services at Sunset
Sunday 9:00 A.M., 5:15 P.M

Fifth Avenue Synagogue (Orthodox) 838-2122
5 East 62nd Street
Sabbath Evening Services at Sunset
Sabbath & Festival Mornings 9:00 A.M.

Temple Emanu-el (Reformed) 744-1400
Fifth Avenue at 65th Street
Friday 5:15 P.M.
Saturday 10:30 A.M.

Lutheran

St. Peter's Lutheran Church   935-2200
Lexington Avenue at 54th Street
    Sunday 8:45 & 11:00 A.M.
    Jazz Vespers: 5:00 P.M.

Holy Trinity Lutheran Church   877-6815
Central Park West at 65th Street
    Sunday 11:00 A.M.

Methodist

Christ Church United Methodist   838-3036
520 Park Avenue
    Sunday 11:00 A.M.
    Sunday School: 9:45 A.M.

Mormon

**Church of Jesus Christ of Latter-Day
    Saints**   595-1825
2 Lincoln Center
    Sunday 8:30 A.M., 10:30 A.M., 12:30 P.M.

Presbyterian

Fifth Avenue Presbyterian   247-0490
Fifth Avenue at 55th Street
    Sunday 11:00 A.M. and 4:00 P.M. (September–June)

First Presbyterian Church   675-6150
Fifth Avenue between 11th and 12th Streets
    Sunday 11:00 A.M.

Reformed

Marble Collegiate Church   686-2770
Fifth Avenue at 29th Street
    Sunday 11:00 A.M.

Unitarian

Church of All Souls   535-5535
Lexington Avenue at 80th Street
    Sunday 11:00 A.M.

Circle in the Square
1633 Broadway (50th St.)   581-0720
159 Bleecker Street   254-6330

Circle Line Sightseeing Yachts, Inc.   563-3200
Pier 83 (42nd St./The Hudson River)

Citicorp Center   559-2330
Lexington Avenue (54th St.)

City Center   246-8989
131 West 55th Street

City Hall   566-4074
Broadway (Murray St.)

City Lights Bar   938-1111
One World Trade Center (107th Floor)

Citykids   620-0120
130 Seventh Avenue (17th/18th Sts.)

Claremont Riding Academy   724-5100
175 West 89th Street

Classic Bookshop
1212 Avenue of the Americas   221-2252
133 World Trade Center Concourse   466-0668

Claridge   1-609-340-3400
Indiana Avenue and the Boardwalk (Atlantic City, NJ)

Clocktower, The   233-1096
108 Leonard Street

Cloisters, The   923-3700
Ft. Tryon Park

CLOTHING, CHILDREN'S

Au Chat Botte   772-7402
903 Madison Avenue (72nd & 73rd Sts.)
Exquisite, exclusive, and expensive dresses for lucky little girls.

Cerutti   737-7540
807 Madison Avenue (67th & 68th Sts.)

Citykids   620-0120
130 Seventh Avenue (17th & 18th Sts.)
Toys and accessories share this meticulous space with the exclusive designs by the in-house staff.

CLOTHING, MEN'S

Barney's   929-9000
Seventh Avenue and 17th Street
    Monday–Friday 10:00 A.M.–9:00 P.M.
    Saturday 10:00 A.M.–8:00 P.M.
    Sunday Noon–5:00 P.M.
They have the best of almost everything but are very expensive. Wait for the annual sales.

Brooks Brothers   682-8800
346 Madison Avenue (44th St.)
    Monday–Saturday 9:15 A.M.–6:00 P.M.
Classic rather than trendy, Brooks Brothers combines high prices with excellent quality and impeccable service.

Paul Stuart   682-0320
Madison Avenue at 45th Street
    Monday–Friday 8:00 A.M.–6:00 P.M.
    Saturday 9:00 A.M.–6:00 P.M.
Serious shoppers will find classic American clothes, and a large, helpful staff here. The women's department features a select assortment from sportswear to suits.

Ralph Lauren   606-2100
867 Madison Avenue (72nd St.)
Reasonable prices, a clubby atmosphere, and always tasteful.

Yves Saint Laurent Men's Boutique   371-7912
859 Madison Avenue (71st St.)
    Monday–Saturday 10:00 A.M.–6:00 P.M.
Well worth the high prices, St. Laurent's men's designs are timeless classics.

CLOTHING, MEN'S, DISCOUNT

Andrew Pallack   242-4412
85 Fifth Avenue
Prices here are about half of the suggested retail price.

BFO   254-0059
149 Fifth Avenue
A wonderland for shirts and ties. American and imported suits are available for approximately 60% below retail.

Eisenberg and Eisenberg   627-1290
85 Fifth Avenue
Free alterations on a full range of clothing at factory prices.

Gorsart Clothes   962-0024
9 Murray Street
Discounts of 20%–25% on suits, tuxedos, raincoats, shirts, and ties.

Harry Rothman   777-7400
200 Park Avenue South
50% markdowns and a good selection of big and tall sizes.

Moe Ginsburg   982-5254
162 Fifth Avenue

Offers a good variety of domestic and imported suits, overcoats, jackets, and slacks.

Saint Laurie, Ltd.   473-0100
897 Broadway
Classic apparel at top discount prices.

Sussex Clothes, Ltd.   279-4610
302 Fifth Avenue
Top quality suits, sports coats, and trousers at almost-wholesale prices.

CLOTHING, WOMEN'S, DISCOUNT

Altman   254-7275
135 Orchard Street
Top quality imports with some designer labels.

Bolton's
225 East 57th Street   755-2527
53 West 23rd Street   924-6860
Lots of closeouts and good discounts available on designer and medium-priced clothes.

Daffy's   529-4477
111 Fifth Avenue
Everything from sportswear to evening gowns at terrific discounts.

Damages   535-9030
768 Madison Avenue
Important European couturier names at unbelievable prices.

Labels for Less
639 Third Avenue   682-3330
130 West 48th Street   997-1032
Catering to young women, Labels for Less discounts clothing from 20% to 35%.

Loehmann's   543-6420
236th Street and Broadway, Riverdale
It's worth the trip out of Manhattan for Loehmann's fantastic savings, although it may take several trips to find the items you need.

S & W   924-6656
165 West 26th Street
Top discounts on a variety of merchandise from well-known manufacturers and American designers. Specialties include coats, gowns, handbags, and blouses.

Stanrose Dress Company   736-3358
141 West 36th Street

Calvin Klein labels are a favorite here. Discounts of 80% on new, seasonal merchandise.

J.S. Suarez   **315-5614**
26 West 54th Street
Sophisticated, top quality domestic and imported handbags and wallets at discounts up to 50%. Their quality is excellent.

Discount Shoes

You can find top-name shoes at discounts of 15%–30% at the following:

Lace-Up Shoe Shop   **475-8040**
110 Orchard Street

CLUBS, PRIVATE

Century Club   **944-0090**
7 West 43rd Street

Columbia Club   **757-2283**
3 West 51st Street

Cornell Club   **302-8238**
155 East 50th Street

Cosmopolitan Club   **734-5950**
122 East 66th Street

Dartmouth Club   **986-3232**
50 Vanderbilt Avenue

Harvard Club   **840-6600**
27 West 44th Street

Knickerbocker Club   **838-6700**
2 East 62nd Street

Metropolitan Club   **838-7400**
1 East 60th Street

New York Athletic Club   **247-5100**
180 Central Park South (Seventh Ave.)

New York University Club   **354-3400**
123 West 43rd Street

New York Yacht Club   **382-1000**
37 West 44th Street

Princeton Club 15 West 43rd Street	840-6400
Racket and Tennis Club 370 Park Avenue (53rd St.)	753-9700
River Club 447 East 52nd Street	751-0100
Union Club 101 East 69th Street	734-5400
Union League 38 East 37th Street	685-3800
University Club 1 West 54th Street	247-2100
Yale Club 50 Vanderbilt Avenue (45th St.)	661-2070

Coach House, The 110 Waverly Place (Washington Square Park/Sixth Ave.)	777-0303
Coach Leatherware 754 Madison Avenue (65th St.)	594-1581
Coast Guard	668-7000

COFFEE AND TEA

**McNulty's Tea and Coffee Company,
      Inc.**   242-5351
109 Christopher Street (Bleecker/Hudson Sts.)
    Monday–Saturday 11:00 A.M.–11:00 P.M.
    Sunday 1:00 P.M.–7:00 P.M.

Bare wooden floors, unadorned walls, and a 95-year-old tin ceiling contribute to the coziness of this Greenwich Village emporium. Probably the most prestigious and complete coffee house in New York, it's where we shop. They also carry a good selection of decaffeinated teas. When we travel, we take our own coffee pot and packages of our special McNulty blend.

Porto Rico Importing Company   477-5421
201 Bleecker Street
    Monday–Wednesday 9:30 A.M.–7:00 P.M.
    Thursday–Saturday 9:30 A.M.–9:00 P.M.
    Sunday Noon–7:00 P.M.

A family business since 1907, Longo's roasts its own beans and supplies such fine restaurants as Odeon and Cafe Luxembourg.

Sensuous Bean, The   724-7725
60 West 70th Street

Even if you can't afford dinner at Lutece, you can still treat yourself to their coffee—The Sensuous Bean's La Semeuse. The 19 different varieties of Swiss water process decaffeinated coffee available here reflect manager Frank Juliano's personal preferences, as do the many flavored coffees.

Balducci's and Zabar's (*See listing under* GOURMET SHOPS) offer an enormous variety of imported coffees. Nobody beats Zabar's prices.

Cohen Optical   751-6652
Lexington Avenue and 60th Street

Cole-Haan   421-8440
61st Street and Madison Avenue

Coliseum Books, Inc.   757-8381
1771 Broadway (57th St.)

Colombia (Consulate of)   949-9898
10 East 46th Street

Columbia Club   757-2283
3 West 51st Street

Columbia–Presbyterian Hospital   694-2500
Broadway and 168th Street

Columbus Raquet Club   663-6900
795 Columbus Avenue

Columbus Video   568-0123
529 Columbus Avenue

Comedy Cellar, The   254-3630
117 MacDougal Street (West 3rd/Bleecker Sts.)

COMEDY CLUBS

Caroline's at the Seaport   233-4900
89 South Street, Pier 17
This glitzy and glamorous room is booking the biggest names in comedy.
Sunday–Tuesday 8:00 P.M.
Wednesday–Thursday 8:00 P.M. & 10:00P.M.
Friday 8:00 P.M. & 10:30 P.M.
Saturday 7:00 A.M., 9:00 A.M., & 11:30 P.M.
Cover: $12.50–$17.50
Two drink minimum
AE, MC, V, & DC

Catch a Rising Star   794-1906
1487 First Avenue (77th/78th Sts.)

Neophytes hoping to launch careers perform here for customers eager to witness someone launching a career.

Sunday–Thursday 9:00 P.M.–1:00 A.M.
Friday 8:30 A.M. & 11:00 P.M.
Saturday 7:30 A.M. & 10:00P.M., 12:30 A.M.
Cover: $7.00–$12.00
Two drink minimum
AE

Chicago City Limits   772-8707
351 East 74th Street (First/Second Aves.)
Primarily an improvisational group, Chicago City Limits plays off audience suggestions.

Wednesday–Thursday 8:30 P.M.
Friday–Saturday 8:00 P.M. & 10:30 P.M.
Cover: $12.50–$15.00
No minimum
All major credit cards accepted

Comic Strip, The   861-9386
1568 Second Avenue
One of the top showcase clubs in Manhattan.

Sunday–Thursday 9:00 P.M.
Friday–Saturday 9:00 P.M. & 11:30 P.M.
Cover: $5.00–$12.00
Free on Monday
Two drink minimum
AE, MC, & V

Dangerfield's   593-1650
1118 First Avenue (61st/62nd Sts.)
Rodney does his cable specials from this smoke-filled hall of jeers.

Sunday–Thursday 9:15 P.M.
Friday 9:00 P.M. & 11:30 P.M.
Saturday 8:00 P.M. & 10:30 P.M., 12:30 A.M.
Cover: $10.00–$15.00
$7.00 minimum
All major credit cards accepted

Duplex   255-5438
61 Christopher Street at Sheridan Square
A tiny village room that once showcased Joan Rivers and David Brenner.

Friday–Saturday Midnight
Cover: $7.00
Two drink minimum

Improvisation   765-8268
358 West 44th Street (Ninth Ave.)

The oldest comedy showcase in Manhattan celebrated its 25th anniversary in 1988.

Sunday–Thursday 9:00 P.M.
Friday 9:00 P.M. & Midnight
Saturday 8:00 P.M. & 10:30 P.M., 12:40 A.M.
Cover: $7.00–$8.00
$7.00–$8.00 minimum
AE

Stand-Up New York   595-0850
236 West 78th Street (Broadway/Amsterdam Ave.)
This nice, clean club draws an Upper West Side crowd with three acts per show. Political comedy every Monday.

Sunday–Thursday 9:00 P.M.
Friday 8:30 A.M. & 11:30 P.M.
Saturday 8:00 P.M. & 10:00P.M., 12:15 A.M.
Cover: $7.00–$12.00
Two drink minimum
AE, MC, & V

Comfort Inn Murray Hill   947-0200
42 West 35th Street (Fifth/Sixth Aves.)

Comic Strip, The   861-9386
1568 Second Avenue

Commodities Exchange   938-2018
Four World Trade Center

Commuter Book Center, Inc.   599-1056
89 East 42nd Street (in Grand Central Station)

COMPACT DISCS
See **RECORDS/TAPES**

Complete Traveller Bookstore, The   679-4339
199 Madison Avenue (35th St.)

Computer Radio   1-718-886-8888

COMPUTERS
See **RENTALS, COMPUTERS**

Con Edison Emergency   683-8830

CONCERT HALLS

Alice Tully Hall   877-2011
Lincoln Center

Avery Fisher Hall   877-2011
Lincoln Center

Brooklyn Academy of Music   1-718-636-4100
30 Lafayette Avenue, Brooklyn

Carnegie Hall   247-7800
57th Street (Seventh Ave.)

Carnegie Recital Hall   247-7800
57th Street (Seventh Ave.)

Grace Rainey Rogers Auditorium   570-3949
Metropolitan Museum of Art, Fifth Avenue (82nd St.)

Kaufmann Auditorium   427-4410
92nd Street YM/YWHA, 1395 Lexington Avenue
(92nd St.)

Meekin Concert Hall   362-8719
127 West 67th Street

Metropolitan Opera House   362-6000
Lincoln Center

Radio City Music Hall   737-3100
1260 Avenue of the Americas

Town Hall   840-2824
123 West 43rd Street

CONCIERGE SERVICES

As any business person will tell you, it isn't easy being on the road all the time. The strain of handling details of actual travel arrangements combined with all the work one is supposed to be doing add enormously to the stress of one's job. The executives we've met who deal most successfully with travel problems have a secret weapon—the concierge. There is nothing mysterious about concierges. They are like any other tool you use—but you have to know how to use them. Like all tools, concierges come in various levels of quality and, in this case, competence. The best way to learn how to use this tool is just to start using it.

Don't be shy or afraid to talk to your concierge. Remember that they are used to dealing with thousands of people just like you. Whether you are the CEO of a major company or a tourist from Topeka, the concierge has dealt with many people who had precisely the same needs as you do. Also remember that because of the number of people they have seen, they can tell very quickly whether you are a tourist or a CEO and adjust their thinking accordingly. It's difficult to fool a concierge. Always take the direct approach.

When you have to travel, call the hotel in your destination city and ask for the concierge. Give the concierge your basic data: name, date of arrival, credit card information, and ask that the details of your visit be taken care of. This is the time to say you are a tourist and don't know the city or that you will find it necessary to entertain executives of another company. It gives the concierge a feeling for the level of service you will need and the amount of money you will spend to get it. If you are on a budget, say so; if money is not important, tell him or her that also. You don't have to mention money in so many words. If you say you want the best restaurant in town to entertain guests and limos to take you to and fro, the concierge will realize that money is no object.

The basic things that a concierge is called upon to arrange are few:

- Hotel reservations. At his or her hotel and at any others where you might stay during your trip—particularly if they are part of the same hotel chain. The concierge can call the concierges at the other hotels, alert them to your arrival and arrange for your needs to be taken care of. The fact that another concierge has called them establishes a challenge that they try very hard to meet.

- Limos to take you to and from the airport and to move you easily from one appointment to another. These are not necessarily a luxury item. In a city like New York, getting from one place to another can take a great deal of time if you don't know how to use public transportation. The expense can be worth it. If you want the convenience of a limo with less expense, ask the concierge if he or she can arrange for a radio car. Indicate that you want something cheaper than a limo and leave it up to the concierge. There's nothing wrong with saving money.

- Reservations at restaurants, shows, theaters, etc. (Give him or her as much leeway as possible with these because space availability is very fluid and he or she cannot be sure of getting your first choice.) When you are talking about tickets to a show, be sure to discuss a top price. It is important to the concierge to know what to spend on your behalf. If you really need tickets to a sold-out show, the concierge can probably get them if he or she can spend several times the face price of the tickets. In New York, it is not unusual to spend several hundred dollars for theater tickets to a popular show. If you want to save money, say so far in advance so they can be bought at the face price and still be the quality of ticket you desire.

- One of the greatest challenges traveling executives
  face involves correspondence from their offices. If
  you are expecting important mail, let the concierge
  know. Hotels get thousands of pieces of mail a day,
  and yours needs special attention. Have your office
  mark it "Hold for arrival" and "Attention Concierge." When you arrive at the hotel, check with
  the concierge to pick up whatever might have arrived and to give him instructions as to what to do
  with mail arriving after you leave.

Just by following these few suggestions, you will elimi-
nate a lot of the basic problems of travel. If you stop at this
level, you will have made your life a lot easier. But you can
go further. How sophisticated you decide to be with your
new tool is up to you. Your first challenge is to find a concierge with whom you feel a rapport. It's not as hard as you
think. It's like hiring a secretary—you want someone who
is not only efficient but who knows what you really want
no matter what you say to them. Once you find this paragon, be sure to give him or her as much information and
feedback as you can. If they are any good at their job they
will record this information and use it to give you the service you require. Most of the first class concierges we have
known prefer guests who are specific about what they
want and articulate about their likes and dislikes. If a restaurant is not up to your standards, tell the concierge. If
your limo service is not satisfactory, tell the concierge. Remember that concierges are in constant contact with the
owners of these companies and will relay complaints and
praise to them. It helps everybody.

You may have friends or business associates for whom
you would like to arrange a special welcome when they
check into a hotel. There are two ways of doing this. You
may call room service at the hotel and arrange for a fruit
basket, bottle of champagne, or wine and cheese tray. You
may also call the concierge and tell him or her what you
want. If the concierge thinks the room service amenities are
not satisfactory, he or she has the additional option of ordering flowers or sending out for balloons and chocolate.

If you have gone this far, you have learned how to get the
most out of your concierge. The nuances will follow natu-
rally. We've had guests who would call for all kinds of
things they needed even when they weren't coming to stay
in our hotel. We've had foreign guests call from other hotels
in our city because they preferred to deal with someone
who knew them rather than a stranger. A good concierge
welcomes and is flattered by this type of treatment. Taking

care of a guest's needs leads to business, both current and future, for the hotel where the concierge works, and both the concierge and the hotel management realize this.

There are a few things you should not do when dealing with a concierge. They are generally rather obvious.

1. Be direct with the concierge. If you want to know about a specific thing ask about that. Don't ask about the best Italian restaurants if you really want an opinion about a specific one. This may seem like a small thing to you, but the concierge has been through this many times each day.
2. Whatever you do, don't be a "no show." If the concierge has made reservations for you and you don't show up or cancel at the last minute he or she is in trouble. The restaurant or limo service holds the concierge responsible, and it affects his or her ability to make reservations in the future. It is a simple thing to call the concierge and cancel your reservation. The concierge realizes that plans change and is happy to accommodate you.
3. Don't forget to tip the concierge. Aside from the fact that people in the service industry are not well paid, the concierge has performed a service for you that has made your life easier and deserves to be recognized. You also must realize that the whole point of tipping is to get better service and more of it. You're competing with many other people for service.

By now you must have realized that the concierge can help you with almost anything if you can verbalize it. The simple rules are don't be shy, be direct, and be appreciative. Remember that people have asked us about everything in this book.

CONSULATES

Argentina	**397-1400**
12 West 56th Street	
Australia	**245-4000**
636 Fifth Avenue	
Austria	**737-6400**
31 East 69th Street	
Belgium	**586-5110**
50 Rockefeller Plaza	

CONSULATES

Bolivia   **687-0530**
211 East 43rd Street

Brazil   **757-3080**
630 Fifth Avenue

Canada   **757-4917**
1251 Sixth Avenue

Colombia   **949-9898**
10 East 46th Street

Costa Rica   **425-2620**
80 Wall Street

Cyprus   **686-6016**
13 East 40th Street

Dominican Republic   **265-0630**
17 West 60th Street

El Salvador   **889-3608**
46 Park Avenue

France   **606-3600**
934 Fifth Avenue

Germany   **940-9200**
460 Park Avenue

Greece   **988-5500**
60 East 79th Street

Haiti   **697-9767**
60 East 42nd Street

Honduras   **889-3858**
18 East 41st Street

Hungary   **879-4125**
8 East 75th Street

Iceland   **686-4100**
370 Lexington Avenue

India   **879-7800**
3 East 64th Street

Indonesia   **879-0600**
5 East 68th Street

Ireland   **319-2555**
515 Madison Avenue

Israel   **697-5500**
800 Second Avenue

Jamaica   **935-9000**
866 Second Avenue

Japan	**986-1600**
280 Park Avenue	
Jordan	**759-1950**
86 United Nations Plaza	
Korea	**752-1700**
460 Park Avenue	
Lebanon	**744-7905**
9 East 76th Street	
Mexico	**689-0456**
8 East 41st Street	
Monaco	**759-5227**
845 Third Avenue	
Morocco	**758-2625**
437 Fifth Avenue	
Netherlands	**246-1429**
1 Rockefeller Plaza	
New Zealand	**586-0060**
630 Fifth Avenue	
Nicaragua	**247-0120**
1270 Fifth Avenue	
Nigeria	**715-7272**
575 Lexington Avenue	
Pakistan	**879-5800**
12 East 65th Street	
Panama	**246-3771**
1270 Sixth Avenue	
Peru	**644-2850**
805 Third Avenue	
Philippines	**764-1330**
556 Fifth Avenue	
Poland	**889-8360**
233 Madison Avenue	
Portugal	**246-4580**
630 Fifth Avenue	
Saudi Arabia	**752-2740**
866 United Nations Plaza	
Spain	**355-4080**
150 East 58th Street	
Sweden	**751-5900**
825 Third Avenue	

Switzerland	**758-2560**
444 Madison Avenue	
Turkey	**247-5309**
821 United Nations Plaza	
United Kingdom	**752-5747**
845 Third Avenue	
Venezuela	**826-1660**
7 East 51st Street	
Yugoslavia	**838-2300**
767 Third Avenue	

Continental Airlines	**1-718-565-1100**
Cooper-Hewitt Museum	**860-6868**
2 East 91st Street	
Cornell Club	**302-8238**
155 East 50th Street	
Cort Theater	**239-6200**
138 West 48th Street	
Cosmopolitan Club	**734-5950**
122 East 66th Street	
Costa Rica (Consulate of)	**425-2620**
80 Wall Street	

COSTUMES

See **RENTALS, COSTUMES**

Crepes Suzette	**581-9717**
363 West 46th Street (Eighth/Ninth Aves.)	
Crime Victims Hotline	**577-7777**
Criterion Cabaret	**239-6200**
1530 Broadway (45th St.)	
Crosstown Tennis	**947-5780**
14 West 31st Street (Fifth Ave.)	
Crouch & Fitzgerald	**755-5888**
400 Madison Avenue	
Cunard Line	**661-7777**
555 Fifth Avenue (46th St.)	
Cyprus (Consulate of)	**686-6016**
13 East 40th Street	

D

D & D Building
979 Third Avenue

International Design Center of
  New York   **1-718-937-7474**
Main Building: 30-20 Thompson Avenue, Long Island
City, Queens
> Hours 9:00 A.M.–5:00 P.M.
> Shuttle Buses to IDCNY
>> 919 Third Avenue (56th St. between Second/Third
>> Aves.)
>>> Departures every 20 minutes from 8:00 A.M.–6:30 P.M.
>>> Dot Zero Store, 22nd Street and Fifth Avenue
>>> Departures every hour on the hour 10:00 A.M.–4:00 P.M.

American Society of Interior
  Designers   **685-3480**

Dakota, The
1 West 72nd Street (Central Park West)

Damages   **535-9030**
768 Madison Avenue

DANCING

Over a dozen new clubs opened in Manhattan in 1989,
ranging in style from the cozy Delia's to the enormous Red
Zone. The popularity of these places is ephemeral, but the
following are our best bets.

Au Bar   **308-9455**
41 East 58th Street
> Every Night 9:00 P.M.–4:00 A.M.
> Cover Charge:
> Sunday–Thursday $10.00
> Friday & Saturday $15.00

Similar in decor to Nell's (fake English country estate)
with a decidedly Uptown clientele.

The Baja   **724-8890**
246A Columbus Avenue (71st/72nd Sts.)
> Tuesday–Saturday 9:30 P.M.–4:00 A.M.
> Admission:
> Tuesday–Wednesday $5.00
> Thursday–Saturday $10.00

A casual, comfortable club catering to a young crowd on the gentrified Upper West Side. Besides an unusually large kidney-shaped dance floor, it features two side wing areas actually conducive to conversation. Music ranges from the 1950s to the 1990s. No minimum. AE credit card accepted at the bar only.

Delia's   254-9184
197 East Third Street
    Tuesday–Saturday 7:00 P.M.–4:00 A.M.
    Admission Friday & Saturday $5.00
Artists, writers, actors, and young professionals frequent this small and romantic club on the Lower East Side.

Heartbreak   691-2388
179 Varick Street (Houston St.)
    Open 7 days 9:30 P.M.–4:30 A.M.
    Admission $15.00
By day a diner, after dinner hour Heartbreak is transformed into a haven for fans of 1950s and 1960s music. There's a live band on Monday.

Limelight   807-7850
660 Avenue of the Americas (20th/21st Sts.)
    Open 7 days 10:00 P.M.–4:00 A.M.
    Admission:
    Sunday–Thursday $15.00
    Friday–Saturday $18.00
Formerly the Episcopal Church of the Holy Communion, Limelight boasts original Tiffany windows and 35 video monitors.

Mars   691-6262
28 Tenth Avenue (13th St.)
    Thursday–Sunday 10:00 P.M.–4:00 A.M.
    Admission:
    Thursday & Sunday $11.00
    Friday & Saturday $16.00
Each floor of this multistory extravaganza offers a different visual theme and style of music, ranging from avant-garde psychedelic to movie soundtracks. The crowd at this former meat-packing plant is as eclectic as the surroundings, so be prepared.

Maxim's   751-5111
680 Madison Avenue (61st St.)
This Belle Epoque restaurant offers dancing to the Maxim's Orchestra.
    Tuesday–Thursday from 9:00 P.M.
    Friday & Saturday from 10:00 P.M.

M.K.   **779-1340**
204 Fifth Avenue
 Monday–Thursday 10:00 P.M.–3:00 A.M.
 Friday–Saturday 10:00 P.M.–4:00 A.M.
 Admission:
 Monday–Thursday $5.00
 Friday–Saturday $15.00
One of the latest hot spots, this is a typical dance club in that the snob appeal of standing in line and hoping they will let you give them your money seems to draw a big crowd and the usual "celebrities" who supposedly frequent these places. We've yet to have one celebrity ask us about a dance club.

Nell's   **675-1567**
246 West 14th (Seventh/Eighth Aves.)
 Open 7 days 10:00 P.M.–4:00 A.M.
 Admission:
 Sunday–Thursday $5.00
 Friday–Saturday $10.00
For a short time this was one of the hottest clubs. Co-owned by Nell Campbell, it had its moment in the sun, and you shouldn't have much trouble getting in now.

Nell's resembles a Victorian gentleman's private club, complete with overstuffed sofas and gilded mirrors. A jazz trio performs upstairs. An understated dance floor occupies the lower level.

Palladium   **473-7171**
126 East 14th Street (Park Ave.)
 Tuesday–Saturday 10:00 P.M.–4:00 A.M.
 Admission:
 Monday–Thursday $15.00
 Friday–Saturday $20.00
Giant murals by some of New York's trendiest young artists adorn the walls of this converted theater. State-of-the-art video screens and disco technology made this one of the instant "in" places. Although still very popular, it no longer is first choice of the night people.

Rainbow Room   **632-5000**
30 Rockefeller Plaza
 Tuesday–Saturday 5:00 P.M.–1:00 A.M.
Restored to 1930s elegance, the Rainbow Room is everyone's dream of a posh supper club. It has been the hottest spot in town since it reopened after a two-year renovation. Dinner reservations are accepted six weeks in advance and sell out immediately.

Red Blazer, Too   262-3112
349 West 46th Street (Eighth/Ninth Aves.)
 Open until 4:00 A.M.
Monday through Wednesday, it's big band music with a
swing beat. Thursday through Saturday, the Dixie combos
take over. On Sunday, dancing starts at the Jazz Brunch
(1:00 P.M.–5:00 P.M.) and continues until 9:00 P.M. There's
never a cover or admission charge; you simply buy a drink
at the bar, or, if you're at a table but not dining, pay a two
drink minimum.

Red Zone   582-2222
440 West 54th Street
 Wednesday–Saturday 10:00 P.M.–4:30 A.M.
 Cover:
 Wednesday–Thursday $10.00
 Friday–Saturday $15.00
 No cover with dinner
Take your choice: you can dance on the ground floor's
10,000 square-foot dance floor complete with lasers,
strobes, and fog machines, or relax upstairs in a sound-
proof, red-walled restaurant. The crowd is eclectic.

Regine's   826-0990
502 Park Avenue (59th St.)
 Monday–Saturday 11:00 P.M.–4:00 A.M.
 Cover:
 Monday–Thursday $15.00
 Friday–Saturday $20.00
 All major credit cards accepted
The most elegant of dance clubs, Regine's is a survivor—
twelve years of successfully appealing to the fickle tastes of
New Yorkers and international visitors. Dinner is served
from 7:30 P.M. until Midnight. At 11:00 P.M., hand-painted
screens are opened to reveal the dance floor.

Roma di Notte   832-1128
137 East 55th Street (Lexington/Third Aves.)
 Monday–Saturday 6:00 P.M.–2:00 A.M.
Enjoy delicious Northern Italian cuisine while being
entertained by a quartet performing songs in four lan-
guages.

Roseland Ballroom   247-0200
239 West 52nd Street
 Ballroom dancing:
 Thursday & Sunday 2:30 P.M.–Midnight
 Saturday 2:30 P.M.–11:00 P.M.
 Disco:
 Friday 10:00 P.M.–4:00 A.M.

Saturday 11:00 P.M.–4:00 A.M.
Admission varies

This enormous landmark dance hall seeks to please both the trendy and the traditionalist.

Stringfellow's   254-2444
35 East 21st Street (Park Ave. & Broadway)

This elegant private supper club opens its doors to non-members nightly at 11:30 P.M. Even if you're old enough to vote, you won't feel out of place here.

1018   645-5157
515 West 18th Street (Tenth Ave.)
    Thursday, Friday, Saturday 10:18 P.M.–5:00 A.M.
    Admission:
    Thursday $10.00
    Friday–Saturday $15.00

This 18,000 square foot dance hall in what used to be the Roxy Theater avoids the usual dance club claustrophobia and features a soundproof lounge and balcony.

Tunnel, The   244-6444
220 Twelfth Avenue (27th St.)
    Wednesday–Sunday 10:00 P.M.–4:00 A.M.
    Admission:
    Wednesday–Thursday $15.00
    Friday–Saturday $20.00
    Sunday $10.00

It's worth a visit just to see the fantastic use of this cavernous space—an old railroad tunnel.

View, The   704-8900
1535 Broadway (45th St.)

As you revolve on the dance floor, the dance floor revolves, too. High above New York, this is the city's only revolving lounge and restaurant. The decor is simple and elegant and does not attempt to compete with the beautiful view. Live entertainment and an upscale crowd make this a good choice to impress that special date.

World Trade Center   938-1111
For a mere $3.50 cover charge, plus whatever you choose to drink, you can glide around the dance floor at either the **City Lights Bar** or the **Hors d'Oeuvrerie**. The views from both are spectacular.

Dangerfield's   593-1650
1118 First Avenue (61st/62nd Sts.)

Darbar   432-7227
44 West 56th Street (Fifth/Sixth Aves.)

Darrow's Fun Antiques	838-0730
309 East 61st Street (First/Second Aves.)	
Dartmouth Club	986-3232
50 Vanderbilt Avenue (50th St.)	
David Webb	421-3030
7 East 57th Street	
Davidoff of Geneva	489-5580
535 Madison Avenue (54th St.)	
Days Inn—New York	581-8100
440 West 57th Street	
Deak International, Inc.	
630 Fifth Avenue	757-6915
1 Herald Square (Sixth Avenue/33rd/34th St.)	736-9790
Dean & DeLuca	431-1691
121 Prince Street	
Delia's	254-9184
197 East Third Street	

DELIS

Carnegie Deli   757-2245
854 Seventh Avenue (54th/55th Sts.)
Our favorite deli anywhere! What a way to gain weight! Aside from our own opinion, everyone agrees that this is the best deli in New York!

New York Delicatessen   541-8320
104 West 57th Street (Sixth Ave.)
There is nothing to recommend this deli except the fact that it is open 24 hours a day. We list it only because tourists do ask for it.

Second Avenue Kosher Delicatessen   677-0606
156 Second Avenue (10th St.)
McDowell lived on their soups one year when he just couldn't get rid of a cold. Fight your way through the crowd waiting at the takeout counter and be prepared for the traditional gruff waiter who's been there forever. The sandwiches are humongous, and the food is delicious.

Stage Deli   245-7850
834 Seventh Avenue (53rd/54th Sts.)
The least of the famous New York delis. Why go here when Carnegie is only a block away?

DELIVERY SERVICES

How did we ever survive before Federal Express? These services are indispensable for today's fast-paced business. Even if you don't have a business account with them, it's possible to charge delivery to a major credit card.

DHL Worldwide Express	**1-718-719-8000**
	1-718-417-3000
	1-718-995-8132

Federal Express
To arrange for pick up call: **777-6500**
The main office, at 42nd Street and Eleventh Avenue, is open weekdays until 9:30 P.M.

Purolator Courier	**333-5560**
	1-800-645-3333
	233-7233

United Parcel Service **695-7500**
643 West 43rd Street
Open daily 8:30 A.M.–5:30 P.M.
$4.00 pick-up charge
$1.90 C.O.D. charge
70 lbs. limit per package
Package size cannot exceed 108 inches, length and girth combined.

Delta Airlines **239-0700**

DEPARTMENT STORES
See also **STORES**

Alexander's **593-0880**
731 Lexington Avenue (59th St.)
Monday–Saturday 10:00 A.M.–9:00 P.M.
Sunday Noon–5:00 P.M.
The most economical of the major department stores.

A & S **594-8500**
33rd Street and Avenue of the Americas
Monday, Thursday, Friday 9:45 A.M.–8:30 P.M.
Tuesday, Wednesday 9:45 A.M.–6:45 P.M.
Saturday 10:00 A.M.–6:45 P.M.
Sunday 10:00 A.M.–6:00 P.M.
The first department store to open in Manhattan in 20 years, A & S is the center of a glittery, art deco retail mall that will eventually house 125 stores. Moderate prices attract loyal customers to browse through eight floors.

Barney's   **929-9000**
106 Seventh Avenue (17th St.)
    Monday–Friday 10:00 A.M.–9:00 P.M.
    Saturday 10:00 A.M.–8:00 P.M.
    Sunday Noon–5:00 P.M.
Long known as one of the city's largest men's clothing
stores, Barney's now has one floor devoted exclusively to
women's clothing. They run the gamut from punk to exclusive designer fashions. Very expensive, except at sale time,
when you can save up to 70%.

Bergdorf Goodman   **753-7300**
754 Fifth Avenue (57th St.)
    Monday–Saturday 10:00 A.M.–6:00 P.M.
    Thursday 10:00 A.M.–8:00 P.M.
There is only one Bergdorf Goodman, and this is it. Designer fashions, gorgeous furs and a branch of the
Kentshire Galleries with antique jewelry are some of the
delights here. Everything is of the highest quality—priced
to match.

Bloomingdale's   **355-5900**
1000 Third Avenue (59th St.)
    Monday & Thursday 10:00 A.M.–9:00 P.M.
    Tuesday, Wednesday, Friday, & Saturday 10:00 A.M.–
    6:30 P.M.
    Sunday Noon–6:00 P.M.
New York's trendiest department store. For a special
treat, call their Personal Shopper (705-3030) for a one-on-
one shopping spree. This is particularly helpful if you are
short on time.

Henri Bendel   **247-1100**
10 West 57th Street
    Monday–Saturday 10:00 A.M.–6:00 P.M.
    Thursday 10:00 A.M.–8:00 P.M.

Lord & Taylor   **391-3344**
424 Fifth Avenue (38th St.)
    Monday–Saturday 10:00 A.M.–6:00 P.M.
    Thursday 10:00 A.M.–8:00 P.M.

Macy's   **971-6000**
34th Street and Sixth Avenue
    Monday, Thursday, Friday 9:45 A.M.–8:30 P.M.
    Tuesday, Wednesday 9:45 A.M.–6:45 P.M.
    Saturday 9:45 A.M.–6:00 P.M.
    Sunday 10:00 A.M.–6:00 P.M.

Occupying an entire city block, Macy's outlasted its competitors and celebrated its 85th year in 1988. From salami to sable, Macy's has it all.

Saks Fifth Avenue   **753-4000**
611 Fifth Avenue (50th St.)
    Monday–Saturday 10:00 A.M.–6:00 P.M.
    Thursday 10:00 A.M.–8:00 P.M.

DHL   **1-718-417-3000**

Dial-a-Secretary   **348-9575**

DIAMOND DISTRICT

This is a fascinating part of town to visit. Few people are immune to the seduction of gemstones and gold, and those are the commodities to be found here. A word of caution—if you are not a jewelry expert, you can easily be cheated. There are many stories of dealers who fleece the unwary, so be sure to get an independent appraisal of expensive stones. The Gemological Institute of America is the most reliable. The appraiser used by the jeweler in question is the least reliable.

Rennie Ellen   **869-5525**
15 West 47th Street (Room 401)
    Monday–Friday 10:00 A.M.–4:30 P.M.
    By appointment only
The first woman diamond dealer in the male-dominated diamond district, Rennie Ellen has built her reputation on scrupulous honesty and integrity. She teaches her customers to analyze color, quality, and grading before making a selection. Rennie's work as a consumer's advocate earned her the unofficial title of "Mayor of 47th Street," and her enormous mail-order business testifies to the absolute faith people have in her. If you visit only one store, make it this one.

Jan Skala   **246-2942**
1 West 47th Street
    Monday–Saturday 9:30 A.M.–5:00 P.M.
One of the few dealers who is not averse to retail customers, Skala offers diamonds, pocket watches, and a good selection of Russian enamels.

Jewelry Exchange, The
15 West 47th Street (between Fifth & Sixth Aves.)
Monday–Saturday 10:00 A.M.–5:30 P.M.

Forty separate shops at one location make your shopping easy. Prices are low as usual in the Diamond District where the middleman is eliminated.

Myron Toback   398-8300
25 West 47th Street (Fifth/Sixth Aves.)
    Monday–Friday 8:30 A.M.–4:00 P.M.
    Closed the first two weeks in July, December 25th, and January 1st.
Located in an arcade that specializes in retail sales, Toback is excellent source for gold, gold-filled, and silver chains sold by the foot. You will find astonishing prices on gold and silver earrings.

DISCOS
See **DANCING**

Dish of Salt   921-4242
133 West 47th Street (Sixth/Seventh Aves.)

Doctors Hospital   870-9000
East End Avenue and 87th Street

Dollhouse Antics   876-2288
1308 Madison Avenue (92nd/93rd Sts.)

DOLLS

**Iris Brown's Victorian Doll and
    Miniature Shop**   593-2882
253 East 57th Street (at Second Ave.)

Dollhouse Antics   876-2288
1308 Madison Avenue (92nd/93rd Sts.)
    Monday–Saturday 11:00 A.M.–5:30 P.M.
    Closed Saturday–Monday in summer

Dollsanddreams   876-2434
1421 Lexington Avenue (92nd/93rd Sts.)
    Monday–Friday 10:30 A.M.–6:00 P.M.

New York Doll Hospital, The   838-7527
787 Lexington Avenue (61st/62nd Sts.)
    Monday–Saturday 10:00 A.M.–6:00 P.M.
The only people in America trusted enough to repair Hazel, the 150-year old doll of one of Adele's favorite guests at The Pierre.

Dollsanddreams   876-2434
1421 Lexington Avenue (92nd/93rd Sts.)

Domenico Bus Service	**1-718-442-8666**

Dominican Republic (Consulate of)   265-0630
17 West 60th Street

Don't Tell Mama   757-0788
343 West 46th Street (Eighth/Ninth Aves.)

Doral Court Hotel   685-1100
130 East 39th Street

Doral Inn   755-1200
Lexington Avenue (49th St.)

Doral Park Avenue   687-7050
70 Park Avenue

Doral Tuscany   686-1600
39th Street (east of Park Ave.)

Dorset Hotel   247-7300
30 West 54th Street

Double Image Repertory Co.   245-2489
304 West 47th Street

Doubleday
724 Fifth Avenue (57th St.)   397-0550
Citicorp Center (Third Ave./53rd St.)   223-3301

Douglas Fairbanks Theater   239-4321
432 West 42nd Street

Dow Jones Report   976-4141

Drake Swissotel   421-0900
440 Park Avenue

Drama Book Shop, Inc.   944-0595
723 Seventh Avenue (2nd Floor, between 48th/49th Sts.)

DRUG STORES, TWENTY-FOUR HOUR

Kaufman Pharmacy   755-2266
Lexington Avenue and 50th Street
    Open 24 hours a day, 7 days a week

Duplex   255-5438
61 Christopher Street at Sheridan Square

Dutchess II, The   242-1408
70 Grove Street (Sheridan Square)

E

East 34th Street Heliport	1-800-645-3494
East 34th Street (East River)	
East Hampton Air	1-516-537-0560
East Side Antiques, Flea & Farmer's	
Market	737-8888
Eastern Airlines	986-5000
Eastern Onion	741-0006
39 West 14th Street	
Eastgate Tower Hotel	687-8000
222 East 39th Street (Second/Third Aves.)	
Edison Hotel	840-5000
228 West 47th Street (Broadway/Eighth Ave.)	
Edwardian Room	759-3000
The Plaza, Fifth Avenue and 59th Street	
Eeyore's Books for Children	
2212 Broadway (79th St.)	362-0634
25 East 83rd Street (Madison Ave.)	988-3404
Egypt Air	581-5600
Eisenberg and Eisenberg	627-12906
85 Fifth Avenue	
El Al	768-9200
El Salvador (Consulate of)	889-3608
46 Park Avenue	
Elaine's	534-8103
1703 Second Avenue (88th/89th Sts.)	
Elizabeth Arden	407-1000
691 Fifth Avenue (54th St.)	
Elysee Hotel	753-1066
60 East 54th Street	

EMBASSIES

Embassies are located in Washington, DC. For the representatives of foreign governments in New York City see the listing under Consulates.

Embassy Suites Times Square	1-800-362-2779
Broadway at 47th Street	

EMERGENCIES

AAA Road Service	757-3356

Ambulance	**911**
Coast Guard	**668-7936**
Con Edison	**683-8830**
Crime Victims Hotline	**577-7777**
Fire	**911**
FBI	**335-2700**
Poison Control Center	**764-7667**
Police	**911**
Rape Hotline	**267-7273**
U.S. Secret Service	**466-4400**

Empire Diner   **243-2736**
210 Tenth Avenue (22nd St.)

Empire Hotel, The   **265-7400**
44 West 63rd Street

Empire State Building   **736-3100**
350 Fifth Avenue (34th St.)

Endicott Booksellers   **787-6300**
450 Columbus Avenue (81st/82nd Sts.)

Enticer Motor Yacht Corporation   **354-8844**
500 Fifth Avenue

Entrepreneur Yacht Charters Corp.   **722-2386**

Epirotiki Lines   **599-1750**
551 Fifth Avenue

Esplanade Hotel, The   **874-5000**
304 West End Avenue (74th St.)

Essex House   **247-0300**
160 Central Park South

Eugene O'Neill Theater   **246-0220**
230 West 49th Street

Eze   **691-1140**
254 West 23rd Street (Seventh/Eighth Ave.)

F

F.A.O. Schwartz   **644-9400**
767 Fifth Avenue (58th St.)

F.R. Tripler	**922-1090**
300 Madison Avenue (46th St.)	
Fanelli Antique Timepieces, Ltd.	**517-2300**
1131 Madison Avenue	
Farrell's Limousines	**860-4200**
Fat Tuesday's	**533-7902**
190 Third Avenue (17th St.)	

FAX

The FAX machine is rapidly replacing the post office for many businessmen and their companies. Most hotels now offer this service to their guests and, while it is expensive, many find the speed of transmitting documents worth the price. Some of the private companies who offer FAX service are listed below.

A-Fax International	**489-7307**
990 Sixth Avenue (36th St.)	
Executive Telex Service, Ltd.	**732-2252**
116 Nassau Street	**1-800-4 A TELEX**
Telex: 226000 ETLX UR	**FAX: 212-619-1545**
12041 XAS NYK	
Cable: TELEXCOM	
Telex and Fax	**949-0722**
237 Park Avenue	
Domestic and International	
24 hours a day, 7 days a week	
Federal Bureau of Investigation (FBI)	**335-2700**
Federal Express	**777-6500**
Eleventh Avenue and 42nd Street	
Federal Hall National Monument	**264-8711**
26 Wall Street	
Federal Reserve Bank of New York	**720-6130**
33 Liberty Street	
Fendi	**767-0100**
720 Fifth Avenue (56th St.)	

FERRIES

Staten Island Ferry	**806-6940**
St. George Ferry Terminal, Battery Park	
Subway: IRT #1 to South Ferry	

Monday through Friday during peak hours, the ferries depart every 20 minutes starting at 7:30 A.M. Saturday and Sunday, the ferry departs every half hour from 9:30 A.M.–9:30 P.M., then every hour on the hour.

Still New York's biggest bargain, the Staten Island Ferry runs 24 hours a day and provides a wonderful view of the Statue of Liberty. Round-trip costs just $.50. Take the boat to Staten Island and back. Don't look at the New York skyline until the return trip. It's a great experience to watch New York gradually loom larger and larger as you get closer. This is one of the best ways to experience the effect of being swallowed by the metropolis. Go to Wall Street as soon as you dock if you want to experience the total feeling of being dominated by tall buildings. It's a feeling you won't get in any other city.

Liberty Ferry	**806-6940**
Battery Park	**269-5755**

Starts at 9:15 A.M. and runs every hour on the hour until 4:00 P.M.
Fares:
Children $1.50 (under 11 Free)
Adults $3.25

Fifth Avenue Presbyterian Church	**247-0490**
Fifth Avenue (55th St.)	

Fifth Avenue Synagogue (Jewish Orthodox)	**838-2122**
5 East 62nd Street	

Fine and Klein	**674-6720**
119 Orchard Street	

Fire Emergency Number	**911**

First Presbyterian Church	**675-6150**
Fifth Avenue (11th/12th Sts.)	

FLEA MARKETS

Annex Antiques and Flea Market	**1-718-965-1076**

Avenue of the Americas at 26th Street
Every Sunday, April–November 10:00 A.M.–6:00 P.M.
Admission $1.00

For over 22 years, dealers have purveyed jewelry, vintage clothing and linens, Oriental rugs, Victoriana, Depression glass, Chinese porcelains, and African art at this outdoor market.

Canal Street Flea Market   226-7541
Canal and Greene Streets
    Saturday & Sunday, year round 10:00 A.M.–6:00 P.M.

Between 50 and 60 dealers set up here with turn-of-the-century quilt tops, 1940s Fiestaware, coins, stamps, records, and the ubiquitous tweed overcoats.

Market I.S. 44   923-5016
Columbus Avenue at 78th Street
    Every Sunday, year round 10:00 A.M.–6:00 P.M.

Considered by many as the place to Sunday browse and buy, this antique, flea, and green market offers nearly 200 dealers. Inside the cafeteria and outside in the schoolyard, you can find new merchandise (blank tapes, tube socks, hats), old jewelry, vintage clothing, Oriental rugs, and English Hallmark silver. Fresh produce, cheeses, and breads are displayed at the colorful greenmarket. Proceeds fund children's after-school projects.

East Side Antiques, Flea & Farmer's
    Market   737-8888
    Every Saturday, year round 9:00 A.M.–5:00 P.M.

There's something for everyone at this eclectic indoor and outdoor market. Fresh fruit, flowers and plants, cheeses, and smoked meats vie for attention with Oriental rugs, used clothing, and jewelry. Books, handwoven rugs, silk scarves, blank tapes, and baked goods complete the assortment.

Florian Papp   288-6770
962 Madison Avenue

FLORISTS

Every hotel has its own arrangement for providing flowers—either there is a florist on the premises or nearby. But there is only one florist open all of the time. They can also provide balloons.

Rialto Florists   688-3234
707 Lexington Avenue (57th/58th Sts.)
    Open 24 hours a day, 7 days a week
    Order by phone
    All major credit cards accepted

Flower Fifth Avenue Hospital   860-8000
Fifth Avenue and 106th Street

Flutie's   693-0777
Pier 17, South Street Seaport

Folk Music Line   666-9605

Footlight Records 113 East 12th Street	**533-1572**
Forbes Galleries 62 Fifth Avenue (12th St.)	**206-5548**
Forbidden Planet 821 Broadway (11th/12th Sts.) 227 East 59th Street	**473-1576** **751-4386**

FOREIGN CURRENCY EXCHANGE

Deak International
630 Fifth Avenue **757-6915**
1 Herald Square (Sixth Ave. between
33rd/34th Sts.) **736-9790**

Chequepoint USA **980-6443**
551 Madison Avenue (55th St.)
Foreign currency exchange services, check cashing, and
sales of bank drafts and cable services.
Monday–Friday 8:00 A.M.–6:00 P.M.
Saturday & Sunday 10:00 A.M.–6:00 P.M.

Harold Reuter & Co., Inc. **661-0826**
Pan Am Building, Third Floor East, Room 332
Monday–Friday 8:30 A.M.–4:00 P.M.

Manfra, Tordella & Brokes, Inc. **621-9555**
Rockefeller Plaza, 59 West 49th Street
Monday–Friday 8:30 A.M.–4:30 P.M.

FORMAL WEAR

See **RENTALS, FORMAL WEAR, MEN** and **RENTALS,
FORMAL WEAR, WOMEN**

Fortune Garden Pavilion 209 East 49th Street	**753-0101**
Fortunoff 681 Fifth Avenue	**343-8787**
47th Street Photo 67 West 47th Street (Sixth/Seventh Aves.)	**398-1410**
Foucher Paris Chocolatier 789 Lexington Avenue (61st St.)	**759-0027**
Foul Play Books of Mystery & Suspense 10 Eighth Avenue (12th St.)	**675-5115**

Four Seasons	**754-9494**
99 East 52nd Street (Lexington/Park Aves.)	
France (Consulate of)	**606-3600**
934 Fifth Avenue	
Franklin Furnace Archive	**925-4671**
112 Franklin Street	
Fraunces Tavern Museum	**425-1778**
54 Pearl Street (at Broad St.)	
Fred Leighton	**288-1872**
781 Madison Avenue (66th St.)	

FREE THINGS

In New York, almost nothing is completely free. If people want something, other people will put a price on it. But while it is undoubtedly most enjoyable to see New York on $500 a day, it's possible to be entertained, educated, and titillated without spending too much. Even jaded native New Yorkers may wish to partake of the Big Apple's free and nearly free offerings. (After all, since you're paying astronomical rents and taxes to live here, you're surely entitled to some compensation.)

AT & T Infoquest Center   **605-5555**
550 Madison Avenue
    Tuesday 10:00 A.M.–9:00 P.M.
    Wednesday–Sunday 10:00 A.M.–6:00 P.M.
    Closed Monday
Learn about the information technologies of the future such as fiber optics, holograms, robotonics, voice recognition, and artificial intelligence.

Beaches
Coney Island and the Rockaways are among the most popular of New York City's fifteen miles of beaches and can easily be reached by public transportation. A stroll along the three-mile boardwalk at Coney Island to Brighton Beach, the Russian enclave called "Odessa by the Sea," is pleasant in any season.

Brooklyn Botanic Garden   **1-718-622-4433**
1000 Washington Avenue
Covering 52 acres, this outstanding botanical garden is especially noted for its Japanese gardens and Fragrance Garden for the blind.

Central Park   **360-1333**
From 59th to 110th Streets between Fifth Avenue and Central Park West

No, this isn't just a piece of land that greedy real estate developers never got their hands on. Central Park was created by Frederick Law Olmstead and Calvert Vaux over a period of sixteen years (1857–1873) on a virtually barren land area. Maps are available at The Dairy Visitor Information Center (65th Street, mid-park). Every Sunday at 2:00 P.M., the Urban Park Rangers lead "theme" tours. (Call 397-3091 for further details.) During the summer, both the New York Philharmonic and the Metropolitan Opera present free concerts to thousands of enthusiastic fans. When exploring the park on your own, do use caution and don't wander off into deserted areas.

Churches: More than havens for prayerful retreat, New York's churches abound with impressive works of art and architecture. We suggest visiting:

Cathedral of St. John the Divine, The   316-7540
Amsterdam Avenue at 112th Street
> Open daily 7:00 A.M.–5:00 P.M.
> Tours Monday–Saturday at 11:00 A.M. and 2:00 P.M.
> The length of two football fields, the Cathedral of St. John the Divine is the world's largest Gothic church. Its magnificent stained glass windows, Biblical garden, Barbarini tapestries, and eclectic gift shop reward the adventurous souls who venture into the outskirts of Harlem. **Insiders' Tip**: Have lunch across the street at the Green Tree Hungarian Restaurant, a great value, frequented by students of Barnard and Columbia. The mulled wine takes the Cathedral's chill from your bones.

Trinity Church   602-0800
74 Trinity Place (Broadway at Wall St.)
> Open daily 7:30 A.M.–9:00 P.M.
> The highest building in New York for nearly 50 years, this Episcopalian Church in Gothic Revival style is the third building (erected in 1846) on the same site since 1697. Alexander Hamilton and Robert Fulton are buried in the adjacent cemetery. Also of interest is nearby St. Paul's Chapel (Broadway and Fulton St.), where Washington worshipped when President, the oldest building in New York in continuous use. **Insiders' Tip**: Free classical music concerts are given here every Tuesday at 12:30 P.M.

Citicorp Center   559-2330
Lexington Avenue and 54th Street
The world's eighth tallest building, distinguished by its slanted roof, Citicorp Center houses "The Market," a three-

level complex of shops and restaurants from around the world. Free entertainment. Call for exact information.

City Hall   566-4074
Broadway and Murray Street
    Open weekdays 10:00 A.M.–3:30 P.M.
Historic portraits and antiques are displayed in this beautiful landmark building, the governing center of the city for such luminaries as Boss Tweed, Fiorello La Guardia, and Ed Koch. City Hall Park was the site of the hanging of Nathan Hale in 1776.

Commodities Exchange   938-2018
Four World Trade Center
    The Visitors' Gallery is open daily from 9:30 A.M. to 3:00 P.M. Catch a fascinating glimpse of the world of pork bellies and soybean futures.

Federal Hall National Monument   264-8711
26 Wall Street
    Open Monday–Friday 9:00 A.M.–5:00 P.M.
This historic marble building, reminiscent of a Doric temple, was the site of George Washington's 1789 inauguration as America's first President. Exhibits stress New York's role in colonial history. Plan your visit for a Wednesday and enjoy the free American Landmark Festivals Concert at 12:30 P.M.

Federal Reserve Bank   720-6130
33 Liberty Street
    With a minimum of seven days advance notice, you can arrange for a free 1-hour guided tour of this important financial institution. Tours are given Monday through Friday at 10:00 A.M., 11:00 A.M., 1:00 P.M. and 2:00 P.M.

Grant's Tomb
Riverside Drive (122nd St.)
    Wednesday–Sunday 9:00 A.M.–4:30 P.M.
Learn the answer to that old question, "Who's buried in Grant's Tomb?" Actually, both Ulysses S. Grant and his wife, Julia are entombed—above ground—here. The colorful mosaic tile benches surrounding the building are a wonderful place to relax and enjoy the view of the Hudson.

New York Botanical Garden, The   220-8700
Fordham Road and Bronx River Parkway
    Open daily 10:00 A.M.–5:00 P.M.
Always a delightful place to walk, the garden is free daily. There is no admission charged to the Enid Haupt Conservatory on Saturday from 10:00 A.M. until Noon.

New York Stock Exchange, The   **656-5168**
See where fortunes are made and lost! The Visitor's Gallery (entrance at 20 Broad St.) is open daily from 9:20 A.M.–4:00 P.M., with free tours every half hour.

Rockefeller Center
Stretching from 47th to 52nd Streets, between Fifth and Seventh Avenues, Rockefeller Center contains a maze of underground shops, restaurants and the city's most famous ice-skating rink (which does charge admission). You can pick up a free brochure at the Visitors Bureau and take a self-guided walking tour.

Trump Tower
725 Fifth Avenue (56th/57th Sts.)
   Open daily 8:00 A.M.–10:00 P.M.
Wander through the six-story atrium while enjoying piano music drifting up from a cafe and the gentle gurgling of an 80-foot high waterfall. Window shopping is a major activity here.

French-American Reweaving
         Company, The   **753-1672**
37 West 57th Street

Frick Collection, The   **288-0700**
1 East 70th Street

Fu's   **517-9670**
1395 Second Avenue (72nd/73rd Sts.)

Fugazy   **1-718-507-7000**

Fugazy Limo   **661-0100**

FURS

The first time a guest asked for a recommendation of a furrier, I thought, "She certainly has an unrealistic idea of a concierge's salary," but I have since come to sympathize with the plight of the would-be-buyer. Misleading advertising and "deals" are rampant. Our advice: find a furrier you can trust and don't be fooled by "Sales." We have found the following companies to be reliable:

Steven Corn Furs, Inc.   **695-3914**
141 West 28th Street
   Open daily 10:00 A.M.–6:00 P.M.
   All major credit cards accepted
In business for over 90 years, Steven Corn Furs offers a complete range from raccoon to sable at wholesale prices. The low-key salesmen advise without pressuring or offering "specials."

I. Wasserman & Son Furs   279-2763
352 Seventh Avenue (29th St.)
   Monday–Friday 10:00 A.M.–6:00 P.M.
   Sunday 11:00 A.M.–3:00 P.M.
   Closed Saturday
   No credit cards accepted

On the recommendation of Florence, my colleague at the Pierre, I scouted out Wasserman when my sister, Dr. Ziminski of Johns Hopkins Hospital, was looking for the perfect coat. Money was no object. Down in Baltimore, she was getting the typical hype, "This coat normally goes for $18,000, but for you, if you take it today, it's only $5,700." I explained to Jack Wasserman that I was not the buyer, asked to see the full range of his line and asked the questions many buyers are afraid to ask, "What makes this coat worth $8,000 and another only $4,000?" Jack brought unlined coats out of the workroom, turned them inside-out, showed me the stitching and finishing, and gave me a mini-course in quality.

Wasserman's specialty is Samink, light and luxurious as sable at half the price. My sister finally bought a "drop-dead" Samink coat for under $12,000. The styling is classic, and Jack guarantees that the fur will last forever.

G

Gallagher's Steakhouse   245-5336
228 West 52nd Street (Broadway/Eighth Ave.)

GALLERIES
See **ART GALLERIES**

GAS STATIONS
Amoco
153 Seventh Avenue (20th St.)   255-9611
   Open 24 hours
1855 First Avenue (96th St.)   289-8832

Atlas Garage   865-3311
303 West 96th Street

Bowery Service Station   674-2827
326 Bowery

Capitol Service Station
1124 First Avenue (East 62nd St.)   759-9334
640 First Avenue (East 36th St.)   679-7585

Gaseteria   245-9830
Eleventh Avenue and 59th Street

Gulf Products   924-1260
500 West 23rd Street

Merit Gasoline Stations   674-9698
250 East Houston Street

Mobil
1132 York Avenue (62nd St.)   308-6250
842 Eleventh Avenue (57th St.)   582-9269

Gaseteria   245-9830
Eleventh Avenue (59th St.)

GAY BARS

All bars have a precarious life-span in the Big Apple. Gay bars are no exception; they come and go fairly fast. Listed below are some of the ones which have exhibited unusual staying power.

Break, The   627-0072
232 Eighth Avenue (22nd St.)

Candle Bar   874-9155
309 Amsterdam Avenue(74th/75th Sts.)
Leather–Western bar.

Dutchess II, The   242-1408
70 Grove Street (Sheridan Square)
The women's bar in New York.

Julius   929-9672
159 West 10th Street (Seventh Ave./Waverly Place)

Monster, The   924-3557
80 Grove Street (Seventh Ave.)

Star Sapphire   688-4711
400 East 59th Street (First Ave.)
The only Asian/Oriental bar in the city.

Trix   265-9240
234 West 50th Street (Broadway/Eighth Ave.)

Ty's   741-9641
114 Christopher Street (Bleecker/Bedford Sts.)

Uncle Charlie's	**255-8787**
56 Greenwich Avenue (East of Seventh Ave.)	
Works, The	**799-7365**
428 Columbus Avenue (81st St.)	

Gene's Bicycles   **249-9218**
242 East 79th Street (Second/Third Aves.)

General Vision Center   **594-2931**
330 West 42nd Street (Eighth/Ninth Aves.)

Georg Jensen   **759-6457**
683 Madison Avenue (61st St.)

George Washington Bridge
178th Street at Ft. Washington Avenue

Georgette Klinger
501 Madison Avenue (52nd St.)   **838-3200**
978 Madison Avenue (76th St.)   **744-6900**

Germany (Consulate of)   **940-9200**
460 Park Avenue

Gershwin Theater   **586-5100**
222 West 51st Street

Gingiss Formalwear   **302-1742**
560 Fifth Avenue (46th St.)

Giordano   **947-3883**
409 West 39th Street (Ninth/Tenth Aves.)

Giorgio Armani   **988-9191**
815 Madison Avenue (67th St.)

Giselle   **673-1900**
143 Orchard Street

Givenchy Boutique   **772-1040**
954 Madison Avenue (75th St.)

Glad Tidings Tabernacle   **563-4437**
325 West 33rd Street

Go Fly a Kite   **472-2623**
153 East 53rd Street (Citicorp Center)

Godiva   **593-2845**
701 Fifth Avenue (55th St.)

Golden Nugget Hotel/Casino   **347-7111**
Boston and Pacific Aves. at the Boardwalk
(Atlantic City, NJ)

Golden Theater   **239-6200**
252 West 45th Street

Goldfield's   **753-3750**
229 East 53rd Street (Second/Third Aves.)

Goldwater Memorial Hospital   750-6800
Roosevelt Island

GOLF COURSES

Kissena Park Golf Course   **1-718-939-4594**
164-15 Boothe Memorial Avenue, Flushing, Queens

Mosholu Golf Course   **655-9164**
Jerome Avenue and Holly Lane, Bronx

Pine Hills Country Club   **1-516-878-4343**
162 Wading River Road, Manorville, NY

Spring Lake Golf Club   **1-516-924-5115**
Route 25 and Bartlett Road, Middle Island, NY

Gorsart Clothes   **962-0024**
9 Murray Street

Gotham Bar & Grill   **620-4020**
12 East 12th Street (Fifth Ave./University Place)

Gotham Book Mart   **719-4448**
41 West 47th Street

GOURMET FOODS

Balducci's   **673-2600**
424 Avenue of the Americas (9th St.)
    Monday–Saturday 7:00 A.M.–8:30 P.M.
    Sunday 7:00 A.M.–6:30 P.M.
Still family-owned, Balducci's is a feast for the senses. Beautiful vegetables, imported cheeses, and homemade cannelloni vie for your attention.

Dean & DeLuca   **431-1691**
560 Broadway (Prince St.)
    Monday–Saturday 10:00 A.M.–7:00 P.M.
    Sunday 10:00 A.M.–6:00 P.M.
200 cheeses, 30 varieties of coffee and bread from 12 bakeries, plus an excellent selection of cookware.

Zabar's   **787-2000**
2245 Broadway (80th St.)
    Monday–Friday 8:00 A.M.–8:00 P.M.
    Saturday 8:00 A.M.–Midnight
    Sunday 9:00 A.M.–6:00 P.M.
The biggest and the best. Every week, Zabar's sells over seven tons of coffee, ten tons of cheese, and three tons of smoked fish to 35,000 happy customers. Add this to another 10,000 browsers and you can imagine how crowded it can be. Choose from among 450 varieties of cheese and 50 kinds

of salami and sausages. Upstairs houses a wide selection of housewares.

Gouverneurs Hospital   374-4000
227 Madison Avenue

Grace Rainey Rogers Auditorium   570-3949
The Metropolitan Museum of Art, Fifth Avenue (82nd St.)

Gracie Mansion   570-4751
East End Avenue (88th St.)

Gracie Square Hospital   988-4400
420 East 76th Street

Gramercy Park Hotel, The   475-4320
2 Lexington Avenue

Grand Central Station   935-3960
42nd Street (Lexington Ave.)

Grand Hyatt Hotel   883-1234
Park Avenue (42nd St.)

Grand Sea Palace   265-8133
346 West 46th Street

Grant's Tomb
Riverside Drive (88th St.)

Gray Line New York Tours, Inc.   397-2620
254 West 54th Street

Greece (Consulate of)   988-5500
60 East 79th Street

Greene Luggage Repair   682-7978
6 East 46th Street

Greene Street Cafe   925-2415
101 Greene Street (Prince/Spring Sts.)

GREENWICH VILLAGE

"The Village," once a small colonial town called Greenwich, really was a rural retreat at one time—a haven from yellow-fever and smallpox epidemics that plagued early settlers. It passed through a phase of being a wealthy residential neighborhood, immortalized by Henry James in *Washington Square*. When the millionaires moved further uptown, their houses were divided into small apartments and studios whose low rents once attracted struggling actors, artists, musicians, writers, and political radicals. Gentrification has driven them away.

Visitors who come to the Village expecting to find a bohemian outpost will be disappointed. On a typical weekend, tourists far outnumber residents. Still, with its large concentration of restaurants, coffee houses, comedy clubs, and bars, plus its unique character, Greenwich Village is a "must-see" for tourists. It is also the center of New York's gay community.

Greyhound	**636-0800**
Gucci	**826-2600**
689 Fifth Avenue (54th St.)	
Guggenheim Museum	**360-3500**
1071 Fifth Avenue (89th St.)	
Gulf Products	**924-1260**
500 West 23rd Street	

H

H. Stern	**688-0300**
645 Fifth Avenue (51st St.)	
Hacker Art Books	**688-7600**
45 West 57th Street	
Haiti (Consulate of)	**697-9767**
60 East 42nd Street	
Halloran House	**755-4000**
525 Lexington Avenue	
Hammacher Schlemmer	**421-9000**
147 East 57th Street	
Hampton Jitney	**267-1392**
Hard Rock Cafe	**489-6565**
221 West 57th Street (Seventh Ave./Broadway)	
Harlem Hospital	**491-1234**
Lenox Avenue and 135th Street	
Harlem Spirituals, Inc.	**302-2594**
1457 Broadway	
Harold Clurman Theater	**594-2370**
412 West 42nd Street	
Harold Reuter & Co., Inc.	**661-0826**
Pan Am Building, Third Floor East, Room 332	
Harrah's Marina	**1-609-441-5000**
1725 Brigantine Boulevard (Atlantic City, NJ)	

Harry Rothman	**777-7400**
200 Park Avenue South	
Harry Winston	**245-2000**
718 Fifth Avenue (56th St.)	
Harvard Club	**840-6600**
27 West 44th Street	
Hatsuhana	**355-3345**
17 East 48th Street (Madison/Park Aves.)	
Heartbreak	**691-2388**
179 Varick Street (Houston St.)	
Hecksher Theater	**534-2804**
1230 Fifth Avenue (104th St.)	
Helen Hayes Theater	**944-9450**
240 West 44th Street	

HELICOPTER CHARTERS

Island Helicopter Corp.   **1-718-895-1626**
34th Street and East River

Helicopter tours of New York City. Service to airports from 34th Street Heliport (at East River) and charter services.

New York Helicopter
Garden City, Long Island   **1-800-645-3494**
Heliport at 30th Street and the
Hudson River   **247-8687**
Service daily 9:00 A.M.–6:00 P.M.

Provide a choice of six tours of New York City. Reservations are not required for groups of less than ten people.

HELICOPTER TOURS

Island Helicopter Corp.   **683-4575**
34th Street and East River
    Daily except Christmas and New Year's Day.
    January–March 9:00 A.M.–6:00 P.M.
    April–December 9:00 A.M.–9:00 P.M.
No reservations necessary.

The world's largest helicopter sightseeing service has five different tours of New York City ranging from 16 miles to over 100 miles. Save $5.00 by buying tickets from your hotel concierge. They also provide service to airports from their convenient midtown location and are available for charters.

102

Manhattan Helicopter Tours   247-8687
Twelfth Avenue at West 30th Street
   Daily except Christmas and New Year's Day.
   October–April 9:00 A.M.–5:00 P.M.
   May–September 9:00 A.M.–7:00 P.M.
You may choose from several flight plans which provide wonderful views of Manhattan and nearby boroughs.

New York Helicopter
Garden City, Long Island   **1-800-645-3494**
Heliport at 30th and the Hudson River   247-8687
Provide a choice of six tours of New York City. Reservations are not required for groups of less than ten people.
   Service daily 9:00 A.M.–6:00 P.M.

HELIPORTS

East 34th Street Heliport   **1-800-645-3494**
34th Street and the East River

East 60th Street Heliport   880-1234
60th Street and the East River

**Pier 6 Heliport (Lower Manhattan
   Heliport)**   248-7230
South of Wall Street on the East River

West 30th Street Heliport   563-4442
30th Street and the Hudson River

Helmsley Middletowne Hotel   755-3000
148 East 48th Street (Lexington/Third Aves.)

Helmsley Palace, The   888-7000
455 Madison Avenue (50th/51st Sts.)

Helmsley Park Lane   371-4000
36 Central Park South (Fifth/Sixth Aves.)

Helmsley Windsor   265-2100
100 West 58th Street (Sixth Ave.)

Henri Bendel   247-1100
10 West 57th Street

Herman's Sporting Goods   73-7400
135 West 42nd Street (Sixth Ave./Broadway)

Hermès   751-3181
11 East 57th Street

Hertz   1-800-654-3131

Hewyler Chocolates   308-1311
510 Madison Avenue (53rd St.)

Hirsch Photo   557-1150
699 Third Avenue (44th St.)

HOCKEY

New York Rangers, The   563-8300
Madison Square Garden, Seventh Avenue
(31st/33rd Sts.)

Holiday Inn Crowne Plaza   840-4000
49th Street and Broadway

Holland Tunnel
Canal Street at Hudson Street

Holy Trinity Lutheran Church   877-6815
Central Park West (65th St.)

Honduras (Consulate of)   889-3858
18 East 41st Street

Horizontal Club, The   826-2922
336 East 61st Street (First/Second Aves.)

Horn & Hordart Automat   599-1665
200 East 42nd Street (Third Ave.)

Hors d'Oeuvrerie   938-1111
One World Trade Center

HORSE-DRAWN CARRIAGES

See **CARRIAGES**

HORSEBACK RIDING

Claremont Riding Academy   724-5100
175 West 89th Street
Monday–Friday 6:00 A.M.–10:00 P.M.
Saturday & Sunday 6:00 A.M.–5:00 P.M.

In the mood for a brisk canter through Central Park? For
years, people have been getting horses from this, the oldest
stable in New York. The horses can be rented for $27.00 per
hour, cash only. The academy staff will evaluate your ability by talking with and listening to you before letting you
out on one of their beauties. They have an indoor ring
where you can practice, and classes and private lessons are
available. If you are interested in jumping, hunting, or dres-
sage, they can accommodate you. You must use an English
saddle.

If you're feeling a little rusty about your equestrian ability, private lessons are also available at the rate of:
$30.00 per half hour
$60.00 per hour

Hospital for Joint Diseases	598-6000
301 East 17th Street	
Hospital for Special Surgery	606-1000
535 East 70th Street	

HOSPITALS

Beekman Downtown	233-5300
170 William Street	
Bellevue	561-4141
First Avenue and 27th Street	
Beth Israel	420-2000
Stuyvesant Square and 17th Street	
Cabrini–Columbia	725-6000
227 East 19th Street	
Columbia–Presbyterian	694-2500
Broadway and 168th Street	
Doctors	870-9000
East End Avenue and 87th Street	
Flower Fifth Avenue	860-8000
Fifth Avenue and 106th Street	
Goldwater Memorial	750-6800
Roosevelt Island	
Gouverneurs	374-4000
227 Madison Avenue	
Gracie Square	988-4400
420 East 76th Street	
Harlem	491-1234
Lenox Avenue and 135th Street	
Hospital for Joint Diseases	598-6000
301 East 17th Street	
Hospital for Special Surgery	606-1000
535 East 70th Street	
Jewish Memorial	569-4700
Broadway and 196th Street	
Lenox Hill	794-4567
Park Avenue and 77th Street	

Manhattan Eye & Ear 210 East 64th Street	838-9200
Medical Arts Center 57 West 57th Street	755-0200
Memorial Sloan Kettering York Avenue and 68th Street	704-7722
Metropolitan First Avenue and 98th Street	360-6262
Mount Sinai Fifth Avenue and 100th Street	650-6500
New York Eye & Ear 310 East 14th Street	598-1313
New York Hospital–Cornell Medical Center 525 East 68th Street	472-5454
New York Infirmary 107 William Street	233-5300
New York University 550 First Avenue	340-7300
Payne Whitney 525 East 68th Street	472-6282
Roosevelt–St. Luke's Ninth Avenue and 59th Street	554-7000
Sloane Hospital for Women 622 West 168th Street	694-2500
St. Luke's Amsterdam Avenue and 114th Street	870-6000
St. Vincent's Seventh Avenue and 11th Street	790-7000
St. Clare's 415 West 51st Street	586-1500
Syndeham Family Care Manhattan Avenue and 123rd Street	686-7500
Veterans' Administration First Avenue and 24th Street	686-7500
Women's–Roosevelt 1111 Amsterdam Avenue	870-6000
Hotalings 142 West 42nd Street (Sixth/Seventh Aves.)	840-1868

HOTELS

Algonquin, The (Comfortable) 59 West 44th Street	**840-6800**
Bedford, The (Inexpensive) 118 East 40th Street	**697-4800**
Beekman Tower, The (Comfortable) First Avenue at 49th Street	**355-7300**
Beverly, The (Comfortable) 125 East 50th Street	**753-5300**
Carlyle, The (Luxury) 35 East 76th Street	**744-1600**
Chelsea Hotel, The (Inexpensive) 222 West 23rd Street (Seventh/Eighth Aves.)	**243-3700**
Comfort Inn Murray Hill **(Inexpensive)** 42 West 35th Street (Fifth/Sixth Aves.)	**947-0200**
Days Inn–New York (Comfortable) 440 West 57th Street	**581-8100**
Doral Court Hotel, The **(Comfortable)** 130 East 39th Street	**685-1100**
Doral Inn, The (Comfortable) Lexington Avenue at 49th Street	**755-1200**
Doral Park Avenue, The **(Comfortable)** 70 Park Avenue (38th Street)	**687-7050**
Doral Tuscany, The (Comfortable) 120 East 39th Street (Lexington/Park Aves.)	**686-1600**
Dorset, The (Comfortable) 30 West 54th Street (Fifth/Sixth Aves.)	**247-7300**
Drake Swissotel, The (First Class) 440 Park Avenue	**421-0900**
Eastgate Tower, The (Comfortable) 222 East 39th Street (Second/Third Aves.)	**687-8000**
Edison, The (Inexpensive) 228 West 47th Street (Broadway/Eighth Ave.)	**840-5000**
Elysee, The (Comfortable) 60 East 54th Street (Park/Madison Aves.)	**753-1066**
Embassy Suites Times Square Broadway at 47th Street Opening Fall 1990	

Empire, The (Inexpensive) **265-7400**
44 West 63rd Street

Esplanade, The (Inexpensive) **874-5000**
304 West End Avenue (74th St.)

Essex House (First Class) **247-0300**
160 Central Park South
Closed until Spring 1991

Gramercy Park, The (Inexpensive) **475-4320**
2 Lexington Avenue

Grand Hyatt, The (First Class) **883-1234**
Park Avenue at 42nd Street

Halloran House, The (Comfortable) **755-4000**
525 Lexington Avenue

**Helmsley Middletowne, The
(Comfortable)** **755-3000**
148 East 48th Street (Lexington/Third Aves.)

Helmsley Palace, The (First Class) **888-7000**
455 Madison Avenue

Helmsley Park Lane, The (First Class) **371-4000**
36 Central Park South (Fifth/Sixth Aves.)

**Helmsley Windsor, The
(Comfortable)** **265-2100**
100 West 58th Street (Sixth Ave.)

**Holiday Inn Crowne Plaza, The
(First Class)** **977-4000**
1605 Broadway (49th St.)

Howard Johnson (Inexpensive) **581-4100**
851 Eighth Avenue (51st St.)

Inter-Continental, The (First Class) **755-5900**
111 East 48th Street

Kitano, The (Inexpensive) **840-3080**
66 Park Avenue

Lexington, The (Comfortable) **755-4400**
Lexington Avenue at 48th Street

Loew's Summit (Comfortable) **752-7000**
Lexington Avenue at 51st Street

✈ **Lombardy, The (Comfortable)** **753-8600**
11 East 56th Street (Park/Lexington Aves.)

Lowell, The (Luxury) **838-1400**
28 East 63rd Street (Madison/Park Aves.)

Macklowe, Hotel (First Class)   **869-5800**
145 West 44th Street (Sixth Ave./Broadway)

Marriott Marquis, The (First Class)   **398-1900**
1535 Broadway (45th/46th Sts.)

Mayfair Regent, The (Luxury)   **288-0800**
Park Avenue at 65th Street

Mayflower, The (Comfortable)   **265-0060**
15 Central Park West (61st St.)

Milford Plaza, The (Inexpensive)   **869-3600**
270 West 45th Street (Eighth Ave.)

Morgan's (First Class)   **686-0300**
237 Madison Avenue

New York Helmsley, The (First Class)   **888-1624**
212 East 42nd Street

New York Hilton, The (Comfortable)   **586-7000**
1335 Avenue of the Americas

**New York Marriott Financial Center
    (First Class)**
West Street
(Opening 1991)

New York Penta, The (Comfortable)   **736-5000**
401 Seventh Avenue

Novotel, The (Comfortable)   **315-0100**
226 West 52nd Street

**Omni Berkshire Place, The
    (Comfortable)**   **753-5800**
52nd Street and Madison Avenue

**Omni Park Central, The
    (Comfortable)**   **484-3300**
870 Seventh Avenue

Paramount, The (Inexpensive)   **764-5500**
235 West 46th Street (Broadway/Eighth Ave.)

Park 51 (First Class)   **765-1900**
152 West 51st Street

Parker Meridien, The (Luxury)   **245-5000**
118 West 57th Street (Sixth/Seventh Aves.)

Peninsula New York, The (Luxury)   **247-2200**
700 Fifth Avenue (55th St.)

Pierre, The (Luxury)   **838-8000**
2 East 61st Street

Plaza, The (First Class)   759-3000
Fifth Avenue at 59th Street

Plaza Athenee, The (Luxury)   734-9100
37 East 64th Street (Madison/Park Aves.)

Ramada Inn, The (Inexpensive)   581-7000
48th Street and Eighth Avenue

Regency, The (Luxury)   759-4100
540 Park Avenue (61st/62nd Sts.)

Rihga Royal, The (First Class)   307-5000
150 West 54th Street (Sixth/Seventh Aves.)

Ritz Carlton, The (First Class)   757-1900
112 Central Park South

**Roger Smith Winthrop, The
(Comfortable)**   755-1400
501 Lexington Avenue

✦ **Roosevelt, The (Inexpensive)**   661-9600
Madison Avenue at 45th Street

Royalton, The (First Class)   869-4400
44 West 44th Street

**St. Moritz on the Park, The
(Comfortable)**   755-5800
50 Central Park South (Sixth Ave.)

St. Regis, The (Luxury)
2 East 55th Street (Fifth Ave.)
    Opening Spring 1991

Salisbury, The (Inexpensive)   246-1300
123 West 57th Street (Sixth/Seventh Aves.)

Sheraton Centre, The (Comfortable)   581-1000
811 Seventh Avenue

**Sheraton City Squire, The
(Comfortable)**   581-3300
Seventh Avenue at 51st Street

**Sheraton Park Avenue, The
(Comfortable)**   685-7676
45 Park Avenue

Sherry Netherland, The (First Class)   355-2800
781 Fifth Avenue (59th St.)

Shoreham, The (Inexpensive)   563-1800
33 West 55th Street

Stanhope, The (Luxury)   288-5800
995 Fifth Avenue (81st St.)

Surry, The (Comfortable)   288-3700
20 West 76th Street (Madison Ave.)

Tudor, The (Inexpensive)   986-8800
304 East 42nd Street (Second Ave.)

United Nations Plaza, The (Luxury)   355-3400
1 United Nations Plaza

Vista International, The (First Class)   938-9100
Three World Trade Center

Waldorf Astoria, The (First Class)   355-3000
Park Avenue at 50th Street

Waldorf Towers, The (Luxury)   355-3100
100 East 50th Street (Park Ave.)

Wales, The (Inexpensive)   876-6000
Madison Avenue at 92nd Street

Warwick, The (Comfortable)   247-2700
65 West 54th Street

Wellington, The (Inexpensive)   247-3900
Seventh Avenue and 55th Street

Wentworth, The (Inexpensive)   719-2300
59 West 46th Street (Fifth/Sixth Aves.)

Westbury, The (Luxury)   535-2000
Madison Avenue at 69th Street

Wyndham, The (Inexpensive)   753-3500
42 West 58th Street (Fifth/Sixth Aves.)

HOTELS, LUXURY

Carlyle, The   744-1600
35 East 76th Street (Madison Ave.)
   Head Concierge: John Neary

Singles: $200–255   Doubles: $220–270   Suites: $425–1,000

Everyone agrees that this is the number one hotel in New York. John Neary has been the concierge here for many years and is responsible for maintaining the high level of service for which the hotel is famous. The rooms are luxuriously furnished and include choice antiques. The clientele is primarily "old money" and upper-level business people. Don't forget to enjoy Bobby Short and his piano in the famous Cafe Carlyle.

Lowell, The   838-1400
28 East 63rd Street (Park & Madison Aves.)
   Head Concierge: Mario Cinti

Singles: $180–200   Doubles: $220–290   Suites: $340–600

One of New York's most elegant "boutique hotels." With only 60 rooms, The Lowell can concentrate on providing the special service that has made it so desirable to its clientele. Many of the cozy rooms have wood-burning fireplaces and some include kitchenettes. The Pembroke Room serves afternoon tea.

Mayfair Regent, The   **288-0800**
610 Park Avenue (65th St.)
    Head Concierge: Bruno Brunelli
Singles: $210–270 Doubles: $230–320 Suites: $550–1,200

Like all of the true luxury hotels, this establishment is small and focuses on personal service for its prized guests. The European atmosphere attracts the crème de la crème of travelers and The Mayfair Regent is giving The Carlyle a run for its money. Recently, the clientele from some of the other fine hotels have been discovering how pleasant it is to stay here.

Parker Meridien   **245-5000**
118 West 56th Street (Sixth/Seventh Aves.)
    Head Concierge: Said Ouriaghli
Singles: $190–245 Doubles: $215–270 Suites: $270–650

Conveniently located near the Russian Tea Room, Carnegie Hall, Tiffany's, and Trump Tower, the Parker Meridien also offers lovely views of Central Park. The penthouse health club includes a track, racquetball courts, and a pool. Its dining room, Maurice, serves superb nouvelle cuisine and has the additional advantage of being open on Sunday.

Peninsula New York, The   **247-2200**
700 Fifth Avenue (55th St.)
Singles: $210–225 Doubles: $225–325 Suites: $525–2,500

New Yorkers are delighted to see the old Gotham back in operation. After a series of unlucky owners, the Peninsula Group has completed renovations and is luring the quality of guest that distinguishes its flagship hotel in Hong Kong. With its prized location in the heart of the city's best shopping, this could become a strong contender in the luxury market.

Pierre, The   **838-8000**
2 East 61st Street (Fifth Ave.)
Singles: $240–335 Doubles: $265–355 Suites: $475–1,500

Plaza Athenee, The   **734-9100**
37 East 64th Street (Madison/Park Aves.)
    Head Concierge: Eugenio Chinigo
Singles: $245–285 Doubles: $275–315 Suites: $550–1,800

One of New York's very special hotels. The best of the Trusthouse Forte Hotels in this country, it is home to the British royal family when they are in town. That says almost everything about the service and accommodations.

Regency, The   **759-4100**
540 Park Avenue (61st/62nd Sts.)
    Concierges: Penny, Kenzo, and Kathleen
Singles: $185–245 Doubles: $205–265 Suites: $450–950

You can judge the caliber of The Regency's clientele by the large number of stretch limos double-parked in front.

St. Regis, The
Fifth Avenue and 55th Street
    Due to reopen in 1991.

Stanhope, The   **288-5800**
995 Fifth Avenue (81st St.)
    Head Concierge: Rick Cook
Singles and doubles: $250–325   Suites: $350–775

Located directly across from the Metropolitan Museum, the Stanhope has just undergone a $30 million renovation. One wonders why, with all this care, they still expect their tea guests to balance cup, saucer, and crumpets from knee-height tables.

United Nations Plaza   **355-3400**
1 United Nations Plaza (44th St.)
    Head Concierge: Kevin Edmund
Singles: $190–225 Doubles: $210–235 Suites: $450–1,100

As one would expect, a large number of diplomats stay here when they're in town. The Ambassador Grill serves a luscious Sunday brunch.

Waldorf Towers, The   **355-3100**
100 East 50th Street (Park Ave.)
    Head Concierge: Herb Tepper
Every U.S. President since Hoover has stayed at the Waldorf Towers. Beautiful suites.

Westbury, The   **535-2000**
15 East 69th Street (Madison Ave.)
    Head Concierge: Anthony Pike
Singles: $210–250 Doubles: $230–270 Suites: $325–1,000

Another fine Trusthouse Forte property. Not in the same league as the Plaza Athenee, but quite good.

HOTELS, FIRST CLASS

Drake Swissotel, The   **421-0900**
400 Park Avenue (56th St.)

Head Concierge: Barbara Van Der Vloed
Singles: $190–220 Doubles: $215–245 Suites: $385–800

Introduce yourself to Barbara. She is the concierge who will make your stay more pleasant and enjoyable in this efficient Swiss hotel. One of the best in our profession, she can ease your way through all of those business and entertainment requirements leaving your time free for fun and shopping. The personal approach is second nature to all of the efficient staff. The decor is European, of course, accented with an oriental flavor. Rooms are comfortable and some include refrigerators. Chef Jean-Georges Vongerichten provides Mediterranean French cuisine in The Lafayette, one of the best hotel restaurants.

Essex House, The   247-0300
160 Central Park South (Sixth and Seventh Aves.)
   (Closed for renovations)

Grand Hyatt, The   883-1234
Park Avenue and 42nd Street
   Head Concierge: Jessica Gibson
Singles: $195–210 Doubles: $220–230 Suites: $350–1,200

With its contemporary architecture and sleek lines, this is typical of the very large chain establishments. No one is surprised to find a tropical setting in the lobby, complete with waterfall and trees. This is the type of environment that appeals to most tourists and to many business people. The super-chains all provide a level of efficiency and service that is quite acceptable and The Grand Hyatt is no exception.

Helmsley Palace, The   888-7000
455 Madison Avenue (50th St.)
   Head Concierge: Jan Sevela
Singles: $210–255 Doubles: $265–325 Suites: $550 and up

We've all seen the pictures of Queen Leona standing guard here. Built over the Villard Houses, this portion of the building is lavishly ornate and well worth the visit. It does not seem to draw the quality of clientele required to be considered a luxury hotel, however. Service is on the same level as all of the other first class establishments and their reputation suffers from too much Leona.

Helmsley Park Lane, The   371-4000
36 Central Park South (Fifth/Sixth Aves.)
   Head Concierge: Tom Murphy
Singles: $180–245 Doubles: $200–265 Suites: $500–1,170

Your standard first class hotel. Good service, good food, nothing outstanding except the views of Central Park from some of the park-side rooms.

Holiday Inn Crowne Plaza   **977-4000**
49th Street and Broadway
An upscale Holiday Inn.

Inter-Continental, The   **755-5900**
111 East 48th Street (Park/Lexington Aves.)
   Head Concierge: Constantine Urso
Singles: $175–275 Doubles: $205–275 Suites: $285–3,500

Quietly attractive rooms, an undistinguished afternoon tea, and an extremely noisy lobby.

Macklowe, The Hotel   **768-4400**
145 West 44th Street (Sixth Ave./Broadway)
Singles/Doubles: $185–225 Suites: $395

Not just a hotel, the Macklowe's 638 First Class rooms will be only a portion of Manhattan's first executive conference center. The center will provide state-of-the-art facilities. The Hudson Theater, a historic landmark, is being renovated for use as a screening center by the major film companies.

Marriott Marquis, The   **398-1900**
1535 Broadway (45th/46th Sts.)
Concierge Manager: Cari Miller
Singles: $220–270 Doubles: $230–280 Suites: $425–3,500

We think this is the best of the First Class hotels—but we're prejudiced. McDowell has worked for two of Marriott's hotels and met Adele when they were both concierges here at the Marquis. This mammoth hotel (New York's largest), in the middle of the theater district, was the first major hotel in the Times Square area and one of the major contributors to the gentrification of Times Square. Designed as a convention hotel, it has 80,000 square feet of meeting space, 1877 guest rooms, an assortment of restaurants and lounges, and an entire floor of shops and stores. With a large lounge serving the special Concierge Levels, Marriott has ample need for the 18 concierges who work in locations on three floors. Business travelers (who have voted Marriott their favorite hotel chain) vie with tourists and sightseers for space in the famous revolving rooftop restaurant and lounge, The View. It is the only New York hotel containing a theater.

Morgan's   **686-0300**
237 Madison Avenue (38th St.)
Singles: $160–195 Doubles: $175–215 Suites: $270–380

A favorite of rock stars. Black-and-white tiled bathrooms, ultramodern decor, and a staff sworn to discretion.

New York Helmsley, The   **490-8900**
212 East 42nd Street (Second/Third Aves.)

Head Concierge: Robert Larey

Singles: $165–210   Doubles: $185–230   Suites: $340

Upholds the reliable Helmsley standards.

New York Hilton, The   586-7000
1335 Avenue of the Americas (53rd/54th Sts.)
    Head Concierge: Zoe Magno
Singles: $150–195   Doubles: $175–220   Suites: $400–550

This enormous hotel caters to every caliber of traveler—
from tour groups to demanding business people. Deal
makers will appreciate the business center with computers,
work stations, fax machines, Dow Jones phone, and 24-
hour dictation services. Pleasure travelers might enjoy
looking out on the Avenue of the Americas from the spacious cocktail lounge, or discoing the night away in Pur-
suits. Any hotel with a branch of H. Stern in the lobby gets
Adele's endorsement.

Park 51   765-1900
152 West 51st Street (Seventh Ave.)
Singles: $235–265   Doubles:$255–285   Suites: $450–900

This hotel has just changed hands again. It was formerly
The Grand Bay, which advertised itself as the only luxury
hotel on the West Side. Under Continental Companies, it
fell short of this goal. Perhaps the new owners can do better.

Plaza, The   759-3000
768 Fifth Avenue (59th St.)
    Head Concierge: Thomas Wolfe
Singles: $195–450   Doubles: $225–450   Suites: $500–1,340

The Plaza has been cleaned and refurbished to a fare-
thee-well. The dark and dowdy look is a thing of the past,
and there will soon be real palm trees in the Palm Court.
Gilding abounds and the glitter of the chandeliers is almost blinding. In short, the magnificience of the public
rooms has been restored. In addition to The Plaza's historical and architectural importance, it has brought us the
myth of Eloise and has been the site of many a glittering
event. Occupying a perfect location, with Fifth Avenue at
its front door and Central Park at its side, it offers easy access to some of the world's best shopping. Tea at the Palm
Court, cocktails at the Oak Bar, and delicious seafood at
the Oyster Bar are well-established Manhattan traditions.
The concierge staff, now 18 strong, includes four members of the Clefs d'Or.

Rihga Royal Hotel, The   307-5000
150 West 54th Street (Sixth/Seventh Aves.)
One Bedroom Suites: $225–405   Two Bedroom Suites: $450–1,500

This is the newest of the all-suites hotels to open recently. Although there is controversy as to whether this is the direction hotels should be going, the Rihga Royal is a beautiful addition to the New York market. Like all new hotels, there will be a shakedown period while it trains and refines its staff, but the future looks bright for both the hotel and its guests.

Ritz Carlton, The   **757-1900**
112 Central Park South (Sixth & Seventh Aves.)
   Head Concierge: Martin Anker
Singles: $200–320 Doubles: $230–350 Suites: $585–1,200

This hotel remains open while extensive renovations are in progress. We'll have more to say when the work is finished.

Royalton, The   **869-4400**
44 West 44th Street (Fifth/Sixth Aves.)
   Head Concierge: Ellen Potter
Singles: $190–230 Doubles: $215–255 Suites: $285–1,200

So much media attention was paid to the Philippe Stark decor, we expected to be dazzled. We weren't. The staff seems to earn extra points for rudeness.

Sherry Netherland, The   **355-2800**
781 Fifth Avenue (59th St.)
   Head Concierge: Peter Kalaf
Singles and doubles: $175–250 Suites: $280–450

Although this is mainly an apartment hotel, a small number of rooms are rented on a transient basis. Extremely elegant.

Vista International, The   **938-9100**
Three World Trade Center
   Head Concierge: Jason Seequin
Singles: $180–245 Doubles: $205–270 Suites: $390 and up

A surprising bargain and the perfect location if you will be doing business in the Wall Street area.

Waldorf Astoria, The   **355-3000**
301 Park Avenue (49th/50th Sts.)
   Concierges: Michael Keilley and Tony Lambert
Singles: $165–230 Doubles: $190–255 Suites: $325–780

This grande dame of the Hilton chain has just had a face-lift, and the result is marvelous.

HOTELS, COMFORTABLE

Algonquin Hotel, The   **840-6800**
59 West 44th Street (Fifth/Sixth Aves.)
Singles: $140–150 Doubles: $150–160 Suites: $280–300

A favorite of theater people. The rooms are acceptable, but the main floor is the real story here. Dorothy Parker, Robert Benchley, and other luminaries of the Round Table once lunched in the Rose Room. Now, Andrea Marcovicci, Liliane Montevecchi, and Harry Conlin Jr. beguile audiences in the Oak Room. We love meeting friends for cocktails in the lobby—it's as close as you can get to a private club.

Beekman Tower, The   355-7300
First Avenue at 49th Street
Singles: $160–170 Doubles: $180–190 Suites: $190–350

This all-suites hotel near the United Nations offers fully equipped kitchens, two restaurants, and coin-operated washers and dryers.

Beverly Hotel, The   753-2700
125 East 50th Street (Lexington Ave.)
Singles: $129–149 Doubles: $139–159 Suites: $139–200

You will enjoy personalized service at this family owned small hotel.

Days Inn–New York   581-8100
440 West 57th Street
Singles: $119–139 Doubles: $124–144 Suites: $225–350
No frills.

Doral Court Hotel, The   685-1100
130 East 39th Street (Lexington Ave.)
Singles: $145–170 Doubles: $165–190 Suites: $275–475

Located in the fashionable Murray Hill area, just three blocks from Grand Central Station, the Doral Court's tastefully decorated large rooms and attentive staff have made it a favorite of seasoned travelers.

Doral Inn, The   755-1200
49th Street & Lexington Avenue
Singles: $114–138 Doubles: $128–152 Suites: $200–600

The most economy-oriented of the many Dorals in New York features a fully equipped laundry room for do-it-yourselfers and a fitness center with squash courts.

Doral Park Avenue, The   687-7050
70 Park Avenue (38th St.)
Singles: $155–175 Doubles: $175–195 Suites: $350–500

A terrific Park Avenue location, sidewalk cafe, and lovely rooms.

Doral Tuscany, The   686-1600
120 East 39th Street (Lexington/Park Aves.)
Singles: $175–200 Doubles: $200–225 Suites: $325–850

This is an appealing, comfortable hotel. It makes you feel good just to be in the lobby. Small and well-decorated, it's the flagship of the Doral chain which is better known for its spectacular resorts and spas in the Miami area. The biggest surprise is the incredibly good restaurant, Time & Again. We would compare it favorably with most of the two-star restaurants where we've eaten.

Dorset, The   247-7300
30 West 54th Street (Fifth/Sixth Aves.)
Singles: $175–235   Doubles: $195–255   Suites: $275–475

We find the Dorset a little lacking in service. There's no concierge, and theater tickets are handled by the small gift shop. However, they do offer a splendid Sunday brunch.

Eastgate Tower, The   687-8000
222 East 39th Street (Second/Third Aves.)
Studios: $165–205   Jr. Suites: $175–215   Suites: $195–330

All-suites hotel. All of its 192 units have fully equipped kitchens.

Elysee, The   753-1066
60 East 54th Street (Park/Madison Aves.)
Singles: $150–210   Doubles: $165–225   Suites: $275–600

A small and gracious midtown hotel.

Halloran House   755-4000
525 Lexington Avenue (49th St.)
Singles: $140–170   Doubles: $155–185   Suites: $300–500

Convenient midtown location with easy access to public transportation, two restaurants, and a lively cocktail lounge make this a favorite of business travelers.

Helmsley Middletowne   755-3000
148 East 48th Street (Lexington/Third Aves.)
Singles: $135–145   Doubles: $145–155   Suites: $195–380

All of this converted apartment house's 192 rooms have kitchenettes, and some have terraces. Minibus service to major airports is provided.

Helmsley Windsor, The   265-2100
100 West 58th Street (Sixth Ave.)
Singles: $135   Doubles: $145   Suites: $215-325

A small (300 room), gracious, quietly elegant hotel one block from Central Park.

Lexington, The   755-4400
Lexington Avenue and 48th Street
Singles: $145–175   Doubles: $160–190   Suites: $325–450

Just a short walk from Saks and Bloomingdale's, the 750-room Hotel Lexington offers fine value. Entering the marble-floored lobby, you immediately feel that the staff here will take good care of you—and they do.

Loews Summit   752-7000
Lexington Avenue and 51st Street
Singles: $125–155   Doubles: $140–170   Suites: $250 and up

Reasonable rates, newly renovated guest rooms, a lively lobby bar, and Maude's restaurant attract guests.

Lombardy, The   753-8600
11 East 56th Street (Park/Lexington Aves.)
Singles: $150   Doubles: $165   Suites: $300

Entering The Lombardy, you will feel as though you've stumbled upon someone's very exclusive residence. A quiet and low-key operation.

Mayflower, The   265-0060
15 Central Park West (61st St.)
Singles: $145–165   Doubles: $160–180   Suites: $235–275

Renovated in 1987, The Mayflower is still rather old-fashioned and dreary.

New York Penta, The   736-5000
Seventh Avenue and 33rd Street
Singles: $125–200   Doubles: $160–240   Suites: $275–950

Once the old Hotel Pennsylvania (across the street from Pennsylvania Station) and then the Statler Hilton, the Penta does big business with tour groups. If it's your choice, you can do better for the money.

Novotel, The   315-0100
226 West 52nd Street (Broadway)
Singles: $135–165   Doubles: $145–175   Suites: $350–600

A good choice if your visit to New York will include lots of theater-going.

Omni Berkshire Place   753-5800
21 East 52nd Street (Madison Ave.)
Singles: $195–200   Doubles: $215–260   Suites: $310–1,700

This nicest of the New York Omnis is conveniently located close to the finest of both Fifth Avenue department stores and chic Madison Avenue boutiques.

Omni Park Central, The   247-8000
Seventh Avenue and 56th Street
Singles: $150–220   Doubles: $190–280   Suites: $200–1,200

The Omni's 1,450 rooms are frequented by flight crews, conventioneers, and undemanding tourists.

Roger Smith Winthrop, The   755-1400
501 Lexington Avenue
Singles: $160–175   Doubles: $175–190   Suites: $250–295

What a find! Just 134 beautifully decorated rooms (some with four-poster beds), plus complimentary continental breakfast on weekends.

St. Moritz on the Park   755-5800
50 Central Park South (Sixth Ave.)

Singles: $145–210   Doubles: $165–220   Suites: $250–600

When McDowell worked at the nearby Essex House, people would come in asking for rooms, complaining that when they got into bed at the St. Moritz, their feet were out the window. Unfortunately, the elegant location on Central Park South and the presence of Rumplemeyer's, New York's premier ice cream parlor, do not compensate for the depressingly small rooms.

Sheraton Centre, The   581-1000
52nd Street and Seventh Avenue

Singles: $135–180   Doubles: $165–210   Suites: $375–755

Frequently bustling with conventioneers and tour groups, both this Sheraton and the City Squire are in the midst of a massive and extensive renovation program in anticipation of hosting the 1992 Democratic Convention.

Sheraton City Squire   581-3300
790 Seventh Avenue (51st St.)

Singles: $135–180   Doubles: $165–210   Suites: $285 and up

A convention midtown location within walking distance of Rockefeller Center and the Theater district, moderate rates and an indoor pool are this Sheraton's attractions.

Sheraton Park Avenue   685-7676
45 Park Avenue (37th St.)

Singles: $175–195   Doubles: $190–220   Suites: $245 and up

A multi-million dollar refurbishment has transformed this Sheraton into a handsome, European-style hostelry.

Surrey, The   288-3700
20 West 76th Street (Madison Ave.)

This all-suites hotel near the Whitney Museum offers large rooms with kitchenettes and an attentive, courteous staff.

Warwick, The   246-2700
65 West 54th Street (Avenue of the Americas)

Singles: $160–190   Doubles: $185–215   Suites: $195–475

Built in 1927 by William Randolph Hearst, the Warwick is in the midst of restoration. We love the old-English look of the lobby with its dark green walls, wood paneling, and marble floors. The cozy cocktail lounge invites relaxation.

121

HOTELS, INEXPENSIVE

Many of the people who come to New York have moderate incomes and are looking for ways to economize. We are listing below a group of hotels which provide various levels of service at low prices. "You get what you pay for," and New York is no exception to the rule.

Bedford, The   697-4800
118 East 40th Street (Lexington/Park Aves.)
Singles: $130–160 Doubles: $150–170 Suites: From $180

All of the Bedford's rooms have fully equipped kitchenettes.

Chelsea Hotel, The   243-3700
222 West 23rd Street (Seventh/Eighth Aves.)
Singles: $65–95 Doubles: $80–95 Suites: $145–175

This Chelsea Landmark has attracted the famous (Dylan Thomas) and infamous (Sid Vicious) for years. The rooms are large, soundproof, and desperately in need of refurbishing.

Comfort Inn Murray Hill   947-0200
42 West 35th Street (Fifth/Sixth Aves.)
Singles: $90–110 Doubles: $105–125

A surprisingly charming, European-style hotel, just a short bus ride away from the Javits Center.

Edison, The   840-5000
228 West 47th Street (Broadway/Eighth Ave.)
Singles: $84–90 Doubles: $97–100 Suites $105–140

Budget-minded travelers eager to be in the Theater District frequent the Edison and its coffee shop, affectionately known as the "Polish Tea Room."

Empire, The   265-7400
44 West 63rd Street
Singles: $95–165 Doubles: $105–185 Suites: $185–300

Located directly across from Lincoln Center, the Empire was recently renovated and promises to maintain high standards without high rates.

Esplanade, The   874-5000
304 West End Avenue (74th St.)
Singles: $75–80 Doubles: $99–119 Suites: $118–168

The Esplanade stands in a residential neighborhood—off the beaten track for most tourists. The rooms are spacious and have kitchenettes.

Gramercy Park, The   475-4320
2 Lexington Avenue (21st St.)
Singles: $100–110 Doubles: $105–115 Suites: $150

This was once *the* neighborhood. Edwin Booth lived at 16 Gramercy Park South, and Winston Churchill's mother, Jennie Jerome, was born nearby. An old-fashioned sense of tranquility remains here, and guests at the Gramercy Park Hotel enjoy this haven amidst the bustle of Manhattan.

Howard Johnson   581-4100
851 Eighth Avenue (51st St.)
Singles: $106–142 Doubles: $118–154 Suites: $208–348

The rooms are cheerful and well-appointed, and the location (on the western border of the Theater District) is convenient. This is only a marginally safe area, however. There are still plenty of porno houses nearby.

? Kitano, The   685-0022
66 Park Avenue (38th St.)
Singles: $110–120 Doubles: $140–150 Suites: $200–320

This Japanese hotel offers the choice of Western-style accommodations or rooms with tatami mats and futons.

Milford Plaza, The   869-3600
270 West 45th Street (Eighth Ave.)
Singles: $95–125 Doubles: $110–140 Suites: $245–430

If your stay in New York will be a constant round of business meetings and theater, the Milford Plaza is an acceptable choice. However, you certainly don't want to spend lots of time either in the rooms or the neighborhood—the western limit of Times Square.

Paramount, The   764-5500
235 West 46th Street (Broadway/Eighth Ave.)
Singles: $95–174 Doubles: $115–195

Hotel as theater: Philippe Starck has cleverly renovated this undistinguished Times Square property into a tribute to minimalism. The very small rooms are imaginatively decorated, and the lobby is a work of art.

Ramada Inn, The   581-7000
48th Street and Eighth Avenue
Singles: $98–128 Doubles: $110–140

This no-frills establishment near the theater district is distinguished only by its outdoor rooftop swimming pool. If your needs extend no further than a clean room and a place to swim, this may be for you.

Roosevelt, The   661-9600
Madison Avenue and 45th Street
Singles: $119–169 Doubles: $139–199
An old standby.

Salisbury, The   246-1300
123 West 57th Street (Sixth/Seventh Aves.)
Singles: $108–118   Doubles: $118–128   Suites: $175–295

The location is great. Business travelers are their target—
no frills their policy.

Shoreham, The   247-6700
33 West 55th Street (Fifth/Sixth Aves.)
Singles: $90–110   Doubles: $100–120   Suites: $150–175

This is an adequate hotel, given the price range, and, as a
bonus, La Caravelle, one of New York's better restaurants is
located on the ground floor. They are not, however, con-
nected in any way to the hotel.

Tudor, The   986-8800
304 East 42nd Street (Second Ave.)
Singles and doubles: $95–110   Suites: $160–175

To be used only as a last resort. Tiny, cramped rooms.

Wales, The   876-6000
1295 Madison Avenue (92nd St.)
Singles: $65–95   Doubles: $96–120   Suites: $85–140

Originally called The Chastaigneray, this turn-of-the-
century hotel has been carefully restored to its original con-
dition. Co-owners Bernard Goldberg and Henry Kallan
(who will be the manager) have brought back the Edwardian decor which blends in perfectly with the staid Carnegie
Hill neighborhood.

Wellington, The   247-3900
Seventh Avenue and 55th Street
Singles: $86–89   Doubles: $96–99   Suites: $140–165

Big, clean, cheap, and very ordinary.

Wentworth, The   719-2300
59 West 46th Street (Fifth/Sixth Aves.)
Singles: $65–75   Doubles: $75–105   Suites: $110–150

Frequented by buyers from all over the world, the
Wentworth's proximity to both the Fashion and Theater
Districts, plus cleanliness and efficient service, provide
good value.

Wyndham, The   753-3500
42 West 58th Street (Fifth/Sixth Aves.)
Singles: $95–105   Doubles: $110–120   Suites: $155–300

One of the finest hotels in the inexpensive category.
Within easy walking distance of Lincoln Center, Carnegie Hall, the Theater District, and elegant Fifth Avenue
stores. You'll save enough on the room to splurge on caviar and champagne at Petrossian. There is, however, no
room service.

Howard Johnson   **581-4100**
851 Eighth Avenue (51st St.)
Hubert's   **826-5911**
575 Park Avenue (63rd St.)
Hudson Guild Theater   **760-9810**
441 West 26th Street
Hudson's   **473-0981**
97 Third Avenue (12th/13th Sts.)
Hungary (Consulate of)   **879-4125**
8 East 75th Street

I

I. Wasserman & Son Furs   **279-2763**
352 Seventh Avenue (29th St.)
Iberia Airlines   **1-800-772-4642**

ICE SKATING

Rockefeller Center Skating Rink   **757-5731**
Rockefeller Center Plaza
Daily (October–April) 9:00 A.M.–10:00 P.M.
Admission:
Monday–Thursday:
Adults $7.00
Children (under 12) $6.00
Senior citizens $6.00
Friday–Sunday:
Adults $8.00
Children (under 12) $6.50
Senior citizens $6.50
Skate rental $3.50 for all

Under the watchful eye of Prometheus, skaters glide by on the 122 by 59 foot block of ice that turns the lower plaza of Rockefeller Plaza into a winter wonderland. Another wonder of this rink is the bar on the same level. You can zip in to get an Irish Coffee every few times around the ice. It certainly loosens you up and does wonders for skating ability. You are also very close to the Sea Grill Restaurant (on the south side of the rink) which has some of the best food in town. Be warned that they require a jacket and tie so be sure to dress appropriately for your skating.

Sky Rink   **695-6556**
450 West 33rd Street (Ninth/Tenth Aves.)

Admission (for all ages):
Day sessions $7.00
Night sessions $7.50
Skate rental $2.50

Year-round skating in the penthouse atop the Maritime Union Building. Said to be the world's highest rink.

Wollman Memorial Ice Skating Rink   517-4800
Open daily November through April
Monday 10:00 A.M.–5:00 P.M.
Tuesday–Thursday 10:00 A.M.–9:30 P.M.
Friday–Saturday 10:00 A.M.–11:00 P.M.
Sunday 10:00 A.M.–9:30 P.M.
Admission:
Adults
Monday–Thursday $4.00
All other times $5.00
Children $2.00
Senior citizens $2.00
Skate Rental $2.50

Beautifully renovated, thanks to Donald Trump, the Wollman Rink reopened in 1986 after a six-year closing. One of the most exotic places in the world to skate. Go at night. You will be enclosed by the New York skyline and will skate in a fairyland of woods and skyscrapers! If you are really lucky, it will snow . . . there's nothing like it. A word of warning—you may have to compete with hundreds of children for the pleasure.

Iceland (Consulate of)   686-4100
370 Lexington Avenue

Il Cantinori   673-6044
32 East 10th Street (University Place/Broadway)

Il Cortile   226-6060
125 Mulberry Street (Canal/Hester Sts.)

Il Mulino   673-3783
86 West 3rd Street (Thompson/Sullivan Sts.)

Il Nido   753-8450
251 East 53rd Street (Second/Third Aves.)

Il Valletto   838-3939
133 East 61st Street (Park/Lexington Aves.)

Imperial Theater   239-6200
249 West 45th Street

Improvisation   765-8268
358 West 44th Street (Ninth Ave.)

Inagiku   355-0440
111 East 49th Street (Park/Lexington Aves.)

India (Consulate of) 3 East 64th Street	879-7800
Indochine 430 Lafayette Street	505-5111
Indonesia (Consulate of) 5 East 68th Street	879-0600
Inflatably Yours 318 West 77th Street	580-2776
Inside Track, The 1011 Second Avenue (53rd/54th Sts.)	752-1940
Intar Theater 420 West 42nd Street	239-0827
Inter-Continental Hotel 111 East 48th Street	755-5900
International Center for Photography 1130 Fifth Avenue (94th St.)	860-1777
International Design Center of New York 30-20 Thompson Avenue (Main Building)	1-718-937-7474
Intrepid Sea-Air-Space Museum Pier 86 (46th Street and the Hudson River)	245-0072
Ireland (Consulate of) 515 Madison Avenue	319-2555
Iris Brown's Victorian Doll and Miniature Shop 253 East 57th Street (Second Ave.)	593-2882
Island Helicopter Corp. 34th Street and the East River	1-718-895-1626
Island Helicopter Sightseeing 34th Street Heliport (the East River)	683-4575
Israel (Consulate of) 800 Second Avenue	697-5500
Israel Sack, Inc. 15 East 57th Street	753-6562
Ivaran Lines 1 Exchange Plaza	809-1220 1-800-451-1631

J

J&R Tobacco Corp.   983-4160
11 East 45th Street

J's   666-3600
2581 Broadway (97th/98th Sts.)

J. S. Suarez   315-5614
26 West 54th Street

J. Sung Dynasty   355-1200
Hotel Lexington, 511 Lexington Avenue (48th St.)

JFK International Airport   **1-718-495-5400**
      Arrivals 1-718-656-4520

J.N. Bartfield   245-8890
30 West 57th Street

Jack Lawrence Theater   307-5452
359 West 48th Street

Jack Silver Formal Wear   582-3298
1780 Broadway (57th/58th Sts.)

Jacob Javits Convention Center   216-2000
Eleventh Avenue (36th St.)
  By Bus: M42 (42nd St. Crosstown)
  Serves both the Javits Center and the Circle Line
  Operates 24 hours a day, 7 days a week
  This is not one of the big sightseeing attractions. If you're
going to Javits, it's because you're here for a convention.
Our experience has been that it's a very comfortable convention center. It's big— very big—with plenty of space for
exhibitors and the huge crowds that attend. We are particularly happy to report that there are plenty of bathrooms and
that they are clean. The layout makes it relatively easy to
find everything.

Jamaica (Consulate of)   935-9000
866 Second Avenue

James II   355-7040
15 East 57th Street

James Robinson   752-6166
15 East 57th Street

James, Michel-Allen (Masseur)   486-6309

Jan Skala   246-2942
1 West 47th Street

Japan (Consulate of)   **986-1600**
280 Park Avenue

Japan Airlines   **838-4400**

JAZZ

New York is a jazz lover's paradise. For information on who's playing where, check the Friday, Weekend section of *The New York Times*, the "Cafes and Clubs" listings in the *Village Voice*, or call the Jazzline 1-718-465-7500.

Angry Squire   **242-9066**
216 Seventh Avenue (23rd Ave.)

Blue Note   **475-8592**
131 West 3rd Street (Sixth Ave.)
Top stars such as Freddie Hubbard, the Herbie Hancock Trio, and Chuck Mangione have performed in this sumptuous, art deco locale. Every Monday evening, there's an "All-Star Session." The jazz brunch on Saturday and Sunday is justly famous.

Bradley's   **228-6440**
70 University Place (11th St.)
    Jazz nightly from 9:30 P.M. to 4:00 A.M.
    Lunch Monday–Friday 11:30 A.M.–3:00 P.M.
    Dinner Daily 6:00 P.M.–12:30 A.M.
Good jazz and good food are a surprisingly difficult combination to find, but at Bradley's you get both.

Fat Tuesday's   **533-7902**
190 Third Avenue (17th St.)
    Sunday 8:00 P.M. & 10:00 P.M.
    Monday 9:00 P.M. & 11:00 P.M.
    Tuesday–Thursday 8:00 P.M. & 10:00 P.M.
    Friday & Saturday 8:00 P.M. & 10:00 P.M., Midnight
Nightly performances at this "mecca of jazz," feature such headliners as Dizzy Gillespie, Les McCann, and Stan Getz. Pianist Michael Wolff plays during the jazz brunch on Saturday and Sunday, from Noon to 4:00 P.M.

Fortune Garden Pavilion   **753-0101**
209 East 49th Street
In this unlikely combination of a good Chinese restaurant and jazz club, the music starts at 8:00 P.M. Tuesday through Saturday, and at 7:00 P.M. on Sunday.

J's   **666-3600**
2581 Broadway (97th/98th Sts.)
    Continuous entertainment

Monday–Thursday 8:00 P.M.–Midnight
Friday–Saturday 9:00 P.M.–1:00 A.M.

Continental cuisine and a distinguished lineup of performers are the hallmarks of this three-year old addition to the jazz scene.

Knickerbocker Saloon   **228-8490**
33 University Place (9th St.)

Michael's Pub   **758-2272**
211 East 55th Street (Third Ave.)
Tuesday–Saturday 9:30 P.M. & 11:30 P.M.
Yes, this is where Woody Allen occasionally performs on Monday nights with his Dixieland band.

Red Blazer, Too   **262-3112**
349 West 46th Street (Eighth/Ninth Aves.)
Specialize in Dixieland and music of the Roaring Twenties. There is a dance floor. Open nightly until 4:00 A.M., this is a great spot for after theater.

Sweet Basil   **242-1785**
88 Seventh Avenue (Bleecker St.)
Presents a wide range of top jazz groups nightly.

Sweetwater's   **873-4100**
170 Amsterdam Avenue (68th St.)
R & B plus soul food are the winning combination here.

Village Gate   **475-5120**
160 Bleecker Street (Thompson St.)

Village Vanguard   **255-4037**
178 Seventh Avenue South (11th St.)
Open daily with shows at 10:00 P.M., 11:30 P.M., & 1:00 A.M.
Perhaps the most famous jazz club in the world, the Village Vanguard's smokey basement has launched such notables as John Coltrane, Miles Davis, Theolonius Monk, and Harry Belafonte. The Mel Lewis Jazz Orchestra's Monday night performances are a New York legend. Concierges love this place because they are open on Sunday, when the theaters are closed.

Zinno   **924-5182**
126 West 13th Street (Sixth/Seventh Aves.)
Italian food and American jazz.

Jazz Line   **1-718-465-7500**

Jet Air International   **233-2282**

Jewelry Exchange, The
15 West 47th Street (Fifth/Sixth Aves.)

Jewelry Patch, Inc, The	840-8279
501 Seventh Avenue (37th/38th Sts.)	
Jewish Memorial Hospital	569-4700
Broadway and 196th Street	
Jewish Museum	860-1888
1109 Fifth Avenue	
Jezebel	582-1045
630 Ninth Avenue (45th St.)	
Jim McMullen's	861-4700
1341 Third Avenue (76th St.)	
Joe Allen	581-6464
326 West 46th Street (Eighth/Ninth Aves.)	
John Clancy's	242-7350
181 West 10th (Seventh Ave. So.)	
John Houseman Theater	967-9077
450 West 42nd Street	
John's Pizzeria	243-1680
278 Bleecker Street (Seventh Ave. So./Jones St.)	
Jordan (Consulate of)	759-1950
86 United Nations Plaza	
Joyce Theater	242-0800
175 Eighth Avenue (17th St.)	
Judith Anderson Theater	736-7930
422 West 42nd Street	
Julius	929-9672
159 West 10th Street (Seventh Ave./Waverly Place)	

K

K B M Rental	354-6888
60 West 39th Street	
K-Paul's New York	460-9633
622 Broadway (Bleecker/Houston Sts.)	
Kaufman Pharmacy	755-2266
Lexington Avenue (50th St.)	
Kaufmann Auditorium	427-4410
92nd Street YM/YWHA, 1395 Lexington Avenue (92nd St.)	
Kenjo	333-7220
40 West 57th Street	

KENNELS

Manhattan Pet Hotel   831-2900
312 East 95th Street (First/Second Aves.)
   Monday–Friday 7:00 A.M.–7:00 P.M.
   Saturday 8:00 A.M.–5:00 P.M.
   Closed Saturday and Holidays

Pedigree Pups   752-1377
989 First Avenue (54rd/55th Sts.)

This is the place to know about if you care about your pet. They can and will handle every problem you might have. They operate a luxury pet estate on Long Island for boarding and will pick up and deliver. They frequently make arrangements for the "rich and famous" who travel with their furry friends and they know all of the ins and outs of shipping, licenses, and foreign travel, among other things.

Kenneth   752-1800
19 East 54th Street (Fifth/Madison Aves.)

Kentshire Galleries   673-6644
37 East 12th Street

Kenzo   737-8640
824 Madison Avenue (69th St.)

King Karol   869-0230
1500 Broadway (43rd St.)

Kissena Park Golf Course   1-718-939-4594
164-15 Boothe Memorial Avenue

Kitano   840-3080
66 Park Avenue

Kitchen Arts & Letters, Inc.   876-5550
1435 Lexington Avenue (93rd St.)

KLM   759-3600

Knickerbocker Club   838-6700
2 East 62nd Street

Knickerbocker Saloon   228-8490
33 University Place (9th St.)

Korea (Consulate of)   752-1700
460 Park Avenue

Korean Airlines   371-4820

Krizia Boutique   628-8180
805 Madison Avenue

132

L

La Boite en Bois   874-2705
75 West 68th Street (Columbus Avenue/Central Park
West)

La Camelia   751-5488
225 East 58th Street (Second/Third Aves.)

La Caravelle   586-4252
33 West 55th Street (Fifth/Sixth Aves.)

La Cote Basque   688-6525
5 East 55th Street (Fifth/Madison Aves.)

La Gauloise   691-1363
502 Sixth Avenue (12th/13th Sts.)

La Grenouille   752-1495
3 East 52nd Street (Fifth/Madison Aves.)

La Guardia (Ground Information)   1-800-AIR-RIDE

La Guardia (Port Authority)   1-718-476-5000

La Guardia Aircraft Charter Services   1-718-476-5366

La MaMa Annex   475-7710
66 East 4th Street

La Reserve   247-2993
4 West 49th Street (Fifth Ave.)

La Ripaille   255-4406
605 Hudson Street (West 12th/Bethune Sts.)

La Tulipe   691-8860
104 West 13th Street (Sixth/Seventh Aves.)

Labels for Less
639 Third Avenue   682-3330
130 West 48th Street   997-1032

Lafayette   832-1565
The Drake Hotel, 65 East 56th Street (Park Ave.)

Lambs Theater   997-1780
130 West 44th Street

LAN Chile   1-800-735-5526

Landmark Tavern   757-8595
626 Eleventh Avenue (46th St.)

Lanvin   838-4330
701 Madison Avenue (62nd St.)

Larry Matthews 24 Hour Beauty Salon   246-6100
536 Madison Avenue

Lattanzi   315-0980
361 West 46th Street (Eighth/Ninth Aves.)

Laura Ashley   735-1010
21 East 57th Street

Laura Fisher   838-2596
1050 Second Avenue

Le Bernardin   489-1515
155 West 51st Street (Sixth/Seventh Aves.)

Le Cirque   794-9292
58 East 65th Street (Madison/Park Aves.)

Le Cygne   759-5941
55 East 54th Street (Madison/Park Aves.)

Le Perigord   755-6244
405 East 52nd Street (First Ave.)

Le Regence   606-4647
The Hotel Plaza Athenee, 37 East 64th Street
(Madison/Park Aves.)

Le Relais   751-5108
712 Madison Avenue (63rd/64th Sts.)

Lebanon (Consulate of)   744-7905
9 East 76th Street

Lee Fordin   840-7799
19 West 44th Street

Lenox Hill Hospital   794-4567
Park Avenue and 77th Street

Leo Castelli   431-5160
420 West Broadway

Lexington Hotel   755-4400
Lexington Avenue (48th St.)

Lexington Luggage   223-0698
793 Lexington Avenue

Liberty Ferry   806-6940
Battery Park

Limelight   807-7850
660 Avenue of the Americas (20th/21st Sts.)

Limited, The   838-8787
691 Madison Avenue (62nd St.)

LIMOUSINES

We have found the following services to be reliable and courteous. Most companies have a one and a half hour minimum per call, so even if you just need a car to take you from the hotel to the theater, it will cost about $60.00. Limo costs are tricky and can be cause for problems. Discuss costs when you make your reservation—don't be surprised later. Remember that tips, tolls, and parking charges are extra. All costs we quote are as of January 1990.

Carey Limo	**517-7010**
Dav-El	**580-6500**
Farrell's	**860-4200**
Fugazy Limo	**661-0100**
London Towncars	**988-9700**

Operate a fleet of 100 vehicles. Cadillac limousines ($50.00 per hour) seat six, Buick sedans ($40.00 per hour) accommodate four, and Buick station wagons ($48.00 per hour) seat either six passengers or lots of luggage.

Smith Limo   **247-0711**

A far less expensive alternative to a limo is a radio car. They have a flat fee per call (no minimum), and are a much more practical way of negotiating the narrow streets of Chinatown or Little Italy. Our favorite of these services is:

Computer Radio   **1-718-886-8888**

Its drivers receive 60 hours of training before starting work. In addition to transporting guests, we have used them for messengering large items around town and retrieving luggage from airports.

Lincoln Center for the Performing Arts   **877-1800**
Broadway (64th/66th Sts.)

Lincoln Tunnel
39th Street at Ninth Avenue

Lionel Madison Trains   **777-1110**
105 East 23rd Street (Park/Lexington Aves.)

LIQUOR STORES

Acker Merrall & Condit   **787-1700**
160 West 72nd Street (Broadway/Columbus Ave.)
Since 1820, they have offered attentive service and a great variety of vintage wines.

Morrell & Company   **688-9370**
535 Madison Avenue (54th/55th Sts.)

You can rely on Peter J. Morrell for expert advice and the very finest in wines. His staff can help you with selections for your own enjoyment or for those difficult gift items. A complete stock of old and rare wines, champagnes, and spirits.

Sherry-Lehman   **838-7500**
679 Madison Avenue (61st/62nd Sts.)

Wine & Liquor Outlet   **308-1650**
1114 First Avenue (61st St.)
   Daily 9:00 A.M.–11:00 P.M.
   Open Sunday
Excellent discounts on the city's largest selection of wines and liquors.

Literary Bookshop, Inc.   **633-1151**
15 Christopher Street

LITTLE ITALY

Although Chinatown is gradually encroaching on what used to be considered "Little Italy, " this area still extends along Mulberry Street between Houston and Canal Streets. Wandering through this area, you have your choice of a number of fine restaurants and pastry shops. On a fine summer's evening, dining outside at S.P.Q.R. or sipping cappucino at Ferrara's is a delight to be savored.

Little People's Theater Company, The   **765-9540**
39 Grove Street

Loehmann's   **543-6420**
236th Street and Broadway, Riverdale

Loew's Summit   **752-7000**
Lexington Avenue (51st St.)

Log_On Computer Services   **674-6446**
611 Broadway (Houston St.), Suite 515

Logos Bookstore   **697-4888**
342 Madison Avenue (43rd/44th Sts.)

Lombardy Hotel   **753-8600**
11 East 56th Street (Park & Lexington Aves.)

London Towncars   **988-9700**

Long Island Railroad   **1-718-454-5477**
LIRR Terminal at Penn Station

   General Information   **1-718-739-4220**

   Lost and Found   **1-718-526-0020**

   Special Services   **1-718-990-7498**

Longacre Theater 220 West 48th Street	**239-6200**
Lord & Taylor 424 Fifth Avenue (38th St.)	**391-3344**

LOST AND FOUND

Bus	**690-9638**
Subway	**1-718-330-4484**
Taxi Commission	**869-4513**
Lotto Results	**976-2020**
Louis Vuitton 51 East 57th Street	**371-6111**
Lowell Hotel 28 East 63rd Street	**838-1400**

LOWER EAST SIDE

This area still retains some of the character of the thousands of refugees from Eastern Europe who settled here at the end of the 19th century. Restaurants such as Sammy's Famous Rumanian, Bernstein-on-Essex Street (Kosher Chinese), Veseleka, and Christine's Polish Kitchen continue to draw crowds for their home cooking and reasonable prices. On Sunday, shopping for bargains at the discount stores on Orchard, Delancey, and Grand Streets is a popular pastime for New Yorkers and visitors alike.

Lower Manhattan Theater Center Two World Trade Center (Mezzanine Level)	
Lucille Lortell Theater 121 Christopher Street	**924-8782**
Lufthansa	**1-718-895-1277**

LUGGAGE REPAIR

See **REPAIRS, LUGGAGE**

Lunt-Fontanne Theater 205 West 46th Street	**575-9200**
Lusardi's 1494 Second Avenue (77th/78th Sts.)	**249-2020**
Lutece 249 East 50th Street (Second Ave.)	**752-2225**
Lyceum Theater 149 West 45th Street	**239-6200**

M

M.K.   779-1340
204 Fifth Avenue

Macklowe Hotel   869-5800
145 West 44th Street (Sixth Ave./Broadway)

Macy's   971-6000
34th Street (Sixth Ave.)

Madison Avenue Baptist Church   685-1377
Madison Avenue at 31st Street

Madison Square Garden   563-8300
Seventh Avenue (32nd St.)

Madison Towers Hotel   685-3700
Madison Avenue (38th St.)

Main Post Office   967-8585
33rd Street and Eighth Avenue

Majestic Theater   239-6200
245 West 44th Street

Mamma Leone's   586-5151
The Milford Plaza Hotel, 261 West 44th Street

Manfra, Tordella & Brookes, Inc.   621-9555
Rockefeller Plaza, 59 West 49th Street

Manhattan Art and Antiques Center   355-4400
1050 Second Avenue

Manhattan Bridge
Canal Street at the Bowery

Manhattan Eye & Ear Hospital   838-9200
210 East 64th Street

Manhattan Helicopter   247-8687
Twelfth Avenue at West 30th Street

Manhattan Marriage License Bureau   269-2900
Municipal Building, 1 Chambers Street

Manhattan Ocean Club   371-7777
57 West 58th Street (Fifth/Sixth Aves.)

Manhattan Pet Hotel   831-2900
312 East 95th Street (First/Second Aves.)

Manhattan Theater Club   645-5848
131 West 55th Street

Manhattan Yacht Charters   772-9430
233 East 81st Street (Second/Third Aves.)

Marble Collegiate Church   686-2770
Fifth Avenue (29th St.)

Marie-Michelle   315-2444
57 West 56th Street (Fifth/Sixth Aves.)

Mark Cross   421-3000
645 Fifth Avenue (51st St.)

Mark Hellinger Theater 757-7064
247 West 51st Street.

Mark, The   744-4300
25 East 77th Street

Market I.S. 44   923-5016
Columbus Avenue (76th/77th Sts.)

Markova, Judy (Masseuse)   891-4328

MARRIAGE LICENSES

Manhattan Marriage License Bureau
Municipal Building, 1 Chambers Street (second floor)

The process of getting married in New York is quite simple. There is no requirement for either a blood test or a physical examination. Just go to the Manhattan Marriage License Bureau, and take with you the following:

• ID—In the form of a driver's license, passport, birth certificate, work ID, or any other legitimate form of identification.

• Divorce papers (if necessary).

You will have to fill out an application, swear that the facts on it are true, and wait for a clerk to type the marriage license. There is a 24-hour waiting period before you can actually get married. If you can't find any place else, there is a chapel next to the License Bureau.

For recorded information call 269-2900.

Marriott Marquis   398-1900
1535 Broadway (45th/46th Sts.)

Mars   691-6262
28 10th Avenue (13th St.)

Martha
475 Park Avenue (58th St.)   753-1511
Trump Tower, 725 Fifth Avenue (56th/57th Sts.)   826-8855

Martin Beck Theater   246-6363
302 West 45th Street

Mary Boone   431-1818
417 West Broadway

MASSAGE

When your shoulders are in a knot and your neck feels like a steel rod, there's nothing like a massage to relax you. But just how do you manage this unless you belong to a health club? The masseurs and masseuses listed below will come to your apartment or hotel room with portable (we finally learned not to call them "collapsible") massage tables. These are no-nonsense professionals. Call to verify rates.

Laura Alexandra Nicholson Pager	**216-0426**
Michel Allen James Pager (Input your phone No.) Pager (Leave a message)	**356-5557** **356-5557**
Renate Vieth Pager	**521-9292**
Judy Markova Pager	**891-4328**

Maurice   245-7788
The Parker Meridien Hotel, 118 West 57th Street
(Sixth/Seventh Aves.)

Maxim's   751-5111
680 Madison Avenue (61st/62nd Sts.)

Mayfair Regent   288-0800
610 Park Avenue (65th St.)

Mayflower Hotel   265-0060
15 Central Park West (61st St.)

McGraw-Hill Bookstore   512-4100
1221 Avenue of the Americas (48th/49th Sts.)

MCM   688-2133
717 Madison Ave

McNulty's Tea & Coffee Company, Inc.   242-5351
109 Christopher Street (Bleecker/Hudson Sts.)

Meadowlands   1-201-935-8500
East Rutherford, NJ

Medical Arts Center   755-0200
57 West 57th Street

Meekin Concert Hall   362-8719
127 West 67th Street

Memorial Sloan Kettering Hospital   704-7722
York Avenue and 68th Street

Merit Gasoline Stations   674-9698
250 East Houston Street

MESSENGER SERVICES

Messenger service is an essential element in the daily activities of the New York businessman. Listed below are our choices of the many available. They have been selected not only because they do good work, but because they have the most important qualification—they are always open.

Airline Delivery Services   687-5145
60 East 42nd Street
They boast that they will deliver anything, anywhere, anytime. Open 24 hours a day, 365 days a year.

Bullit Courier
42 Broadway (Wall St.)   952-4343
405 Lexington Avenue (Chrysler Bldg.)   983-7400
203 West 38th Street (Broadway)   221-7900
Service is available 24 hours a day, 7 days a week, even on holidays.

Metro Bicycle Store   427-4450
1311 Lexington Avenue(88th St.)

Metro North   532-4900
  Information   736-4545
  Lost and Found   560-7534
  Package Express/Baggage   560-7534

Metropolitan Club   838-7400
1 East 60th Street

Metropolitan Hospital   360-6262
First Avenue and 98th Street

Metropolitan Museum of Art, The   879-5500
Fifth Avenue and 82nd Street

Metropolitan Opera House   362-6000
Lincoln Center, Broadway (64th/66th Sts.)

Mexico (Consulate of)   689-0456
8 East 41st Street

MGM Grand Air   1-800-933-2646

Michael's Pub   758-2272
211 East 55th Street (Third Ave.)

Mickey Mantle's   688-7777
42 Central Park South

Midtown Tennis Club	**989-8572**
341 Eighth Avenue (27th St.)	
Midway Airlines	**1-800-621-5700**
Midwest Express Airlines	**1-800-452-2022**
Mikimoto	**586-7153**
608 Fifth Avenue (49th St.)	
Milford Plaza	**869-3600**
270 West 45th Street (Eighth Ave.)	
Minetta Lane Theater	**420-8000**
18-22 Minetta Lane	
Mini Bus (Airports)	**355-1992**
Minskoff Theater	**869-0550**
200 West 45th Street	
Mitsukoshi	**935-6444**
461 Park Avenue (57th St.)	
Mitzi Newhouse Theater	**787-6868**
Lincoln Center	
Mobil	
1132 York Avenue (62nd St.)	**308-6250**
842 Eleventh Avenue (57th St.)	**582-9269**
Moe Ginsburg	**982-5254**
162 Fifth Avenue	
Monaco (Consulate of)	**759-5227**
845 Third Avenue	
Mondrian	**935-3434**
7 East 59th Street (Fifth/Madison Aves.)	

MONEY MACHINES

There are thousands of money machines in New York—almost every branch bank has them. We have listed below a selection of them located in the areas most frequented by tourists. They are listed by street to make it easy for you to find them on this list. The exact address follows the street. Remember that in New York the streets normally run east to west and the avenues north to south. All of the following are in both the NYCE and Cirrus systems:

204 West 4th Street (at Grove St.)
8th Street (756 Broadway)
8th Street (2 Fifth Ave.)
17th Street (201 Park Ave. So.)
18th Street (130 Fifth Ave.)

33rd Street (960 Avenue of the Americas)
34th Street (349 Fifth Ave.)
34th Street (358 Fifth Ave.)
38th Street (1400 Broadway)
39th Street (1411 Broadway)
39th Street (530 Seventh Ave.)
41st Street (1441 Broadway)
42nd Street (40 East 42nd St. at Madison Ave.)
42nd Street (Grand Central Terminal, main level)
43rd Street (510 Fifth Ave.)
43rd Street (422 Lexington Ave.)
44th Street (1 United Nations Plaza, at First Ave.)
44th Street (530 Fifth Ave.)
45th Street (360 Madison Ave.)
47th Street (401 Madison Ave.)
48th Street (500 Lexington Ave.)
49th Street (301 Park Ave.)
50th Street (1251 Avenue of the Americas)
50th Street (30 Rockefeller Plaza–Fifth Ave.)
51st Street (1275 Avenue of the Americas)
51st Street (1633 Broadway)
51st Street (850 Third Ave.)
11 West 51st Street (Fifth Ave.)
52nd Street (488 Madison Ave.)
54th Street (641 Lexington Ave.)
55th Street (1350 Avenue of the Americas)
55th Street (425 Park Ave.)
57th Street (711 Lexington Ave.)
57th Street (741 Fifth Ave.)
57th Street (970 Eighth Ave.)
59th Street (640 Madison Ave.)
60th Street (770 Lexington Ave.)
65th Street (1934 Broadway)
72nd Street (260 Columbus Ave.)
74th Street (940 Madison Ave.)
200 West 79th Street (Amsterdam Ave.)
79th Street (2219 Broadway)
59 West 86th Street (Columbus Ave.)
126 East 86th Street (Lexington Ave.)
352 East 86th Street
180 Canal Street (Mott Street, Chinatown)
40 Wall Street (William St.)
Pennsylvania Station
Long Island Railroad Concourse, 33rd Street &
Seventh Avenue
1 Penn Plaza, Lower Level (33rd Street &
Seventh Ave.)
100 World Trade Center, Main Level

Those of us who bank with Citibank know that they are not part of another system. However, their 24-hour banking centers are scattered all around town and an be found at:

250 Broadway (City Hall)
55 Wall Street (near William St.)
World Trade Center Concourse
111 Wall Street (near Water St.)
160 Varick Street (Van Dam St.)
75 Christopher Street (near Sheridan Square)
72 Fifth Avenue (13th St.)
250 Fifth Avenue (28th St.)
One Park Avenue (32nd St.)
334 Fifth Avenue (33rd St.)
580 Second Avenue (32nd St.)
201 West 34th Street (Seventh Ave.)
1430 Broadway (40th St.)
401 West 42nd Street (Ninth Ave.)
717 Avenue of the Americas (23rd St.)
Citicorp ((Lexington Ave. at 53rd St.)
1740 Broadway (56th St.)
175 West 72nd Street (Broadway)
2350 Broadway (86th St.)
162 Amsterdam Avenue (67th St.)

Monster, The   924-3557
80 Grove Street (Seventh Ave.)

Montrachet   291-2777
239 West Broadway (North Moore/White Sts.)

Morgan Library   685-0008
29 East 36th Street (Madison Ave.)

Morgan's Hotel   686-0300
237 Madison Avenue (38th St.)

Mormon Visitors Center   595-1825
2 Lincoln Square

Morocco (Consulate of)   758-2625
437 Fifth Avenue

Morrell & Company   688-9370
535 Madison Avenue (54th/55th Sts.)

Morris-Jumel Mansion   923-8008
Edgecomb Avenue (West 160th St.)

Morton, The Interior Design Bookshop   421-9025
983 Third Avenue (59th St.)

Mosholu Golf Course   655-9164
Jerome Avenue and Holly Lane

Mount Sinai Hospital	650-6500
Fifth Avenue and 100th Street	
Murder, Ink.	362-8905
271 West 87th Street (Broadway/West End Ave.)	
Museum of American Folk Art	581-2475
49 West 53rd Street	
Museum of Broadcasting	752-4690
1 East 53rd Street	
Museum of Modern Art	708-9400
11 West 53rd Street	
Museum of the American Indian	283-2420
Broadway and 155th Street	
Museum of the City of New York	534-1672
Fifth Avenue at 103rd Street	

MUSEUMS

American Craft Museum   956-6047
40 West 53rd Street
  Wednesday–Sunday 10:00 A.M.–5:00 P.M.
  Tuesday 10:00 A.M.–8:00 P.M.
  Closed Monday and National Holidays
  Admission:
  Adults $3.50
  Children/Senior citizens $1.50
  By subway: E or F train to 53rd Street
  By bus: M1, M2, M3, M4, or M5
Now housed in new quarters, this museum features the best this country has produced and continues to create in the crafts field. The new galleries make it possible for the curators to mount shows which continue to delight all of us who remember our parents and grandparents laboring over quilting frames and working so diligently to give beauty to the everyday objects they used. Don't miss it.

American Museum of Immigration   422-2150
The Statue of Liberty
  Monday–Friday 9:00 A.M.–6:00 P.M.
  Saturday & Sunday 9:00 A.M.–7:00 P.M.
  By subway: #1 train to South Ferry

**American Museum of Natural
    History**   769-5000
Central Park West at 79th Street
  Monday, Tuesday, Thursday, & Sunday 10:00 A.M.–5:45 P.M.

Wednesday, Friday, & Saturday 10:00 A.M.–9:00 P.M.
Closed on Christmas and Thanksgiving
Suggested Admission:
Adults $4.00
Children $2.00
Senior citizens $3.00
Friday & Saturday 5:00 P.M.–9:00 P.M. Free
By subway: IND C train to 81st Street
By bus: M7, M10, or M11 to 79th Street

This place has the most complex system of hours and fees we've encountered in New York. While it's obvious that none of the museums has any real consideration for the public (except as a source of money) this operation takes the cake. Theodore Roosevelt would have had a fit. Although the collections are important and the research performed here even more so, we have never had a pleasant visit. Unlike the city's other museums, this one seems to be used as a nursery, with ill behaved children and toddlers running through the hallways and exhibit areas. The gem collection is housed in a darkened multilevel room that has never heard of the handicapped. In fact, if you look up from the floor as you walk along, you'll become one of the handicapped.

Asia Society Galleries   **288-6400**
725 Park Avenue (70th St.)
Tuesday–Saturday 11:00 A.M.–6:00 P.M.
Sunday Noon–5:00 P.M.
Closed Monday
Admission:
Non-Members $2.00
Senior citizens/Children $1.00
By subway: #6 train to 68th Street
By bus: M1, M2, M3, or M4

Brooklyn Museum   **1-718-638-5000**
300 Eastern Parkway, Brooklyn
Wednesday–Monday 10:00 A.M.–5:00 P.M.
Closed Tuesday
Admission:
Adults $3.00
Students $1.50
Senior citizens $1.00
By subway: #2 or #3 train to Eastern Parkway

Contains one of the most outstanding collections of Egyptian Art.

Children's Museum of Manhattan   **721-1234**
The Tische Building, 212 West 83rd Street
(Broadway/Amsterdam Ave.)

Tuesday–Sunday 10:00 A.M.–5:00 P.M.
Admission:
Children & Adults $4.00
Thursday 3:00 P.M.–5:00 P.M. Free to students

Not really a museum, CMOM could be called a learning center. Built around a theme of "self-discovery" for children, exhibits and workshops contribute to a creative approach that draws 150,000 kids a year. Just reopened in new and larger quarters, the museum has four floors of exhibits in which children can actually participate. The most prominent of the permanent exhibits is The Brainatarium. This is a multimedia amphitheater in which visitors are introduced to the brain and how it works in conjunction with the five senses. There is a Media Center where children make their own video programs, an art studio, and a fascinating series of exhibits about patterns and how they affect us and our world.

Cloisters, The   923-3700
Ft. Tryon Park
Tuesday–Sunday 9:30 A.M.–4:45 P.M.
Closed Monday
Suggested admission:
Adults $5.00
Students/Senior citizens $2.50
Includes admission to main museum at Fifth Avenue and 82nd Street
Children (under 12) free if accompanied by an adult
By subway: A train to 190th Street, walk through Ft. Tryon Park
By bus: M4 to the Cloisters

A branch of the Metropolitan Museum, The Cloisters sits on a hilltop overlooking the Hudson River. It is composed of parts of various European cloisters and other architectural features dating from the 12th through the 15th centuries. The collection is from the same period and includes such rare and wonderful things as the Belles Heures, those incredible illuminated manuscripts of Jean, Duke du Barry. Robert Campin's Annunciation Altarpiece is here and Adele's favorites, the Unicorn Tapestries. Don't miss the chance to rest in the courtyard and listen to music of the Middle Ages. Finish your visit with a stroll through the herb gardens and along the battlements overlooking the river.

Cooper–Hewitt Museum   860-6868
2 East 91st Street (Fifth Ave.)
Tuesday 10:00 A.M.–9:00 P.M.
Wednesday–Saturday 10:00 A.M.–5:00 P.M.
Sunday Noon–5:00 P.M.
Closed Monday

Admission:
Adults $3.00
Students/Senior citizens $1.50
Tuesday 5:00 P.M.–9:00 P.M. Free
By subway: #4, #5, or #6 train to 96th Street, or
#6 train to 86th Street
By bus: M1, M2, M3, or M4

Housed in the renovated Carnegie Mansion, the Smithsonian Institution's national museum of design features changing exhibitions on the decorative arts. Its permanent collection contains more than 165,000 objects representing many cultures throughout the history of civilization.

Forbes Galleries   206-5548
62 Fifth Avenue (12th St.)
Hours:
Tuesday, Wednesday, Friday, & Saturday 10:00 A.M.–4:00 P.M.
Thursday: Groups by advance reservation only
Admission: Free
By subway: B, D, L, N, R, #4, #5, or #6 train to Union Square
By bus: M2, M3, or M5

This is where you can see Malcolm Forbes's fabulous collection of Faberge Easter eggs and over 12,000 toy soldiers.

Fraunces Tavern Museum   425-1778
54 Pearl Street (Broad St.)
Monday–Friday 10:00 A.M.–4:00 P.M.
Sunday Noon–5:00 P.M. (October–May)
Admission:
Adults $2.50
Children/Senior citizens $1.00
Free on Thursday
By subway: #4 or #5 train to Bowling Green
#1 train to South Ferry
#2 or #3 train to Wall Street
N or R train to Whitehall Street
E train to World Trade Center
By bus: M1, M6, or M15 to South Ferry

Built in 1719 and converted into a tavern in 1762, Fraunces Tavern was the site of George Washington's farewell address to his officers after the Revolutionary War. The upper two stories house an early American museum.

After viewing the exhibits, you can dine in the lovely Colonial rooms downstairs.

Frick Collection   288-0700
1 East 70th Street
Tuesday–Saturday 10:00 A.M.–6:00 P.M.

Sunday 1:00 P.M.–6:00 P.M.
Closed Monday
Admission:
Adults $2.00
Students/Senior citizens $.50
By subway: #6 train to 68th Street and Lexington
Avenue
By bus: M1, M2, M3, or M4

Once the home of Henry Clay Frick, the steel magnate, this is one of the most beautiful old buildings in the city. It also houses a wonderful collection of fine and decorative art. Since this was Frick's home, it follows that his collection of art is highly personal. That is part of the enjoyment of it. With the advice of the greatest of art dealers of his era, Lord Duveen, Frick bought the very best of the "Old Masters" which were on the market in those days. If you possibly can, visit this house. It is a wonderful experience to see how business tycoons of a bygone era lived and to see the things with which they chose to live.

Guggenheim Museum   360-3500
1071 Fifth Avenue (89th St.)
Tuesday 11:00 A.M.–8:00 P.M.
Wednesday–Sunday 11:00 A.M.–5:00 P.M.
Closed Monday
Adults $4.50
Students/Senior citizens $2.50
Children (under 7) Free
Tuesday 5:00 P.M.–8:00 P.M. Free for everyone
By subway: #4, #5, or #6 train to 86th Street
By bus: M1, M2, M3, or M4 Madison and Fifth Avenue
buses

The only building in New York designed by noted architect Frank Lloyd Wright, The Guggenheim owns and exhibits in rotation some 5,000 modern paintings. Kandinsky, Mondrian, Chagall, and Pollock are well represented.

Note: Much of the building will be closed for renovation until Fall of 1991. Call for specific information.

International Center for Photography   860-1777
1130 Fifth Avenue (94th St.)
Tuesday Noon–8:00 P.M.
Wednesday–Friday Noon–5:00 P.M.
Saturday–Sunday 11:00 A.M.–6:00 P.M.
Closed Monday
Admission:
Adults $3.00
Students/Senior citizens $1.50

Children (under 12) $.50
By subway: #6 train to 96th Street and Lexington
Avenue
By bus: M1, M2, M3, or M4

Devoted to supporting photography, the ICP has developed a prominent permanent collection and arranges exhibitions which supplement and enhance it. Due to the boom in camera enthusiasts, this is a very popular museum. If you are interested in books on photography, the bookstore probably has what you are looking for. It's one of the best.

Intrepid Sea–Air–Space Museum   **489-6900**
Pier 86 (46th St. and the Hudson River)
Wednesday–Sunday 10:00 A.M.–5:00 P.M.
Closed Monday and Tuesday
Admission:
Adults $4.75
Children $2.75
Senior citizens $4.00
By subway: A, B, C, D, E, N, #1, #2, #3, or #7 train to
42nd Street
By bus: M42 Crosstown to the Hudson River

Veteran of World War II, Vietnam, and NASA recovery missions, the 910-foot aircraft carrier *Intrepid* is now a technology museum highlighting man's achievements in naval, aviation, and aerospace sciences. Continuous movies and multimedia shows as well as rockets, satellites, capsules, and many historic aircraft. If you are interested in modern man's involvement with space and war, this is a must.

Jewish Museum   **860-1888**
1109 Fifth Avenue (92nd St.)
Monday, Wednesday, & Thursday Noon–5:00 P.M.
Tuesday Noon–8:00 P.M.
Tuesday 5:00 P.M.–8:00 P.M. Free
Sunday 11:00 A.M.–6:00 P.M.
Closed Friday, Saturday, major Jewish and legal
holidays.
Admission:
Adults $4.00
Children/Senior citizens $2.00
By subway: #4 or #5 train to 86th Street; #6 train to
96th Street
By bus: M1, M2, M3, or M4

Operated under the auspices of The Jewish Theological Seminary of America, the museum's collections survey 4000 years of Jewish heritage. The largest of its kind in the Western Hemisphere, it has more than 14,000 artifacts and works of art.

Metropolitan Museum of Art   879-5500
Fifth Avenue & 82nd Street
> Sunday & Tuesday–Thursday 9:30 A.M.–5:15 P.M.
> Friday–Saturday 9:30 A.M.–9:00 P.M.
> Closed Monday
> Suggested Admission: Adults $5.00
> Students/Senior citizens $2.50
> By subway: #4 or #5 train to 86th Street; #6 train to 79th Street
> By bus: M1, M2, M3, or M4

One of the world's greatest and largest (32 acres) museums, the Metropolitan features the remains of the Egyptian temple at Dendur; Impressionist masterpieces; galleries of Asian, Islamic, Assyrian, Greek, Roman, primitive and medieval art; and much more. The Costume Institute's exhibits are always jammed. The Lila Acheson Wallace wing is devoted to 20th century art. From May 1st to November 1st, visitors may visit the Iris and B. Gerald Cantor Roof Garden. Designed to accommodate large 20th century sculptures, it also offers a breathtaking view of the city.

Museum of American Folk Art   977-7298
2 Lincoln Square
Broadway (65th/66th Sts.)
> Hours:
> Daily 9:00 A.M.–9:00 P.M.
> Admission: Free
> By subway: #1 train to 66th Street
> By bus: M5, M7, or M104

A combination of miracles! Open all day every day and free! In the New York museum world this is unheard of, and of course, the collections and changing exhibitions are a welcome addition to the art scene. The craftsmanship and ingenuity of our forefathers takes on new meaning as it is beautifully displayed in the museum's new quarters. Located in the Lincoln Center area, it's the perfect foil for an evening at the opera or before a concert.

Museum of the American Indian   283-2420
Broadway & 155th Street
> Hours:
> Tuesday–Saturday 10:00 A.M.–5:00 P.M.
> Sunday 1:00 P.M.–5:00 P.M.
> Closed Monday
> Admission:
> Adults $3.00
> Children/Senior citizens $2.00

By subway: #1 train to 157th Street
By bus: M4 or M5

This museum has had as bad a time as the native Americans it is designed to represent. Long in danger of closing and covered with scandal, the collection is fantastic and represents all the best of the American Indian. Not only will you see their art and the craftsmanship they put into their functional items, you will leave with an understanding of the history of these people and their daily lives.

Museum of Broadcasting   **752-7684**
23 West 52nd Street
Tuesday Noon–8:00 P.M.
Wednesday–Saturday Noon–5:00 P.M.
Admission:
Adults $4.00
Children/Senior citizens $2.00
By subway: E or F train to 53rd Street; #6 train to 51st Street
By bus: M1, M2, M3, M4, M5, or M32

Founded in 1975 by the legendary William Paley, this museum is one of the most unique and successful. It is difficult to convey, in a short space, all of the activities and goals that make up its mission. Basically, it collects, preserves, interprets, and exhibits radio and television programs and makes them available to the general public. The collection is comprehensive, and there are few things you can ask for that won't be there. The Beatles' American debut on "The Ed Sullivan Show" and Sid Caesar's "Your Show of Shows" are favorite selections. You can view the program of your choice in specially built consoles which seat two. Special programs and workshops are available for children on Saturday.

Museum of the City of New York   **534-1672**
Fifth Avenue at 103rd Street
Tuesday–Saturday 10:00 A.M.–5:00 P.M.
Sunday and Holidays 1:00 P.M.–5:00 P.M.
Closed Monday
Suggested Admission:
Adults $3.00
Senior citizens $1.50
Children $1.00
Families $5.00
By subway: Lexington Avenue #6 train to 103rd Street, then walk west three blocks.
By bus: M1, M2, M3, or M4 to 104th Street

The primary goal of this museum is the preservation of the history of New York City. Of the many things one can see here, we are particularly fond of the Costume Collection, which features clothing worn by New Yorkers or designed by them. It is easy to be fascinated by the Theater Collection, the most comprehensive history of the New York theater ever assembled. Children will enjoy the Toy Collection.

Museum of Modern Art   708-9400
11 West 53rd Street
    Thursday 11:00 A.M.–9:00 P.M.
    Friday–Tuesday 11:00 A.M.–6:00 P.M.
    Closed Wednesday
    Admission:
    Adults $5.00
    Students $3.50
    Senior citizens $2.00
    By subway: E or F train to 55th Street and Fifth Avenue
    By bus: M1, M2, M3, M4, M5, or M32
Although recently remodeled into a cold and unwelcoming environment primarily to make money from the air rights above it, this is the place to see modern art in this country. Keep in mind that "modern" is not contemporary art. MOMA offers the best the world produced from the late 1800s through the late 1950s. Don't miss the sculpture Garden—not as nice as it used to be, it still is a great place to rest and look at some of the best modern work.

New York City Fire Museum   691-1303
278 Spring Street
    Monday–Friday 10:00 A.M.–4:00 P.M.
    Group tours by appointment
    Suggested donation:
    Adults $3.00
    Children $.50
    By subway: #6 train to Spring Street
A complete history of fire fighting in New York City. Tools from Colonial times to the present, examples of the old pumpers, ladder trucks and steamers, and even a horse-drawn sled for winter use make for an interesting sightseeing trip. All of the paraphernalia that was used by the volunteers and, since 1865, the New York City Fire Department, is here to see and touch.

New York Historical Society   873-3400
170 Central Park West
    Tuesday–Saturday 10:00 A.M.–5:00 P.M.
    Sunday 1:00 P.M.–5:00 P.M.
    Closed Monday

Admission:
Adults $2.00
Children $1.00
By subway: B or C train to 81st Street
By bus: M10

A neglected jewel of a museum, the Historical Society contains a comprehensive display of Tiffany lamps and the definitive collection of works by John James Audubon.

South Street Seaport Museum   669-9400
207 Front Street
Tuesday–Friday 11:00 A.M.–4:00 P.M.
Saturday & Sunday 11:00 A.M.–5:00 P.M.
Closed Monday
Admission:
Adults $5.00
Senior citizens $4.00
Students $3.00
Children $2.00
By subway: 2, 3, 4, or 5, to Fulton Street
By bus: M15 (South Ferry) down Second Avenue to Fulton Street

Housed in several locations throughout the seaport, the museum includes three guided walking tours, the tall ship Peking, historical films, and a working re-creation of a 19th century print shop.

Whitney Museum of American Art   570-3600
945 Madison Avenue (75th St.)
Tuesday 1:00 P.M.–8:00 P.M.
Wednesday–Saturday 11:00 A.M.–5:00 P.M.
Sunday Noon–6:00 P.M.
Closed Monday
Admission:
Adults $4.50
Senior citizens $2.50
College students (with ID) Free
Tuesday 6:00 P.M.–8:00 P.M. Free
By subway: #6 train to 77th Street
By bus: M1, M2, M3, or M4

While it has a collection of modern art, it is the Whitney's continuing interest in contemporary artists that keeps New Yorkers flocking to its exhibitions. There is no other museum which does so much to put the stamp of approval on new work—culminating in the famous biennial which selects what its curators feel is the best currently being produced. Since a lot of people (and artists) disagree, this is always an interesting event.

Whitney Museum at the Equitable
    Center   **544-1000**
787 Seventh Avenue (52nd St.)
   Monday–Friday 11:00 A.M.–6:00 P.M.
   Thursday 11:00 A.M.–7:30 P.M.
   Saturday Noon–5:00 P.M.
   Closed Sunday
   Admission: Free
   By subway: N or R train to 49th Street; #1 train to
   50th Street
   By bus: M6, M7, or M104

One of several locations the Whitney uses to bring selections from its permanent collection to the public. Of necessity small, it gives New Yorkers a chance to see art on their lunch hour and, in this case, is conveniently located near many of the midtown hotels.

Music & Dance Booth   **382-2323**
Bryant Park, 42nd Street (Avenue of the Americas)

Music Box Theater   **239-6200**
239 West 45th Street

Myron Toback   **398-8300**
25 West 47th Street (Fifth/Sixth Aves.)

Mysterious Book Shop, The   **765-0900**
129 West 56th Street

N

Nat Sherman   **751-9100**
711 Fifth Avenue (55th St.)

National Car Rental   **1-800-328-4567**

NBC Studio Tour   **664-4000**
GE Building, 30 Rockefeller Plaza

Neil Simon Theater   **757-8646**
250 West 52nd Street

Nell's   **675-1567**
246 West 14th Street (Seventh/Eighth Aves.)

Netherlands (Consulate of)   **246-1429**
1 Rockefeller Plaza

New Jersey Transit   **1-201-762-5100**

New York Athletic Club	247-5100
180 Central Park South (Seventh Ave.)	
New York Botanical Garden, The	220-8700
Fordham Road and Bronx River Parkway, Bronx	
New York Bound Bookshop	245-8503
50 Rockefeller Plaza (50th/51st Sts.)	
New York Delicatessen	541-8320
104 West 57th Street (Sixth Ave.)	
New York Doll Hospital, The	838-7527
787 Lexington Avenue (61st/62nd Sts.)	
New York Eye & Ear Hospital	598-1313
310 East 14th Street	
New York Helicopter	1-800-645-3494
New York Helmsley	490-8900
212 East 42nd Street (Second/Third Aves.)	
New York Hilton	586-7000
1335 Avenue of the Americas (53rd/54th Sts.)	
New York Historical Society	873-3400
170 Central Park West	
New York Hospital–Cornell Medical	
Center	472-5454
525 East 68th Street	
New York Infirmary	233-5300
107 William Street	
New York Marriott Financial Center	
(Opening 1991)	
New York Penta	736-5000
Seventh Avenue (33rd St.)	
New York Public Library	
Fifth Avenue (42nd St.)	930-0501
Reference	340-0849
New York Stock Exchange	656-5167
20 Broad Street (Wall St.)	
New York University Club	354-3400
123 West 43rd Street	
New York University Hospital	340-7300
550 First Avenue	
New York Yacht Club	382-1000
37 West 44th Street	
New Zealand (Consulate of)	586-0060
630 Fifth Avenue	

Newark Airport	1-201-961-2000
Newell Art Galleries	758-1970

425 East 53rd Street

NEWSSTANDS

Hotalings   840-1868
142 West 42nd Street (between Sixth & Seventh Aves.)
Hours:
Monday–Friday 7:30 A.M.–9:00 P.M.
Saturday–Sunday 7:30 A.M.–8:00 P.M.

Carries an enormous selection of foreign and out-of-town newspapers.

24-hour Newsstands
Broadway at 72nd, 79th, 94th, 96th, & 104th Streets
First Avenue at 65th & 86th Streets
Second Avenue at St. Mark's Place & 50th & 53rd Streets
Third Avenue at St. Mark's Place & 54th Street
Lexington Avenue at 64th & 89th Streets
Sixth Avenue at 8th, 48th, & 57th Streets
Eighth Avenue at 23rd, 42nd, & 46th Streets

Nicaragua (Consulate of)	247-0120

1270 Fifth Avenue

Nicholson, Laura Alexandra (Masseuse)	216-0426

Nigeria (Consulate of)	715-7272

575 Lexington Avenue

NIGHTCLUBS

Five years ago, we would have had a terrible time listing nightclubs—the grand era of such places as the Persian Room was long gone, and our guests often refused to believe that the glittering New York nightlife they'd seen in movies was no more. Happily, it's back.

Ballroom, The   244-3005
253 West 28th Street (Eighth Ave.)

Eartha Kitt, Blossom Dearie, and the legendary Peggy Lee indicate the caliber of performer you can expect at The Ballroom. Chef Felipe Rojas-Lombardi serves up Continental cuisine and offers Spanish hors d'oeuvres at the tapas bar. Tuesday–Saturday. Two drink minimum; cover charge varies with performer. All major credit cards accepted.

Cafe Carlyle, The   744-1600
Madison Avenue at 76th Street

Bobby Short has been holding forth for years in this chic and elegant room. When he leaves town for a well-earned rest, stars like George Shearing or "Designing Women's" Dixie Carter appear. Closed Sunday and Monday. Cover charge varies with performer. All major credit cards accepted.

Criterion Cabaret   239-6200
1530 Broadway (45th St.)

This new nightclub located in the theater district promises to feature major stars. So far, Ben Vereen, Chita Rivera, and David Brenner have appeared here. Doors open one hour before show time, with simple dining and cocktails before and during the shows. Closed Monday. Cover charge ranges from approximately $15.00 to $30.00. Two drink minimum. All major credit cards accepted.

Don't Tell Mama   757-0788
343 West 46th Street (Eighth/Ninth Aves.)

A place to discover tomorrow's star singers and comedians, this cozy Restaurant Row club hopes to be a launching pad for new talent. Most shows are $10.00–12.00. Two drink minimum. No credit cards accepted.

Oak Room at The Algonquin   840-6800
59 West 44th Street (Fifth/Sixth Aves.)

Michael Feinstein rose to fame here, and this continues to be one of Manhattan's best and most intimate cabaret rooms, presenting Andrea Marcovicci, Liliane Montevecchi, Margaret Whiting, and the young jazz pianist Harry Connick Jr. Closed Sunday. $15.00 minimum at all times. Music charge varies from $15.00–20.00. All major credit cards accepted.

Rainbow and Stars   632-5000
GE Building, 30 Rockefeller Center

Tony Bennett opened this glittering new cabaret and supper club atop the GE building, and performers such as Rosemary Clooney, Lisa Kirk, and Theodore Bikel have appeared here. Dinner is served before the early show, and a supper menu is available after 10:30 P.M. Closed Sunday and Monday. $35.00 cover charge. AE credit card only.

Northwest Airlines   736-1220

Notes   247-8000
The Omni, Seventh Avenue (55th St.)

Novotel   315-0100
226 West 52nd Street (Broadway)

O

O'Neal's Balloon	**399-2353**
48 West 63rd Street	

O.K. Harris	**431-3600**
383 West Broadway	

Oak Room at The Algonquin	**840-6800**
59 West 44th Street (Fifth/Sixth Aves.)	

OBSERVATION DECKS

Empire State Building   **736-3100**
350 Fifth Avenue (34th St.)
    Open Daily 9:30 A.M.–Midnight
    Admission:
    Adults $3.25
    Children & Senior citizens $1.75
Outdoor promenade on the 86th floor; enclosed 102nd floor observatory. Tickets sold until 11:25 P.M.

World Trade Center   **466-7377**
Two World Trade Center
    Open Daily 9:30 A.M.–9:30 P.M.
    Admission:
    Adults $2.95
    Children & Senior citizens $1.50
Adele's first stop with out-of-town visitors is the enclosed deck on the World Trade Center's 107th floor. They are invariably dazzled. The rooftop promenade is the world's highest open-air viewing platform.

Odeon	**233-0507**
145 West Broadway (Thomas St.)	

Olympia Bus Service	**964-6233**

Olympic Airways	**838-3600**

Omni Berkshire Place	**753-5800**
21 East 52nd Street (Madison Ave.)	

Omni Park Central	**247-8000**
Seventh Avenue (56th St.)	

One if by Land, Two if by Sea	**255-8649**
17 Barrow Street (Seventh Ave. So./West 4th St.)	

One Night Stand	**772-7720**
905 Madison Avenue	

ORCHARD STREET

Years ago, Orchard Street was the place to get real bargains in clothing, shoes, yard goods, and leather items such as purses, jackets, and luggage.

This was the past.

We have found that there are no longer any important bargains, and the quality of goods is such that it is no longer a viable place to shop. One can get the same prices (or better) at sales in department stores. We were interested to see that there were no tourists in the area.

We regret to say that another New York landmark is a thing of the past. We cannot, in good conscience recommend Orchard Street for either shopping or sightseeing.

Orpheum Theater   **477-2477**
126 Second Avenue (8th St.)

Orso   **489-7212**
322 West 46th Street (Eighth/Ninth Aves.)

OTB (Off-Track Betting)   **Racing Results: 976-2121**
There are 109 locations for legalized gambling around town. Hotel guests are most likely to frequent those at:

42nd Street & Broadway

**48th Street between Fifth & Sixth
    Avenues**

**52nd Street between Fifth &
    Madison Avenues**

56th Street & Seventh Avenue

For a more refined atmosphere, try:

Inside Track, The   **752-1940**
1011 Second Avenue (between 53rd & 54th Sts.)
    Open Daily 11:30 A.M.–5:00 P.M. & 7:00 P.M.–11:30 P.M.
    Tuesday 7:00 P.M.–11:30 P.M. only
For a $5.00 admission fee, bettors can order drinks, have lunch or dinner in the rustic English pub restaurant, and watch the races on two giant TV screens and 19 monitors. Jacket required.

Skyward, The Select Club   **704-5262**
165 Water Street
Located two blocks south of the South Street Seaport, at the intersection of Water Street and Maiden Lane, this combined betting parlor/restaurant simulcasts live New York Racing Association (NYRA) thoroughbred races in the af-

ternoon and harness races in the evening onto three large screens and 56 TV monitors. Also displayed are tickers from the New York and American Stock Exchanges as well as a quotron with commodities quotes. Admission $5.00 per person. Jacket required.

   Monday–Friday 11:00 A.M.–11:00 P.M.
   Saturday–Sunday 11:00 A.M.–5:30 P.M.

Oyster Bar, The   460-6650
Grand Central Station/Lower Level

Ozark Airlines   1-201-433-6967

P

P.J. Clarke's   759-1650
915 Third Avenue (55th St.)

Pace Gallery   421-3292
32 East 57th Street

Pakistan (Consulate of)   879-5800
12 East 65th Street

Palio   245-4850
151 West 51st Street (Sixth/Seventh Aves.)

Palladium   473-7171
126 East 14th Street (Park Ave.)

Palm Court, The   759-3000
The Plaza Hotel, Fifth Avenue and Central Park South

Palm, The   687-2953
837 Second Avenue (44th/45th Sts.)

Pan Am Water Shuttle   1-800-54-FERRY
From Wall Street to La Guardia Airport

Pan American   687-2600

Pan American Shuttle   1-718-803-6600

Panama (Consulate of)   246-3771
1270 Sixth Avenue

Paragon Athletics   255-8036
867 Broadway (17th/18th Sts.)

Paramount Hotel, The	**764-5500**
235 West 46th Street (Broadway/Eighth Ave.)	
Parioli Romanissimo	**288-2391**
24 East 81st Street (Fifth/Madison Aves.)	
Park 51	**765-1900**
152 West 51st Street	
Park East 56	**418-0400**
128 East 56th Street	
Park Events	**360-1333**
Parker Meridien	**245-5000**
118 West 56th Street (Sixth/Seventh Aves.)	
Parking Violations Bureau	**477-4430**

PARKS

Central Park

New York's biggest and best. Almost 900 acres of trees, lakes, and entertainment facilities in the heart of the city. Many of the business people who stay in midtown or the luxury hotels which fringe the park use it for their early morning jogging. It's reasonably safe in the daytime as long as you don't wander off by yourself. Pay a visit to the zoo (*See* ZOOS) and enjoy the new facilities for our favorite animals who call the city home. In the winter, enjoy the magic of ice skating at night (*See* ICE SKATING) surrounded by the beauty of the city's lights. It you're lucky, maybe it will snow. This is also where you ride if you rent horses from the Claremont Riding Academy (*See* HORSE-BACK RIDING).

Washington Square Park

Once a wonderful park, this is now a haven for drug pushers and ghetto blasters brought on by New York University and its ready market of students. In spite of the city's repeated attempts to physically rebuild, nothing really helps this tired park. Skip it.

Passenger Ship Terminal	**246-4650**
PATH Trains	**1-201-963-2558**
Paul Stuart	**682-0320**
Madison Avenue at 45th Street	
Paula Cooper	**674-0766**
155 Wooster Street	

Payne Whitney Hospital   472-6282
525 East 68th Street

PC Express Rentals   685-6919

Peacock Alley   355-3000
Waldorf Astoria Hotel, 49th Street and Park Avenue

Pearl Theater Co., Inc.   645-7708
125 West 22nd Street

Pearl's   221-6677
38 West 48th Street

Pedigree Pups   752-1377
989 First Avenue (54th/55th Sts.)

Pembroke Room   838-1400
The Lowell, 28 East 63rd Street (Madison Ave.)

Peninsula, The   247-2200
700 Fifth Avenue (55th St.)

Pennsylvania Station (see RAILROADS)
Seventh Avenue (33rd St.)

Periyali   463-7890
35 West 20th Street

Peru (Consulate of)   644-2850
805 Third Avenue

Perugina Chocolate   688-2490
636 Lexington Avenue (54th St.)

Peter Luger's Steak House   1-718-387-7400
178 Broadway (Driggs/Bedford Aves., Brooklyn)

Petrossian   245-2214
182 West 58th Street (Seventh Ave.)

PHARMACIES

Kaufman Pharmacy   755-2266
Lexington Avenue and 50th Street
   Open 24 hours a day, 7 days a week

Philippines (Consulate of)   764-1330
556 Fifth Avenue

Phillips Fine Art Auctioneers   570-4830
406 East 79th Street

PIANO BARS

Bemelman's Bar   744-1600
The Carlyle Hotel, Madison Avenue at 76th Street

Jazz pianist Barbara Carroll is featured Tuesday–Saturday, 9:45 P.M.–1:00 A.M. $5.00 cover charge. Earlier in the evening, from 5:30–8:00 P.M., enjoy Michael Devine.

Cafe Carlyle   744-1600
The Carlyle Hotel, 35 East 76th Street (Madison Ave.)
Bobby Short—need we say more?

Chez Josephine   594-1925
414 West 42nd Street (Ninth/Tenth Aves.)
Jean Claude Baker's relatively new, but already famous, bistro. Two great pianists knock out show tunes to the encouragement of a mixed crowd of actors, business people, and the international set.

Fortune Garden Pavilion   753-0101
209 East 49th Street
First rate jazz artists perform in this stunning Chinese restaurant.

Grand Sea Palace   265-8133
346 West 46th Street
In the unlikely setting of a Thai restaurant, the almost-legendary Danny Apolinar performs Wednesday through Sunday, starting at 9:00 P.M.

La Camelia   751-5488
225 East 58th Street
Elegant Italian restaurant featuring a singer/pianist. Monday–Saturday, 10:00 P.M.–2:00 A.M.

Notes   247-8000
The Omni Hotel, Seventh Avenue at 55th Street
Buck Buchholz performs Tuesday–Thursday 8:30 P.M.–12:30 A.M.

One if by Land, Two if by Sea   255-8649
17 Barrow Street (Seventh Ave.)
On a cold winter's evening, it's hard to top this ultra-romantic Greenwich Village restaurant. The perfect end to a day: sitting at the bar, bathed in the flickering light from two fireplaces, listening to old favorites.

Peacock Alley   355-3000
Waldorf Astoria Hotel, 49th Street and Park Avenue
Jimmy Lyon and Penny Brook play on Cole Porter's piano to entertain an international crowd in one of the city's most celebrated rooms.

Pickwick Arms Hotel   355-0300
230 East 51st Street (Second/Third Aves.)

Pier 6 Heliport	248-7230
South of Wall Street on the East River	
Pierre Deux	243-7740
369 Bleecker Street	
Pierre, The	838-8000
2 East 61st Street (Fifth Ave.)	
Pine Hills Country Club	1-516-878-4343
162 Wading River Road, Manorville, NY	
Pipeworks and Wilke	956-4820
16 West 55th Street (Fifth/Madison Aves.)	
Place des Antiquaires	758-2900
125 East 57th Street	
Plaza, The	759-3000
768 Fifth Avenue (59th St.)	
Plaza Athenee	734-9100
37 East 64th Street (Madison/Park Ave.)	
Plaza Watch & Jewelry	755-6638
826 Lexington Avenue (63rd/64th Sts.)	
Plymouth Theater	239-6200
237 West 45th Street	
Poison Control	340-4494
Poland (Consulate of)	889-8360
233 Madison Avenue	
Police Emergency	911
Port Authority Bus Terminal	564-8484
42nd Street and Eighth Avenue	
Porto Rico Importing Company	477-5421
201 Bleecker Street	
Portugal (Consulate of)	246-4580
630 Fifth Avenue	
Post House, The	935-2888
28 East 63rd Street (Madison/Park Aves.)	

POST OFFICES

Main Post Office	967-8585
33rd Street (Eighth Ave.)	

The salvation of those who file their income tax at midnight on April 15th, the Main Post office is open 24 hours. No registered mail and limited service for packages after regular hours.

POSTAGE

The following are the standard rates for postage:

    Letters (U.S.) $.25 per half ounce (a normal letter)
    Postcards (U.S.) $.15 each
    Letters (Overseas) $.45 per half ounce (a normal letter)
    Postcards (Overseas) $.36 each

Rate increases are anticipated for 1991, however, data is not available as we go to press.

Pret-a-Party   696-9260
238 Madison Avenue, #1-D

Primavera   861-8608
1578 First Avenue (82nd St.)

Primola   758-1775
1226 Second Avenue (64th/65th Sts.)

Princeton Club   840-6400
15 West 43rd Street

Printed Matter   925-0325
7 Lispenard Street

Promenade Theater   580-1313
2152 Broadway (76th St.)

Provincetown Playhouse   477-5048
133 MacDougal Street

Prunelle   759-6410
18 East 54th Street (Fifth/Madison Aves.)

Public Theater   598-7150
425 Lafayette Street

Puppet Company, The   741-1646
31 Union Square West, Loft 2-B

Purolator Courier   333-5560

Q

Qantas   1-800-227-4500

Quatorze   206-7006
240 West 14th Street (Seventh/Eighth Aves.)

Queens Midtown Tunnel
36th Street at Second Avenue

Queensboro Bridge
59th Street at Second Avenue

Quilted Giraffe, The   593-1221
550 Madison Avenue (55th/56th Sts.)

R

RACETRACKS Racing results: 1-914-968-4200

Aqueduct   1-718-641-4700
Rockaway Boulevard at 106th Street, Brooklyn
> By subway: A train to Brooklyn
> First race at 1:00 P.M.
> January 1–May 7, 1990
> Closed Tuesday except April 8th and Easter Sunday
> October 31–December 31, 1990
> Closed Wednesday except November 7th and December 24th

Belmont Park   1-718-641-4700
Hempstead Turnpike at Plainfield Avenue
> Long Island Railroad (LIRR) runs special trains on the days of races.
> $3.50 one-way
> By car take the Cross Island Parkway to Hempstead Turnpike and follow the signs to Belmont.
> May 9th through July 30th, 1990
> August 29th through October 29th, 1990
> Gates open at 11:00 A.M. First race at 1:00 P.M.
> Closed on Tuesday

For the big races reservations are recommended. Call the New York Racing Association at 1-718-641-4700. Seats must be reserved for the Belmont Stakes which is run on June 11.

Meadowlands (Harness Racing)   1-201-935-8500
East Rutherford, NJ
> From the Lincoln Tunnel, follow Route #3 West to the Sports Complex (four miles).
> From the Holland Tunnel or Brooklyn/Staten Island bridge crossings, take the New Jersey Turnpike Extension to the New Jersey Turnpike. Go North on the New Jersey Turnpike to Exit 16W.

Load-and-Go bus service is available for all events from the Port Authority Bus Terminal (Eighth Avenue at 42st St.). It's a 15 minute ride.

A major operation, the track can host approximately 40,000 spectators. It includes three restaurants, 500 color TV monitors, and parking for 22,000 vehicles. For placing your bets there are 538 pari-mutuel windows located in the grandstand area.

Yonkers (Harness Racing)   1-914-968-4200
Yonkers and Central Avenues, Yonkers, NY

Subways: IRT #4 train to the last stop. Go down stairs
and take a #20 White Plains bus to the track.
Jerome Avenue line to Woodlawn Station
Sixth Avenue IND line to Bedford Park Boulevard
Station
White Plains Avenue Line to 238th Street
Van Cortland Park Line to 242nd Street Station
Post time 8:00 P.M., eleven races nightly

Completely prepared to handle the requirements of the
more than 13,000 spectators who frequently fill the grand-
stands. Restaurants, parking facilities, and closed circuit
TV systems are first class.

Racing Results	**976-2121**
Racket & Tennis Club	**753-9700**
370 Park Avenue (53rd St.)	
Radio City Music Hall	**247-4777**
Avenue of the Americas at 50th Street	
Radio City Music Hall Productions	**246-4600**
Raft Theater	**947-8389**
432 West 42nd Street	
Raga	**757-3450**
57 West 48th Street (Fifth/Sixth Aves.)	

RAILROADS

AMTRAK	**582-6875**
Metroliner Information	**582-6387**
Package Express	**560-7385**
Baggage	**560-7636**
Lost and Found	**560-7388**

Trains depart from Penn Station, 33rd Street and Seventh
Avenue. In addition to regular service, there is also the
faster but more expensive Metroliner.

Trains to Washington, DC, depart weekdays on the hour
starting at 7:00 A.M.
Reservations are necessary for the Metroliner.

There is also AMTRAK service from Grand Central Station but on a more limited basis. All service is to be moved
to Penn Station within the next few years.

Long Island Railroad	**1-718-454-5477**
Special Services	**1-718-990-7498**
General Information	**1-718-217-5477**
Lost and Found	**1-718-526-0020**

Trains depart from LIRR Terminal at Penn Station.

Metro North	**532-4900**
Information	**736-4545**
Package Express/Baggage	**560-7534**
Lost and Found	**560-7534**

Trains depart from Grand Central Station, 42nd Street and Park Avenue

Services Westchester, Dutchess, and Putnam Counties and Connecticut.

New Jersey Transit	**1-201-762-5100**
Trains depart from Penn Station	**1-800-772-2222**
PATH Trains	**1-201-963-2558**

A commuter service between New York and New Jersey. Fare is $1.00.

Rainbow and Stars	**632-5000**
30 Rockefeller Center	
Rainbow Room, The	**632-5000**
30 Rockefeller Plaza	
Ralph Lauren/Polo	**606-2100**
867 Madison Avenue (72nd St.)	
Ramada Inn	**581-7000**
48th Street (Eighth Ave.)	
Rape Helpline	**267-7273**
Record Hunter	**697-8970**
507 Fifth Avenue (42nd/43rd Sts.)	

RECORDS/TAPES

Broadway Hal's Big Hit Oldies	**475-9516**
170 Bleecker Street at Sullivan	
Footlight Records	**533-1572**
90 Third Avenue	
113 East 12th Street	

A collectors paradise for out of print and hard-to-find records.

King Karol	**869-0230**
1500 Broadway (43rd St.)	
Sam Goody's	
51 West 51st Street (6th Ave.)	**246-8730**
666 3rd Avenue (43rd St.)	**986-8480**
Record Hunter	**697-8970**
507 Fifth Avenue (42nd/43rd Sts.)	
Tower Records	
692 Broadway (4th St.)	**505-1500**
1967 Broadway (66th St.)	**496-2500**
4th and Lafayette Streets	**505-1505**

Red Blazer, Too   262-3112
349 West 46th Street (Eighth/Ninth Aves.)

Red Zone   582-2222
440 West 54th Street

Regency, The   759-4100
540 Park Avenue (60th/61st Sts.)

Regent Air   1-800-538-7587

Regine's   826-0990
502 Park Avenue (59th St.)

Rene Pujol   246-3023
321 West 51st Street (Eighth/Ninth Aves.)

Rennie Ellen   869-5525
15 West 47th Street, Room 401

RENTALS, AUDIO VISUAL

K.B.M. Rental   354-6888
60 West 39th Street

Columbus Video   568-0123
529 Columbus Avenue

Video Shack   581-6260
1608 Broadway (49th St.)

RENTALS, AUTOMOBILE

All of the major agencies have branches here. Unfortunately, none will pick up or deliver a car for you. Call the 800 number for the location closest to your hotel.

Avis   1-800-331-1212

Budget   807-8700

Hertz   1-800-654-3131

National   1-800-328-4567

Vogel's Eurocars, Inc.   1-914-968-8200
In the mood for something more upscale? Try Vogel's Eurocars, Inc. and rent a Mercedes. A $2,500 security deposit is required on all rentals. American Express, Carte Blanche, Diners Club, cash, or certified check only.

RENTALS, BICYCLE

On a cool spring or brisk autumn day, the idea of renting a bike and pedaling through Central Park is irresistible. All of these firms require an ID and/or a substantial deposit.

A & B Bicycle World   866-7600
663 Amsterdam Avenue

Bicycles Plus   794-2979
1400 Third Avenue (79th/80th Sts.)
   Daily 10:00 A.M.–6:00 P.M., 8:00 P.M. in summer

Bikes in the Park   861-4137
Loeb Boathouse, Park Drive North at 72nd Street in
Central Park
   $5.00 per hour/$25.00 per day

Gene's Bicycles   249-9218
242 East 79th Street (Second/Third Aves.)

Metro Bicycle Store   427-4450
1311 Lexington Avenue (88th St.)

West Side Bicycle Store   663-7531
231 West 96th Street (Broadway)
   $3.00 per hour/$5.00 per hour for a 10-speed bike

Stuyvesant Bicycle   254-5200
349 West 14th Street (Eighth/Ninth Aves.)

RENTALS, COMPUTER

On some occasions, for the last-minute updating of a report or preparation of a speech, it is necessary to rent a computer. These companies provide excellent equipment on short notice.

All Service Computer Rentals, Inc.   524-0003
600 West 58th Street
Always courteous and reliable, with the latest equipment and competitive fees.

Log_On Computer Services   674-6446
611 Broadway, Suite 515
Complete computer services—rent computers by the hour and printers by the page. They do not deliver equipment—you work on their premises. Dan Arnowitz's help was invaluable in the preparation of this book.

PC Express Rentals   807-8234
IBM, Apple, and Compaq computers, plus laser printers available 24 hours a day, 7 days a week. We have had extremely bad experiences dealing with these people and recommend that you do not use them except in dire emergency.

RENTALS, COSTUME

Animal Outfits for People   840-6219
252 West 46th Street
   Monday–Friday Noon–6:00 P.M., by appointment only
The name tells it all. Don't come here looking for Kermit the Frog—Animal Outfits rents only original creations. Prices average $75.00 for three days.

Universal Costumes, Co.   239-3222
535 Eighth Avenue
   Monday–Friday 9:30 A.M.–5:30 P.M.
Manhattan's largest costume rental shop for adults caters to your every whim. A hotel guest wishing to appear as "a knight in shining armor" fulfilled his wish here.

RENTALS, FORMAL WEAR, MEN

Gingiss Formalwear   302-1742
560 Fifth Avenue (46th St.), Second Floor
Gingiss has a complete rental department as well as tuxedos, shirts, and accessories for sale. After Six, Lord West, Bill Blass, Cardin, Dior, Perry Ellis, Lanvin, and Ralph Lauren are among the famous labels offered.

Jack Silver Formal Wear   582-3298/582-3389
1780 Broadway (57th/58th Sts.)

Ted's Fine Clothing   966-2029
83 Orchard Street
   Open Sunday

Zeller Tuxedos   355-0707
201 East 56th Street (Second/Third Aves.)

RENTALS, FORMAL WEAR, WOMEN

At last there's a solution for women who need a "drop-dead" dress for a special occasion, yet don't want to spend a month's salary for something they'll wear only once. Both companies offer a selection in a wide range of sizes. Deposit required and minor alterations included.

One Night Stand   772-7720
905 Madison Avenue

Pret-a-Party   696-9260
238 Madison Avenue, #1-D
Honora Horan is the owner of one of the first rental shops offering evening wear for women. A deposit of $100–250 is required and the rental fees run $75–150. She carries

sizes 4 through 12 in a variety of styles and a selection of costume jewelry to match.

RENTALS, STROLLER

When you come to the big city with the little one, you may very well need a stroller. We have had very good luck with the company listed below.

AAA-U-Rent	**923-0300**
861 Eagle Avenue, Bronx	**665-6633**

REPAIR SERVICES, CIGARETTE LIGHTERS

No need to despair when your favorite gold lighter needs repair. Take it to the dependable staff at:

Authorized Repair Service   **586-0947**
30 West 57th Street (Fifth/Sixth Aves.), Second Floor
    Monday–Friday 8:30 A.M.–5:30 P.M.
Stocks many obsolete parts for lighters no longer being made, and Richard Weinstein will make any parts he can't otherwise obtain. A good place to know about if you need really difficult repairs.

Beny's Authorized Sales & Service   **226-8437**
86 Canal Street (Eldridge St.)
    Sunday–Friday 6:30 A.M.–3:30 P.M.
The oldest of the shops we know about, Beny's has been in business for over 50 years. Jerry Cohen, the owner, can repair almost anything.

**Goldfield's Jewelers & Repair
    Service**   **753-3750**
229 East 53rd Street (Second/Third Aves.)
    Monday–Friday 8:30 A.M.–5:30 P.M.
Real experts at repairing all types of lighters. Antiques and heirlooms get special care and attention.

REPAIR SERVICES, CLOTHING
Alice Zotta   **840-7657**
2 West 45th Street, Room 1504
    Hours:
    Monday–Friday 8:00 A.M.–6:00 P.M.
    Saturday 8:00 A.M.–2:00 P.M.

173

You have to be good to work for the likes of Burberry's and Paul Stuart.

French-American Reweaving
Company, The   753-1672
37 West 57th Street
  Hours:
  Monday–Friday 9:30 A.M.–6:00 P.M.
  Saturday 11:00 A.M.–2:00 P.M.
Reweaving done so well you can't find the damaged area. Cigarette burns, tears, and moth holes quickly disappear.

Superior Weaving & Mending
Company, The   929-7208
41 Union Square West (17th St.)
Suite 423
  Hours:
  Monday–Friday 8:00 A.M.–4:45 P.M.
  Closed Saturday
Another one of the best. Brooks Brothers and Saks Fifth Avenue trust them with their repair work.

REPAIR SERVICES, EYEGLASSES

Cohen Optical   751-6652
Lexington Avenue and 60th Street
A lifesaver! Open Saturday until 6:45 P.M.

General Vision Center   594-2831
330 West 42nd Street (Eighth/Ninth Aves.)
  Monday–Saturday 9:00 A.M.–5:30 P.M.

REPAIR SERVICES, JEWELRY

Jewelry Patch, Inc., The   840-8279
501 Seventh Avenue (37th/38th Sts.)
  Open Monday–Saturday

Rissin's Jewelry Clinic, Inc.   575-1098
4 West 47th Street
  Gemologist–Fine Stones
  Repairs and alterations
  Closed Wednesday & Friday

REPAIR SERVICES, LUGGAGE

Travelers frequently encounter problems with broken or damaged luggage, particularly if they're flying. The following are some of the more helpful and efficient repair shops.

A-Z Luggage   **686-6905**
425 Fifth Avenue (38th/39th Sts.)
  Closed Saturday; open Sunday

Green Luggage Repair   **682-7978**
6 East 46th Street (Fifth/Madison Aves.)
One day repair service Monday through Friday.

Lexington Luggage   **223-0698**
793 Lexington Avenue (61st/62nd Sts.)
One day repair service Monday through Friday.

Resorts International   **972-4444**

REST ROOMS

See **"BATHROOMS"**

RESTAURANTS

Every city has plenty of restaurant guides. Books, along with reviews in weekly and monthly magazines, abound. We love to read them and often do. Our experience with travelers, however, is that they want only a limited amount of information about restaurants and they want it fast. We are giving you, therefore, the same amount and type of information for which our hotel guests ask. Our comments are based upon a combination of our personal experience and guest comments. The majority of the restaurants included here are the best and most popular in New York (reservations are a must at most of them), but we also note some which are only recommended for their atmosphere and others which should be avoided altogether. We have used a key (as shown in margin) to indicate the restaurants which have found the most favor with our guests or which we particularly enjoy.

L = Late (service after Midnight)   S = Open Sunday

Akbar (Indian) S (Moderate)   **838-1717**
475 Park Avenue (57th/58th Sts.)
  Dress code: None
  All major credit cards accepted
Newly refurbished, Akbar maintains its reputation as one of New York's best Indian restaurants. The tandoor-cooked mixed grill, chicken jalfrezie, and Akbar Special Biryani are all winners here.

American Festival Cafe
    (American) L/S (Moderate)   **246-6699**
20 West 50th Street (Fifth/Sixth Aves.)
    Dress code: None
    All major credit cards accepted
The Cafe's food is nothing to write home about, but it's such fun to dine outdoors in the middle of Rockefeller Center or watch the skaters in the winter, that the cafe is always packed. Children especially enjoy having "Breakfast with Santa" during the holidays.

An American Place (American)
    (Expensive)   **684-2122**
2 Park Avenue (32nd St.)
    Dress code: Jacket preferred
    All major credit cards accepted
Chef-owner Lawrence Forgione cooks exclusively with American ingredients. When these include Ipswich clams, Walla Walla onions, Michigan morels, fresh fish from Long Island waters, and Black Angus steaks, the results are imaginative and delicious.

Angelo's of Mulberry Street
    (Italian) (Moderate)   **966-1277**
146 Mulberry Street (Grand/Hester Sts.)
    Dress code: None
    All major credit cards accepted
One of the most famous restaurants in Little Italy. While the food quality is uneven, tourists and New Yorkers still seem to flock here. Expect to wait on line.

Aquavit (Scandinavian) (Expensive)   **307-7311**
13 West 54th Street (Fifth/Sixth Aves.)
    Dress code: Formal in the Atrium, Informal in the Cafe
    Credit cards: AE, MC, & V
If you're looking for Scandinavian food, this is the only place to go. Nelson Rockefeller's former residence has been turned into a handsome restaurant, where the cuisine and service are of the highest quality.

Arcadia (American) (Very Expensive)   **223-2900**
21 East 62nd Street (Fifth/Madison Aves.)
    Dress code: Jacket and tie
    All major credit cards accepted
Anne Rosensweig, the chef/owner, prepares some of the very best and most original "Americana" style cuisine. After a stint at The "21" Club, she's back at her own place, to the delight of her many fans.

Arizona 206 (Nouvelle Southwestern)
    L (Moderate)   **838-0440**
206 East 60th Street (Second/Third Aves.)

Dress code: None
All major credit cards accepted

One of the superstars in the trendy nouvelle south-western sky. The fabulous food may make up for all of the problems such as long waits for tables (in spite of reservations), a very high level of noise, and overcrowding.

Aureole (American) (Very expensive)   **319-1660**
34 East 61st Street (Madison/Park Aves.)
Dress code: Jacket and tie
Credit cards: AE, MC, & V

Chef Charles Palmer (formerly of The River Cafe) had an instant hit in this elegant, two-tiered restaurant, just a short walk from some of the Upper East Side's best hotels.

Aurora (French) (Very expensive)   **692-9292**
60 East 49th Street (Madison/Park Aves.)
Dress code: Jacket
All major credit cards accepted

Renowned restaurateur Joe Baum had better get back here quickly. If the quality of the food continues to slide, the sun will soon set on this Aurora. Lunch only.

Au Tunnel (French Bistro) (Moderate)   **582-2166**
250 West 47th Street (Broadway/Eighth Ave.)
Dress code: None
Credit cards: AE, MC, & V

A delightful French bistro in the heart of the Theater District.

Barbetta (Italian) L (Expensive)   **436-9171**
321 West 46th Street (Eighth/Ninth Aves.)
Dress code: Jacket and tie
All major credit cards accepted

This old standby in the Theater District is more notable for its romantic surroundings than the food.

Bellini by Cipriani (Italian) L/S
(Expensive)   **265-7770**
777 Seventh Avenue (50th/51st Sts.)
Dress code: Jacket
Credit cards: AE, MC, V, & DC

This was an "in" place for a very, very short time. The quality of the food doesn't measure up to the propaganda.

Ben Benson's (Steaks) L/S (Expensive)   **581-8888**
123 West 52nd Street (Sixth/Seventh Aves.)
Dress code: None
All major credit cards accepted

This is a popular steakhouse that has survived for years on location and satisfactory food. Not good—satisfactory. It's close to the theater district and can get you out in time for the curtain. After 6:00 P.M., valet parking is available.

Benihana of Tokyo (Japanese Steakhouse) S (Moderate)   581-0930

47 West 56th Street (Fifth/Sixth Aves.)
    Dress code: None
    All major credit cards accepted

Benihana's signature tabletop cooking continues to delight children, tourists, and the occasional New Yorker. While the cooking may not be authentically Japanese, the show is always entertaining.

Bice (Italian) L/S (Expensive)   688-1999

7 East 54th Street (Madison/Fifth Aves.)
    Dress code: None
    Credit cards: AE & DC

Good, but not one of the great Italian restaurants that we are blessed with here in the Big Apple. Go to see the trendy crowd and sublime Milanese decor.

Bouley (French) (Very expensive)   608-3852

165 Duane Street (Hudson/Greenwich Sts.)
    Dress code: Jacket and tie
    All major credit cards accepted

You'll feel transported to an elegant European inn when you're seated in this beautiful, flower-filled room, sampling David Bouley's delicate nouvelle cuisine. Treat yourself to the eight-course tasting menu ($65.00) for a memorable evening.

Box Tree, The (Continental) S (Very expensive)   758-8320

250 East 49th Street (Second/Third Aves.)
    Dress code: Jacket and tie
    Credit cards: AE

Intimate, romantic, and very expensive.

Brasserie, The (French/Alsatian) L/S (Moderate)   751-4840

100 East 53rd Street (Lexington/Park Aves.)
    Dress code: None
    All major credit cards accepted
    Open 24 hours

We've sent many people here in the dead of night when they couldn't be fed anywhere else. Onion soup is the only notable item on the menu, but at 4:00 A.M., no one seems to mind.

B. Smith's (International) L/S (Moderate)   247-2222

771 Eighth Avenue (47th St.)
    Dress code: None
    All major credit cards accepted

In response to the question, "Where shall we go before or after the theater?" we have sent many guests to B. Smith's.

They always seem to be pleased. Owned by former fashion model Barbara Smith, this is a lively and spacious establishment with large windows that look out on the bustling neighborhood. Ms. Smith is a serious restaurateur —breads are baked on the premises, salads are large and elaborate, and desserts positively sinful.

Bukhara (Indian) S (Moderate)   838-1811
148 East 48th Street (Lexington/Third Aves.)
   Dress code: None
   All major credit cards accepted

Bukhara's cuisine consists of hearty meats and spiced breads prepared in a clay tandoor oven. Platters of grilled meat, chicken, or seafood are accompanied by dal and eight varieties of bread. Although knives and forks will be provided on request, guests at Bukhara are encouraged to just dig in and eat with their fingers.

**Cafe de Bruxelles (Belgian) S
   (Moderate)**   206-1830
118 Greenwich Avenue (13th St.)
   Dress code: None
   All major credit cards accepted

Not many people approach us asking, "Where can we find great Belgian food?" However, we happily direct those seeking "something different" to this cheery, sophisticated bistro. The mussels, bouillabaisse, and carbonnade flamande are outstanding, as are the crisp, golden fries. (*Please* don't call them French.) For dessert, there are those wonderful waffles we learned to love at the 1964 World's Fair, topped with vanilla ice cream and hot chocolate sauce.

**Cafe Des Artistes (French) L/S
   (Expensive)**   877-3500
1 West 67th Street (Central Park West)
   Dress code: Jacket after 5:00 P.M.
   All major credit cards accepted

One of the most frequently requested restaurants in our concierge experience. The food has consistently received reasonably high ratings. If it were equal to the romantic decor, this would be the best restaurant in New York. At the moment, we feel no qualms about a strong recommendation.

**Cafe Luxembourg (Continental)
   L/S (Expensive)**   873-7411
200 West 70th Street (Amsterdam/West End Aves.)
   Dress code: None
   All major credit cards accepted

This lively art deco bistro, just a short walk from Lincoln Center has maintained its high quality despite the departure of chef Patrick Clark to start his own restaurant, Metro.

Cafe Pierre (French) L/S (Expensive)   **940-8185**
The Pierre Hotel, 2 East 61st Street (Fifth Ave.)
  Dress code: Jacket and tie
  All major credit cards accepted

Cafe Un Deux Trois   (French Bistro)
          L/S (Moderate)   **354-4148**
123 West 44th Street (Sixth Ave./Broadway)
  Dress code: None
  Credit cards: AE, MC, & V
To be used only as a last resort for a post-theater bite.
What can you possibly expect from a restaurant that gives
you crayons for drawing on the tablecloth?

Cameo's (Continental) S (Moderate)   **874-2302**
169 Columbus Avenue (68th St.)
  Dress code: None
  All major credit cards accepted
One of our favorites in the Lincoln Center area. Cameo's
simple American cuisine and lively atmosphere attract
crowds from both Lincoln Center and the neighborhood.
There's piano music on Friday and Saturday nights and
during Sunday brunch. A second- floor restaurant with no
elevators, this is not for the handicapped.

Canton (Chinese) S (Moderate)   **226-4441**
45 Division Street (Bowery/East Broadway)
  Dress code: None
  No credit cards accepted
For years we've been sending guests to Canton for some
of the best Cantonese food in New York. You'll dine better if
you ask the owner's advice.

Captain's Table, The   (Seafood)
          (Expensive)   **697-9538**
860 Second Avenue (46th St.)
  Dress code: Jacket requested
  All major credit cards accepted
In a city blessed with fine seafood restaurants, the com-
petition is fierce. Although lacking the decor and culinary
subtleties to rank with the leaders, The Captain's Table is
certainly a high quality establishment. Occasionally, they
outdo themselves; their baby lobster tails are the best we've
ever eaten.

Carlyle Restaurant, The
          (Continental) S (Expensive)   **744-1600**
The Carlyle Hotel, 983 Madison Avenue
(76th/77th Sts.)
  Dress code: Jacket and tie
  All major credit cards accepted

One of the nicest and prettiest hotel dining rooms in the city. The cuisine ranks among the better but not the best French. And, as usual at The Carlyle, service is perfect.

Carnegie Deli (Deli) L/S (Inexpensive)   757-2245
854 Seventh Avenue (54th/55th Sts.)
   Dress code: None
   No credit cards accepted

Our favorite deli. The sleazy surroundings (elbow-to-elbow tables, old-fashioned coat hooks on the walls) are offset by incredible pastrami sandwiches, potato pancakes to put your grandmother's to shame, and their house special ruglach cheesecake. They also deliver from 6:30 A.M. to 4:00 A.M.

Cellar in the Sky   (Continental)
(Very expensive)   938-1111
One World Trade Center (107th Floor)
   Dress code: Jacket and tie
   All major credit cards accepted

The best of the many restaurants in the World Trade Center, it is based on an interesting concept: seven courses designed around five wines and served to just 36 guests. The menu changes twice each month. Dinner is served at 7:30 P.M. and, as we went to press, was $77.00 per person. If you find this concept intriguing, put down the book and call *right now*. Space is very limited, and they are usually booked well over two months in advance.

Cent' Anni (Italian) S (Expensive)   989-9494
50 Carmine Street (Bleecker/Bedford Sts.)
   Dress code: None
   Credit cards: AE

One of the handful of top Italian restaurants, Cent' Anni is informal, comfortable (one might almost say plain) and very friendly. The pastas are superb and the wide range of daily specials expertly prepared. It is also extremely popular so reservations are essential.

Chalet Suisse (Swiss) (Moderate)   355-0855
6 East 48th Street (Fifth/Madison Aves.)
   Dress code: Jacket
   Credit cards: AE, DC, MC, & V

Swiss cuisine is not unlike Austrian cuisine, so Adele, who spent five years in Vienna, was delighted to find old friends like deep-fried Emmenthaler and Wiener Schnitzel on the menu here. There's a rumor that fondues are coming back in style, and this would be a fine place to order one.

Chanterelle (French) (Very expensive)   966-6960
6 Harrison Street (Hudson St.)
   Dress code: Jacket and tie

All major credit cards accepted

Now housed in spectacular new surroundings, Karen and David Waltuck continue to provide elegant, sophisticated cuisine to connoisseurs expecting the best and willing to pay ($73.00 *prix fixe*) for it.

Chez Josephine (French Bistro) L
     (Moderate)   594-1925
414 West 42nd Street (Ninth/Tenth Aves.)
     Dress code: Eclectic
     Credit cards: AE, MC, & V

Hearty bistro fare served in an atmosphere reminiscent of Paris in the 1920s makes this *the* place to go before or after theater. Jean-Claude Baker, adopted son of the legendary Josephine Baker, is one of New York's hardest working hosts, making everyone feel like a guest at a wonderful party. Chef Jean-Claude Teulade's daily specials expand a menu that includes steak au poivre, roasted monkfish, and Adele's favorite appetizer, goat cheese ravioli. Although the serving staff is diligent about getting pre-theater customers out on time, we prefer to linger and listen to the fabulous jazz pianists. A tap dancer and fortuneteller add to the general merriment.

China Grill (French/Chinese/Eclectic)
     L/S (Expensive)
                                                     333-7788
60 West 53rd Street (Sixth Ave.)
     Dress code: None
     All major credit cards accepted

Certainly one of New York's most spectacular-looking restaurants, the block-long China Grill draws inspiration (and some employees) from Wolfgang Puck's Chinois on Main in Santa Monica. You may order either individually or communally, as you would in a Chinese restaurant. Appetizers and desserts are the strong points here; main courses can be disappointing.

Chin Chin (Chinese) S (Moderate)   888-4555
216 East 49th Street (Second/Third Aves.)
     Dress code: None
     All major credit cards accepted

The Chin brothers offer creative Taiwanese cuisine in a sleek, trendy setting.

Christ Cella (Steak) (Expensive)   697-2479
160 East 46th Street (Lexington/Third Aves.)
     Dress code: Jacket and tie
     All major credit cards accepted

A no-nonsense, no-frills steak and chop house that has been pleasing customers since Prohibition days.

C.J. Blanda (Italian) S (Moderate)   **206-7880**
209 Seventh Avenue (22nd St.)
  Dress code: None
  All major credit cards accepted
In an area where cuisine is virtually nonexistent, C.J.'s is an oasis. Primarily a quiet, neighborhood establishment, its Italian food is quite good and its atmosphere charming.

Coach House, The (Southern/American)
  S (Expensive)   **777-0303**
110 Waverly Place (Washington Square Park/
Sixth Ave.)
  Dress code: Jacket
  All major credit cards accepted
Traditional Southern dishes nicely served. Nothing to startle or to thrill.

Crepes Suzette (French) S
  (Inexpensive)   **581-9717**
363 West 46th Street (Eighth/Ninth Aves.)
  Dress code: None
  All major credit cards accepted
A hidden treasure of the theater district with old-style French fare lovingly prepared. The boeuf bourgignon is outstanding, as are the handmade truffles that cap each meal.

Darbar (Indian) S (Moderate)   **432-7227**
44 West 56th Street (Fifth/Sixth Aves.)
  Dress code: None
  All major credit cards accepted
Our favorite Indian restaurant. First-rate cuisine served in beautiful surroundings. Whether you're in the booths downstairs or on the second floor balcony, the atmosphere exudes the richness of old India.

Dish of Salt (Chinese/Cantonese)
  (Expensive)   **921-4242**
133 West 47th Street (Sixth/Seventh Aves.)
  Dress code: Jacket
  Credit cards: AE & DC
Not your average Chinese restaurant. You will either love or hate this glitzy, theater district Cantonese. This is another instance where money spent on decor could have been better used in the kitchen.

Edwardian Room (French) S
  (Very expensive)   **759-3000**
The Plaza, Fifth Avenue and Central Park South
  Dress code: Jacket and tie
  All major credit cards accepted
Chef Kerry Simon is turning the Edwardian Room into a restaurant of true stature. His inventive American cuisine

is expertly prepared, exquisitely presented on beautiful china, and served by a discretely attentive staff. Combined with the palatial grandeur of the famous room, it's altogether a wonderful experience.

Elaine's (Italian) L/S (Moderate)   **534-8103**
1703 Second Avenue (88th/89th Sts.)
    Dress code: None
    All major credit cards accepted
This is the restaurant people love to hate. Bad food and rude service. But for a bad restaurant it sure is popular. Elaine is a favorite with the "in" crowd and can be a warm and caring hostess. Great for star-gazing.

Empire Diner (American) L/S
    (Inexpensive)   **243-2736**
210 Tenth Avenue (22nd St.)
    Dress code: None
    Credit cards: MC & V
This classic art deco diner is a popular late-night snack spot. Eggs, steaks, and burgers are good choices and can be washed down with any of 16 beers or with wine. In addition to listing food for eating, the menu offers food for thought as well, such as, "If at first you don't succeed—so much for skydiving."

Eze (French Provencal) (Expensive)   **691-1140**
254 West 23rd Street (Seventh/Eighth Aves.)
    Dress code: Jacket and tie preferred
    All major credit cards accepted
    Closed Sunday and Monday and August through Labor Day
In a restored town house in Chelsea, chef Gina Zarrilli serves inspired French cooking. Depending on the season, her *prix fixe* menu may feature braised whole red snapper, rack of lamb, cassoulet, or venison with cranberry compote. The creme brulee is one of the best in town. This is definitely a place to linger—don't just rush in for a quick pretheater bite.

Flutie's (Steaks/Seafood) L/S
    (Moderate)   **693-0777**
Pier 17, South Street Seaport
    Dress code: Jacket preferred
    All major credit cards accepted
Go for the marvelous view of Brooklyn and the bargain ($26.50 all you can eat plus champagne) seafood brunch. The bar attracts young Wall Streeters and also serves up immaculately fresh clams and oysters.

Four Seasons (American) L
    (Very expensive)   **754-9494**
99 East 52nd Street (Lexington/Park Aves.)
    Dress code: Jacket and tie
    All major credit cards accepted

The Four Seasons has come to symbolize the best New York has to offer. Philip Johnson and Mies Van der Rohe were responsible for the architecture and interior design that have qualified it as a registered landmark. Originals by Picasso, Miro, and Rauschenberg grace the walls. James Beard and Albert Stockli contributed to the menu concepts. The menu is almost daunting in its variety, the wine list dazzling, and the service truly professional. Lighter Spa Cuisine is also available.

Fu's (Chinese) L/S (Moderate)   **517-9670**
1395 Second Avenue (72nd/73rd Sts.)
    Dress code: Jacket
    All major credit cards accepted

Certainly a contender for "Best Chinese restaurant in New York," Fu's draws raves for its Peking Duck and Grand Marnier shrimp.

Gallagher's Steak House (Steak)
    L/S (Expensive)   **245-5336**
228 West 52nd Street (Broadway/Eighth Ave.)
    Dress code: None
    All major credit cards accepted

The famous eatery with all those steaks in the window, Gallagher's continues to please those seeking hearty meat-and- potatoes fare.

Giordano (Italian) L (Expensive)   **947-3883**
409 West 39th Street (Ninth/Tenth Aves.)
    Dress code: Jacket
    All major credit cards accepted

This is one of those places that New Yorkers love to spring on unsuspecting visitors. You taxi through the Ninth Avenue market district, the only signs say "Lincoln Tunnel to New Jersey," and suddenly you notice a Rolls Royce parked outside a tiny restaurant. You have arrived. Aside from the opulence of the cars, the exterior gives nothing away. Once inside, however, you are greeted with characteristic Italian gusto. The dining room is built around an interior courtyard, and the food, while not trendy, is always of reliable quality.

Gotham Bar & Grill (American) S
    (Expensive)   **620-4020**
12 East 12th Street (Fifth Ave./University Place)
    Dress code: Jacket

All major credit cards accepted

The combination of Chef Alfred Portale's innovative American cuisine and the knockout decor have earned the Gotham a well-deserved reputation as one of the city's most consistently excellent establishments. Their wine list is extensive and reasonably priced.

**Greene St. Cafe   (American Nouvelle)
L/S (Moderate)**   925-2415
101 Greene Street (Prince/Spring Sts.)
    Dress code: Casual
    All major credit cards accepted
Another loft converted into dining for young professionals. A huge, open space with palm trees and wicker furniture, it has the requisite number of actors and artists working as waiters when they would rather be someplace else. The food is undistinguished in a pleasant way.

**Hard Rock Cafe   (Hamburgers) L/S
(Moderate)**   489-6565
221 West 57th Street (Seventh Ave./Broadway)
    Dress code: None
    Credit cards: AE, MC, & V
Not for the faint-hearted. Long lines of people wait outside to experience this temple of rock'n'roll, where Elvis and Beatles memorabilia decorate the walls. If you can endure the blaring music, you can order a fairly decent burger and wash it down with a milk shake or float.

Hatsuhana (Japanese) (Moderate)   355-3345
17 East 48th Street (Madison/Park Aves.)
    Dress code: None
    All major credit cards accepted
New York's best Japanese restaurant. Marvelous sushi, sashimi, and teriyaki. Those in a hurry are advised to sit at the sushi bar, where they may also sample exotic treats that never make it to the tables.

Hubert's (French) S (Expensive)   826-5911
575 Park Avenue (63rd St.)
    Dress code: Jacket and tie
    Credit cards: AE, MC, & V
The quietly elegant dining room, a blend of oriental and art deco, was designed by noted architect Adam Tihany, and features shoji screens, gold-stippled walls, and graciously separated tables. Chef Len Allison's imaginatively eclectic cuisine blends Italian, French, and Japanese influences into something totally his own.

Il Cantinori (Italian) L/S (Expensive)   673-6044
32 East 10th Street (University Place/Broadway)

Dress code: None
All major credit cards accepted
Closed Sunday in July and August

Once one of the city's best Tuscan restaurants, Il Cantinori could use more attention from its owners. The pasta and game dishes are still superb, but the service is lacking. However, the rustic atmosphere and terrace continue to draw crowds—particularly during the summer.

Il Cortile (Italian) L/S (Expensive)   **226-6060**
125 Mulberry Street (Canal/Hester Sts.)
Dress code: None
All major credit cards accepted

The combination of an airy, skylight room and delicious pastas make this one of Little Italy's most popular spots.

Il Mulino (Italian) L (Expensive)   **673-3783**
86 West 3rd Street (Thompson/Sullivan Sts.)
Dress code: Jacket
All major credit cards accepted

For years, when people asked us, "What's the best Italian restaurant?" we sent them to Il Mulino. It was the best then, and it's the best now. Popularity has made overbooking a problem so don't expect to be seated immediately, even if you have reservations.

Il Nido (Italian) (Expensive)   **753-8450**
251 East 53rdStreet (Second/Third Aves.)
Dress code: Jacket and tie
All major credit cards accepted

If you can't get into Il Mulino, go here.

Il Valetto (Italian) L (Expensive)   **838-3939**
133 East 61st Street (Park/Lexington Aves.)
Dress code: Jacket and tie
All major credit cards accepted

Over the years, this restaurant has developed a following for its solid Northern Italian cooking.

Inagiku (Japanese) S (Moderate)   **355-0440**
111 East 49th Street (Park/Lexington Aves.)
Dress code: Jacket
All major credit cards accepted

While it is not among the very best of our many Japanese restaurants, dining at Inagiku can be a most pleasurable experience. In elegant surroundings (a replica of a 15th century shrine), kimono-clad waitresses serve sushi, sashimi, tempura, shabu shabu, and the multi-course gourmet Kaiseki.

Indochine (Vietnamese) L/S
   (Moderate)   **505-5111**
430 Lafayette Street (4th Street/Astor Place)
Dress code: Casual but neat

All major credit cards accepted
Dinner only

Problems with overbooking and indifferent service don't seem to have dimmed the appeal of this still-trendy restaurant. While the food quality tends to be uneven, it can be some of the best Vietnamese food in town.

Jezebel (Southern/Soul) L
    (Moderate)   **582-1045**
630 Ninth Avenue (45th St.)
    Dress code: None
    Credit cards: AE

Yes, it looks like a New Orleans bordello. You will discover wonderful spareribs, fried chicken, garlic shrimp, and other southern specialties here.

Joe Allen (Hamburgers) L/S
    (Moderate)   **581-6464**
326 West 46th Street (Eighth/Ninth Aves.)
    Dress code: None
    Credit cards: MC & V

The best burgers in the theater district, delicious salads served by aspiring actors, and moderate prices combine to make this a perennial favorite. Astound your friends by pointing out that the billboards on the side wall commemorate Broadway's illustrious flops, from "Nefertiti" to "Breakfast at Tiffany's".

John Clancy's (Seafood) L/S
    (Expensive)   **242-7350**
181 West 10th Street (Seventh Ave. So.)
    Dress code: None
    All major credit cards accepted

One of New York's best seafood restaurants. You can feel virtuous by eating their wonderful mesquite-grilled tuna, sword fish, or Norwegian salmon, then splurge on a rich dessert. We should point out, however, that after a negative experience with their management, McDowell had to assume they would be equally rude to any guests he might send them. So he didn't.

John's Pizzeria (Pizza) L/S
    (Inexpensive)   **243-1680**
278 Bleecker Street (Seventh Avenue So./Jones St.)
    Dress code: None
    No credit cards accepted

Many's the time we've tromped through a blizzard for John's brick-oven pizza. They don't take credit cards, they don't deliver, and they don't mind the long line of people waiting to get in. This is New York's *very best. Tell them we sent you.*

J. Sung Dynasty (Chinese) S
(Moderate)   355-1200
Hotel Lexington, Mezzanine (Lexington Avenue & 48th St.)
  Dress code: None
  Credit cards: AE & DC
Hearty Manchurian specialties share the menu with spicy Hunanese dishes at this elegant and well-run establishment. Jimmy Sung is a gracious and attentive host, and his employees reflect this attitude. Not as well known as it deserves to be. Go now before it's discovered.

K-Paul's New York (Cajun) (Expensive)   460-9633
622 Broadway
  Dress code: None
  All major credit cards accepted
  Open Tuesday–Saturday 5:30–11:30 P.M.
Paul Prudhomme's legendary Cajun cuisine has come to New York. Be prepared to wait on line, sit with strangers, and drink your Cajun martinis from jelly glasses while waiting to sample blackened tuna, Cajun popcorn, and other standards. If you have a reservation, be sure that your entire party arrives at the same time. You will not be seated until everyone is there, and since there is no indoor waiting area, you will be forced to stand outside regardless of the weather.

La Boite en Bois (French) L/S
(Expensive)   874-2705
75 West 68th Street (Columbus Avenue/Central Park West)
  Dress code: None
  No credit cards accepted
One of the best in the Lincoln Center area. This tiny restaurant is packed until curtain time, deservedly so. After 8:00 P.M., when the din dies down, you may even be able to hear your dining partner.

La Camelia (Northern Italian) L
(Expensive)   751-5488
225 East 58th Street (Second/Third Aves.)
  Dress code: Jacket
  All major credit cards accepted
Luciano has always treated Adele's guests as though they were members of his own family. This is a terrific place for a late supper. The fine Northern Italian food and piano accompaniment are a wonderful combination. Don't get run over by the stretch limos.

La Caravelle (French) L
(Very expensive)   586-4252
33 West 55th Street (Fifth/Sixth Aves.)
  Dress code: Jacket and tie

All major credit cards accepted

Another of the classic French restaurants with its attendant elegant decor, it was once the favorite of President Kennedy. Although uneven over the years, its star is again on the rise, due to the careful attention of owner Andre Jammet. While La Caravelle may be temporarily overshadowed by bigger names, its quality is already so high that little is required to put it back on top.

La Cote Basque   (French)
(Very Expensive)   688-6525
5 East 55th Street (Fifth/Madison Aves.)
   Dress code: Jacket and tie
   All major credit cards accepted

It's no exaggeration to say that we have sent thousands of guests to La Cote Basque. They loved the food; they loved the decor; they loved the location; they frequently complained of snobbish service.

Lafayette   (French)   (Very expensive)   832-1565
Drake Hotel, 65 East 56th Street (Park Ave.)
   Dress code: Jacket and tie
   All major credit cards accepted

We're running out of superlatives. However, we think we can dredge up a few more on behalf of Lafayette. As concierges, we were seldom called upon to send hotel guests to other hotel dining rooms. Lafayette is one of two that we have frequently recommended, always with good results. It ranks with the very best of the fine French restaurants and will not disappoint you.

La Gauloise   (French Bistro)   S
(Expensive)   691-1363
502 Sixth Avenue (12th/13th Sts.)
   Dress code: None
   Credit cards: AE, MC, & V

This comfortable bistro is beloved for its moderate prices (especially the $19.50 *prix fixe* dinner served Tuesday through Friday from 5:30 P.M. to 6:45 P.M.), charming setting, and attentive service. Also an excellent choice for Saturday or Sunday brunch.

La Grenouille   (French)   L
(Very expensive)   752-1495
3 East 52nd Street (Fifth/Madison Aves.)
   Dress code: Jacket and tie
   Credit cards: AE & V

Beautiful, elegant, and delicious as befits one of New York's finest classic French restaurants. The sublime decor and attentive service make dining a real treat.

Landmark Tavern (Pub) L/S
     (Moderate)   **757-8595**
626 Eleventh Avenue (46th St.)
     Dress code: None
     All major credit cards accepted
Built in 1868, the Landmark Tavern was originally an
Irish waterfront saloon. Soda bread is still baked on the
premises every hour, and if you're overcome by a sudden
longing for bangers and mash, this is one of the few restaurants that can accommodate you. In addition, the Landmark
specializes in roast prime ribs with Yorkshire pudding,
chops, and grilled fresh fish. It is within easy walking distance of the Jacob Javits Convention Center, the Intrepid Museum, and the Circle Line Terminal. The bar carries one of
the city's finest selections of single malt Scotch whiskeys.

La Reserve (French) (Expensive)   **247-2993**
4 West 49th Street (Fifth Ave.)
     Dress code: Jacket and tie
     All major credit cards accepted
Adele still cherishes a letter from a grateful guest who
claims Adele saved her marriage by arranging a last-minute
table at La Reserve. While we can't guarantee the same results
for you, we can guarantee chef Dominique Payradeau's consistently fine cuisine. This is formal dining at its best.

La Ripaille (French Bistro) L
     (Expensive)   **255-4406**
605 Hudson Street (West 12th/Bethune Sts.)
     Dress code: None
     All major credit cards accepted
Comfortable, romantic, and rustic as befits their Greenwich Village location.

Lattanzi (Italian/Jewish Roman)
     (Expensive)   **315-0980**
361 West 46th Street (Eighth/Ninth Aves.)
     Dress code: Jacket preferred
     Credit cards: AE
Our guests have been consistently pleased with this
small and extremely popular theater-district Italian restaurant. After 8:00 P.M., when the theater crowd has departed,
Lattanzi offers the classic cuisine of the Italian Jews.

La Tulipe (French Bistro) S
     (Very expensive)   **691-8860**
104 West 13th Street (Sixth/Seventh Aves.)
     Dress code: Jacket and tie
     All major credit cards accepted
This intimate, gracious, and romantic restaurant occupies the ground floor of a Greenwich Village brownstone.

Innovative French bistro style cuisine at premium prices—considered the best by those who can afford it.

♣
♀ **Le Bernardin   (Seafood/French)**
      (Very expensive   489-1515
   155 West 51st Street (Sixth/Seventh Aves.)
      Dress code: Jacket and tie
      Credit cards: AE, MC, & V
New York's best seafood—so popular that it's necessary to reserve at least two weeks in advance. Gilbert and Maguy Le Coze have created a haven of warmth, tranquility, and good taste with their flawlessly executed cuisine and beautifully decorated room.

♣
♀ **Le Cirque   (French)   (Very expensive)   794-9292**
   58 East 65th Street (Madison/Park Aves.)
      Dress code: Jacket and tie
      Credit cards: AE & DC
The epitome of chic New York. Everybody who is anybody at all is here, feasting on chef Daniel Boulud's superb cuisine. Our international VIPs were always delighted with the attentions of owner and host Sirio Maccione. Their creme brulee is the best in the whole world.

♣
♀ **Le Cygne   (French)   (Very expensive)   759-5941**
   55 East 54th Street (Madison/Park Aves.)
      Dress code: Jacket and tie
      All major credit cards accepted
Superb classical French cuisine in a luscious setting. Definitely one of the very best. The chef, Jean-Michel Bergougnous, was formerly Chef de Cuisine at Lutece.

♣
♀ **Le Perigord   (French)   (Very expensive)   755-6244**
   405 East 52nd Street (First Ave.)
      Dress code: Jacket and tie
      All major credit cards accepted
In a city where a restaurant's life can be ephemeral, Le Perigord has lured a loyal clientele for over 26 years. Both haute and nouvelle cuisines are offered, and the spectacular, made-to-order hot desserts bring your meal to a memorable conclusion.

♣
♀ **Le Regence   (French)   S**
      (Very expensive)   606-4647
   Hotel Plaza Athenee, 37 East 64th Street
   (Madison/Park Aves.)
      Dress code: Jacket and tie
      All major credit cards accepted
The combination of superb food and incredibly opulent surroundings make dining at Le Regence a grand theatrical event, and one that can be enjoyed at breakfast, lunch, or dinner.

Le Relais (French Bistro) S
    (Expensive)   **751-5108**
712 Madison Avenue (63rd/64th Sts.)
   Dress code: None
   Credit cards: AE, MC, & V

A sidewalk cafe, fine for people-watching, but avoid the food.

Lusardi's (Italian) S (Expensive)   **249-2020**
1494 Second Avenue (77th/78th Sts.)
   Dress code: Jacket and tie requested
   All major credit cards accepted

After a hectic period of being a "trend-setter," Lusardi's has settled into being merely wonderful.

♛
  Lutece (French) (Very expensive)   **752-2225**
249 East 50th Street (Second Ave.)
   Dress code: Jacket and tie
   Credit cards: AE, CB, & DC

For many years New York's best restaurant, Lutece now shares this accolade with several others. But Andre Soltner's temple of haute cuisine just seems to improve with age, and the very name has become synonymous with dining at its best. Reservations are accepted up to one month in advance. Closed Saturday during the summer and the entire month of August.

Mamma Leone's (Italian) L/S
    (Moderate)   **586-5151**
Milford Plaza Hotel, 261 West 44th Street (Eighth Ave.)
   Dress code: Jacket requested
   All major credit cards accepted

It's places like this that give Italian cooking a bad name. Once a New York landmark, Mamma Leone's has deteriorated into one of the worst restaurants in the city. Mamma is probably turning in her grave. Recently relocated to the first and second floors of the Milford Plaza Hotel, they took the same dreadful food with them and seem to have no qualms about serving it to unsuspecting tourists. New Yorkers wouldn't dream of going there. There are plenty of really good Italian restaurants for the same price. Find one.

♛
  Manhattan Ocean Club (Seafood)
    L/S (Expensive)   **371-7777**
57 West 58th Street (Fifth/Sixth Aves.)
   Dress code: Jacket requested
   All major credit cards accepted

Only Le Bernadin has better seafood, but we feel that the stark modern decor and bare tables detract from the total dining experience. McDowell fondly remembers them as a place that never, ever, turned him down, even when they had to set up special tables in the bar for his guests.

Marie-Michelle (French) S
(Expensive)   315-2444
57 West 56th Street (Fifth/Sixth Aves.)
Dress code: Jacket requested
All major credit cards accepted

Everyone who eats out all the time has a favorite restaurant and this is ours. Owned by former Dior model Marie-Michelle Rey, it attracts an obviously upscale crowd who come back again and again. We particularly enjoy having working lunches here. Secure in the knowledge that everything will be perfect, we are free to conduct business. In a subdued monochromatic setting, the service is quiet and attentive and the French cuisine is delicious. A favorite with businesspeople at lunch, it becomes softly romantic at night. Marie-Michelle moves from table to table, always with something personal to say to her old friends and an interested welcome for newcomers. It's one of the best French restaurants in New York, and more people have stopped by to tell us they had a wonderful time here than at any other restaurant in this book.

Maurice (French) S
(Very expensive)   245-7788
The Parker Meridien Hotel, 118 West 57th Street (Sixth/Seventh Aves.)
Dress code: Jacket and tie
All major credit cards accepted

As we go to press Maurice is closed. We hope they will have re-opened by the time you are reading this. It has been one of the most important French restaurants in the city and one which a concierge could always confidently send his or her guests. We look forward to another wonderful restaurant.

Maxim's (French) L
(Very expensive)   751-5111
680 Madison Avenue (61st/62nd Sts.)
Dress code: Jacket and tie; Tuxedos on Saturday night
Credit cards: AE, DC, & MC

When it originally opened, people went here only for the elegant Art Nouveau decor which reminded one of its namesake in Paris. And for the dancing, of course. The quality of the food has improved, however, and we no longer have qualms about recommending it. Even other restaurant owners are saying complimentary things. Go for the total experience, not just the food. It's one of the very few places with both dinner and dancing.

Mickey Mantle's   (American)
      L/S   (Moderate)   **688-7777**
42 Central Park South (Fifth/Sixth Aves.)
      Dress code: None
      All major credit cards accepted

Although the food is good, this is primarily a sports bar, where you can enjoy hearty American fare (Philadelphia Cheese Steak, Chicken Fried Steak, Chicken Pot Pie) while watching important games on eight TVs. Mickey is often on hand and gladly signs autographs. Children may order from the "Little League" menu, and single women should note that this place is crawling with men.

Mitsukoshi (Japanese) (Expensive)   **935-6444**
461 Park Avenue (57th St.)
      Dress code: None
      All major credit cards accepted

Entering, you're sure you've misread something and have walked into a department store by mistake. The restaurant is downstairs. In a serene and tranquil atmosphere, kimono-clad waitresses serve up some of the best sushi in New York. It's one of the few restaurants where you have the option of buying a pearl necklace on your way out.

Mondrian   (Very expensive)   **935-3434**
7 East 59th Street (Fifth/Madison Aves.)
      Dress code: Jacket and tie
      All major credit cards accepted

The Dutch-born painter Piet Mondrian once had his studio in this building, which now houses this elegant, low-key American restaurant. The *prix fixe* menu ($34.00 at lunch, $56.00 at dinner) accents imaginatively prepared fish, lobster, and fowl, accompanied by a well-chosen wine list.

Montrachet   (French Nouvelle)
      (Very expensive)   **291-2777**
239 West Broadway (N. Moore/White Sts.)
      Dress code: None
      Credit cards: AE

Montrachet has created waves ever since its doors opened. Critics consistently give it two and three star ratings and praise not only its food but owner Drew Nieporent's philosophy: modern French cuisine in a soft and unpretentious setting. Our discriminating guests concur.

Odeon   (American Nouvelle)
      L/S   (Expensive)   **233-0507**
145 West Broadway (Worth/Duane Sts.)
      Dress code: None
      All major credit cards accepted

This once trendy TriBeCa (**Tri**angle **Be**low **Ca**nal) hot spot has declined drastically. Poor food and sloppy service leave only people-watching as an attraction, and interesting people don't tolerate poor food and sloppy service.

O'Neal's Balloon (Hamburgers)
        L/S (Moderate)   **399-2353**
48 West 63rd Street (Columbus Ave.)
    Dress code: None
    All major credit cards accepted
Located right across the street from The New York State Theater, this is a good place for a quick burger or sandwich before going to Lincoln Center for a performance. Stick to simple items.

One if by Land, Two if by Sea   (Continental)
        L/S (Expensive)   **228-0822**
17 Barrow Street (Seventh Avenue/W. 4th St.)
    Dress code: Dressy casual
    All major credit cards accepted
One of New York's most romantic restaurants, this restored carriage house was formerly owned by Aaron Burr. The individual beef Wellington is sure to please. Two fireplaces plus piano music nightly from 4:00 P.M. add to the appeal of this perennial favorite.

Orso (Italian) L/S (Moderate)   **489-7212**
322 West 46th Street (Eighth/Ninth Aves.)
    Dress code: None
    Credit cards: MC & V
We find it difficult to understand the enormous popularity of this pleasant but unremarkable locale. The little pizzas are adequate (and expensive)—nothing more. If post-theater star- gazing interests you, Orso is a good bet.

Oyster Bar, The (Seafood) (Moderate)   **490-6650**
Grand Central Station, Lower Level
    Dress code: None
    All major credit cards accepted
    Closed Saturday and Sunday
Who would believe that the nether regions of Grand Central Station would house one of the best and certainly most interesting seafood restaurants in New York? Inside the cavernous main dining room, one can feast on a dozen varieties of oyster, impeccably fresh fish, and huge desserts. If you're in midtown, this is a wonderful place for lunch.

Palio (Italian) L (Expensive)   **245-4850**
151 West 51st Street (Sixth/Seventh Aves.)
    Dress code: Jacket and tie (Ladies–No jeans or sneakers!)
    All major credit cards accepted

The beautiful mural at the downstairs bar depicts Sienna's famous race. Upstairs, Chef Andrea Hellrigl puts new twists on old favorites and offers "Farmer's, Hunter's, or Fisherman's" menus as special treats.

Palm, The (Steaks/Seafood) L
        (Expensive)   687-2953
837 Second Avenue (44th/45th Sts.)
   Dress code: None
   All major credit cards accepted
   No reservations
Although their "no reservations" policy is infuriating, many consider The Palm Manhattan's best steakhouse. Don't expect elegance, however. Caricatures on the walls and sawdust on the floors are a trademark here.

Palm Court, The (Desserts/Tea)
        L/S (Moderate)   759-3000
The Plaza Hotel, Fifth Avenue and Central Park South
   Dress code: Jacket, no jeans or sneakers
   All major credit cards accepted
Long the stronghold of little old ladies, there seems to be little reason to anticipate changes in clientele. Occupying The Plaza's main courtyard, its ambience is perfect for lunch or tea. We have confidently sent many guests to Sunday brunch, and they have invariably been pleased. The new decor is a little too harsh and bright for our personal taste—especially the carpet.

Parioli Romanissimo (Italian)
        (Very expensive)   288-2391
24 East 81st Street (Fifth/Madison Aves.)
   Dress code: Jacket and tie
   Credit cards: AE & DC
A beautiful setting, professional service, great truffle dishes, and sky-high prices are the hallmark of this sophisticated townhouse restaurant.

Pearl's (Chinese) S (Moderate)   221-6677
38 West 48th Street (Fifth/Sixth Aves.)
   Dress code: Jacket and tie
   Credit cards: AE
As concierges at the Marriott Marquis, we were responsible for finding restaurants for their thousands of guests. Pearl's was a perfect spot for Cantonese, Hunan, or Szechuan cuisine. Right in the middle of the theater district, it's a great place for people-watching.

Periyali (Greek) (Moderate)   463-7890
35 West 20th Street (Fifth/Sixth Aves.)
   Dress code: None

Credit cards: MC, V, & AE

Feast on immaculately fresh fish, souvlaki, arnisio, moussaka, and baklava in an atmosphere reminiscent of a private house in Greece. (The name is Greek for "seashore.")

Peter Luger's Steakhouse (Steaks)
     S (Expensive)   **1-718-387-7400**
178 Broadway (Driggs/Bedford Aves.), Brooklyn
    Dress code: Jacket preferred
    No credit cards accepted

It's generally agreed that to experience "New York's Best Steak," you must cross over the bridge to Brooklyn. The "beer-hall" atmosphere is not to everyone's taste, but the steaks are.

Petrossian (French/Caviar) L/S
    (Very expensive)   **245-2214**
182 West 58th Street (Seventh Ave.)
    Dress code: Jacket and tie
    All major credit cards accepted

Say "Petrossian" and think "caviar." It's a great place for a little snack of those wonderful fish eggs and champagne after theater. In addition, Chef Marc Salonsky's cuisine is receiving well-earned raves.

P.J. Clarke's (Pub) L/S (Moderate)   **759-1650**
915 Third Avenue (55th St.)
    Dress code: None
    Credit cards: AE & DC

Really a singles bar, Clarke's offers solid burgers in a clubby atmosphere.

Post House, The (Steaks) S
    (Expensive)   **935-2888**
28 East 63rd Street (Madison/Park Aves.)
    Dress code: Jacket and tie
    All major credit cards accepted

One of the better steak houses, The Post House has a devoted following and is particularly popular with business people. Like most steakhouses, portions are huge and service is attentive.

Primavera (Italian) L/S
    (Expensive)   **861-8608**
1578 First Avenue (82nd St.)
    Dress code: Jacket and tie
    All major credit cards accepted

One of New York's top Italian restaurants, Primavera is beloved by concierges because it's one of the few top restaurants open on Sunday night. If you can get in here, do.

Primola (Italian) L/S (Expensive)   **758-1775**
1226 Second Avenue (64th/65th Sts.)
 Dress code: None
 Credit cards: AE & DC
Friendly and dependably first rate.

Prunelle (French) S (Expensive)   **759-6410**
18 East 54th Street (Fifth/Madison Aves.)
 Dress code: Jacket and tie
 All major credit cards accepted
The burled wood interior reminds you of a grand ocean liner. Unfortunately, the not-quite-great food and patronizing attitude of the staff don't do justice to the elegant setting.

Quatorze (French Bistro) L/S
 (Moderate)   **206-7006**
240 West 14th Street (Seventh/Eighth Aves.)
 Dress code: None
 Credit cards: AE
Hearty Alsatian specialties prepared with care and served with panache. Located on the Northern edge of Greenwich Village, Quatorze is a good choice if you're attending a performance at the nearby Joyce Theater.

Quilted Giraffe, The (American)
 (Very expensive)   **593-1221**
AT & T Building Arcade, 15 East 55th Street
(Fifth/Madison Aves.)
 Dress code: None
 Credit cards: AE, MC, & V
This restaurant bears the distinction of being the most expensive in New York. It seems to be worth it since we've always had trouble getting tables for guests. Critics wax fulsome in their praise for the Japanese influenced Nouvelle cuisine, and service is always perfect. Quality is obviously uppermost in the minds of owners Barry and Susan Wine, and success is the result. Make your reservations well in advance.

Raga (Indian) L/S (Moderate)   **757-3450**
57 West 48th Street (Fifth/Sixth Aves.)
 Dress code: None
 All major credit cards accepted
Not among the very best of our many Indian restaurants, it is notable mainly for the reliable quality of its tandoori selections, comfortable decor, and its Rockefeller Center location.

Rainbow Room, The (Continental)
 L/S (Very expensive)   **632-5000**
30 Rockefeller Plaza, 65th Floor (49th/50th Sts.)
 Dress code: Jacket and tie

Credit cards: AE

Like a number of our most noted "big names," the food here leaves something to be desired. But you're not coming here just for the food. Nothing matches an evening in this art deco make-believe world in the sky, where you can return to the glamour and elegance of the Fred Astaire era for a wonderful dining and dancing experience. Make reservations several weeks in advance.

Red Blazer, Too (American/Continental)
     L/S (Moderate)   **262-3112**
349 West 46th Street (Eighth/Ninth Aves.)
     Dress code: None
     All major credit cards accepted

While the food here can best be characterized as "better than you'd expect," Red Blazer, Too attracts with its nightly jazz (and Sunday jazz brunch) with no cover charge. A small dance floor adds to its appeal.

Rene Pujol (French Bistro) L
     (Moderate)   **246-3023**
321 West 51st Street (Eighth/Ninth Aves.)
     Dress code: None
     All major credit cards accepted

Country French decor, good service, and reliable, no-nonsense bistro fare are the hallmarks of this theater district standby.

River Cafe, The (American) L/S
     (Expensive)   **1-718-522-5200**
1 Water Street (East River), Brooklyn
     Dress code: Jacket and tie
     All major credit cards accepted

One of the most frequently requested of New York restaurants, it's located on a barge under the Brooklyn Bridge. The view of Manhattan is breathtaking, and the cuisine has become quite superior. Perfect for a romantic evening.

Rosa Mexicano (Mexican) L/S
     (Moderate)   **753-7407**
1063 First Avenue (58th St.)
     Dress code: None
     All major credit cards accepted

There are only two really good Mexican restaurants in New York, and this is one of them. Fresh guacamole prepared at table-side presages the authentic cuisine to follow. You can do no wrong in your choices and need not fear the customary overuse of peppers and camouflaging hot sauces.

Rosemarie's (Italian) (Expensive)   **285-2610**
145 Duane Street (West Broadway/Church St.)

Dress code: None
Credit cards: AE, MC, & V

Rosemarie Verderame is one of the nicest but shyest restaurateurs we have encountered. We are always delighted to enter her tiny TriBeCa establishment and do so as often as possible. Chef James Bergen won McDowell's heart forever with his "pesce spada olivata," sword fish coated with crushed olives and grilled to perfection. The setting and dress code are casual, service is fine, and it's altogether an enchanting evening.

Rumplemeyer's (Desserts) L/S
(Moderate)   775-5800
50 Central Park South (Fifth/Sixth Aves.)
   Dress code: None
   All major credit cards accepted

THE New York ice cream parlor. For years, we've gone here after ice skating at Wollman Rink. Be prepared for kids stuffing themselves with goodies. Cuisine is not an issue here, although they have sandwiches and light meals. Stuffed animals provide a unique decor.

Russian Tea Room, The (Russian)
L/S (Expensive)   265-0947
150 West 57th Street (Sixth/Seventh Aves.)
   Dress code: Jacket required for dinner
   All major credit cards accepted

One of the most prestigious of New York institutions, The Russian Tea Room was founded by members of the Imperial Russian Corps de Ballet who were fleeing the Russian Revolution. It's been in its current location next to Carnegie Hall since 1926 and has become so renowned for celebrity-watching, one tends to forget how good the food can be. Blini, borscht, and chicken Kiev are worth every delicious calorie.

San Domenico (Italian) S
(Very expensive)   265-5959
240 Central Park South (East of Columbus Circle)
   Dress code: Jacket and tie
   All major credit cards accepted

Traditional Italian elements refined into haute cuisine by chef Paul Bartolotta. This light, airy (and very expensive) restaurant, located just east of Columbus Circle, provides a memorable dining experience.

Sardi's (Continental) L/S   221-8440
234 West 44th Street (Broadway/Eighth Ave.)
   Dress code: None
   All major credit cards accepted

Sardi's has been a legend, and we all keep hoping it will be one again. It is currently closed and back in the hands of

Vincent Sardi, the original owner. There is certainly a need in the theater district for a reincarnation of his original establishment.

Sea Grill, The (Seafood) S
    (Expensive)   246-9201
  19 West 49th Street (Fifth/Sixth Aves.)
    Dress code: Jacket, no sneakers, no jeans
    All major credit cards accepted
This subdued subterranean setting is so luscious, it seems almost superfluous that it offers some of New York's best seafood. Watch the skaters at Rockefeller Center while feasting on salmon poached in Schramsberg court bouillon.

Second Avenue Kosher
  Delicatessen
    (Deli) L/S (Inexpensive)   677-0606
156 Second Avenue (10th St.)
    Dress code: None
    No credit cards accepted
Our choice for the second best deli in town. Don't be put off by the sleazy decor. Fight your way through the crowd waiting at the takeout counter and be prepared for the traditional gruff waiter who's been there forever. The sandwiches are humongous, and the food is delicious.

Serendipity (Desserts) L/S
  (Moderate)   838-3531
225 East 60th Street (Second/Third Aves.)
    Dress code: None
    All major credit cards accepted
A late-night favorite with the many guests we've sent there. If you're in town with the kids, this is a great place to go for hot dogs and burgers. Kids love the desserts, especially the frozen hot chocolate, and so will you.

Seryna (Japanese) L (Expensive)   980-9393
11 East 53rd Street (Fifth/Madison Aves.)
    Dress code: Jacket
    All major credit cards accepted
Set so far back from the street that they place a sign near the sidewalk, Seryna is a much-overlooked treasure. Within walking distance of all the major hotels, this is one of the very top Japanese restaurants. The house specialty, steak cooked on hot stones, always pleases.

Sfuzzi (Italian) S (Moderate)   873-3700
58 West 65th Street (Columbus Ave./Central Park West)
    Dress code: Casual elegance—no sloppy jeans or
    sneakers
    All major credit cards accepted

Sfuzzi is Italian slang for "fun food," and this is a fine, if extremely noisy, place to go for pizza or pasta if you're attending a performance at Lincoln Center.

Shun Lee Palace (Chinese) L/S
     (Moderate)   **371-8844**
155 East 55th Street (Lexington/Third Aves.)
     Dress code: Jacket
     Credit cards: AE, DC, & CB

Vying with Canton for the title of "New York's best Chinese restaurant," Shun Lee Palace has the advantage of its midtown location and elegant decor. The many guests we've sent there have invariably returned smiling and patting their stomachs. If you're a Chinese food freak (and who isn't?), you will find their cuisine mouth-watering.

Sign of the Dove (American) S
     (Expensive)   **861-8080**
1110 Third Avenue (65th St.)
     Dress code: Jacket and tie
     All major credit cards accepted

We're delighted that this beautiful and romantic restaurant finally has a chef whose food is equal to the setting.

Smith & Wollensky
     (Steak/Seafood)
     L/S (Expensive)   **753-1530**
201 East 49th Street (Third Ave.)
     Dress code: Jacket
     All major credit cards accepted

Our favorite, and we think, the perfect steakhouse. Enormous portions of steaks, chops, and lobsters are served in a bustling "men's club" setting. An extensive wine list offers a wide range of tastes and prices, and Thomas Hart, the manager, takes perfect care of his guests. What more can one ask?

Spark's Steakhouse (Steaks)
     (Expensive)   **687-4855**
210 East 46th Street (Second/Third Aves.)
     Dress code: Jacket
     All major credit cards accepted

Everybody has a favorite steakhouse—and this may become yours. It's certainly one of the two or three tops. If you take advantage of the great wine list, you won't mind the crowd and the noise, and will enjoy the usual enormous steak or your choice of seafood.

Spirit of New York (American)
     L/S (Moderate)   **279-1890**
Pier 11, Wall Street
     Dress code: None
     Credit cards: AE, MC, & V

One of several companies that provide lunch, dinner, and moonlight cruises. Don't go for the food; it's the wonderful panorama of the Big Apple, live entertainment (singing waiters and a Salute-to-Broadway review), and dancing that are the draws here. If you enjoy the frenetic cruise ship ambience, this is for you.

S.P.Q.R. (Italian) L/S (Expensive)   **925-3120**
133 Mulberry Street (Hester/Grand Sts.)
   Dress code: None
   All major credit cards accepted
The menu at this converted factory includes specialties of both Northern and Southern Italian cooking, and all are deliciously prepared. Unlike most restaurants in Little Italy, it's extremely spacious.

Stage Deli (Deli) L/S (Inexpensive)   **245-7850**
834 Seventh Avenue (53rd/54th Sts.)
   Dress code: None
   No credit cards accepted
The lesser of the famous New York delis. Why go here when Carnegie is only a block away?

Tavern on the Green (American)
   L/S (Expensive)   **873-3200**
Central Park West at 67th Street
   Dress code: Jacket requested
   All major credit cards accepted
One of the most asked-for restaurants in New York, "The Tavern" has mundane food that is fortunately offset by its spectacular location. (Although why anybody from out-of-town comes to New York to see trees is beyond us.) It is the only restaurant allowed in Central Park and Warner LeRoy's magic touch has made it an awesome visual experience. In any city that had more space, this place would be out of business.

Terrace, The (French) (Expensive)   **666-9490**
400 West 119th Street (Amsterdam Ave./
Morningside Dr.)
   Dress code: Jacket and tie
   All major credit cards accepted
Sitting at the top of Butler Hall at Columbia University is an unlikely find: a really good French restaurant. It is one of the more elegant dining rooms in town and we have frequently recommended it when asked for a "romantic" spot. In addition to the wonderful food, one has a beautiful view of both the Hudson and East rivers.

Terrace V (American) (Expensive)   **371-5030**
Trump Tower, 725 Fifth Avenue, Level Five
(56th/57th Sts.)

Dress code: None

All major credit cards accepted

A lovely place for a break from shopping, Terrace V tempts with simple but imaginative dishes and sinful desserts.

Time and Again   (American/French)
(Expensive)   **685-8887**
The Doral Tuscany Hotel, 116 East 39th Sts.
(Park/Lexington Aves.)

Dress code: Jacket and tie

All major credit cards accepted

When we had lunch with the General Manager and the Chairman of the Board of Doral Hotels, we discovered that they were sitting on one of the better restaurants in New York. Hidden away in the Doral Tuscany Hotel, this French–American restaurant offers superior cuisine in an elegant atmosphere that invites one to relax and linger. With better advertising, this place would be mobbed.

Tre Scalini (Italian) L/S (Expensive)   **688-6888**
230 East 58th Street (Second/Third Aves.)

Dress code: Jacket and tie

All major credit cards accepted

Good, solid Northern Italian served with professional aplomb.

Tropica (American) (Expensive)   **867-6767**
Pan Am Building Concourse, 200 Park Avenue

Chef Ed Brown, formerly at Marie-Michell's, has combined forces with Phillip Darrow to bring us a delightful, new restaurant in the Grand Central Station complex. Mr. Darrow, who maintained such high standards as manager of the Sea Grill, has developed a small but outstanding wine list to accompany the marvelous American/Caribbean seafood that Ed Brown is creating. The combination of their talents promises great things and we intend to follow their progress closely. We suggest that you do too.

Tse Yang (Chinese) L/S (Expensive)   **688-5447**
34 East 51st Street (Madison/Park Aves.)

Dress code: Jacket

Credit cards: AE & V

Guests usually refer to this as "that Chinese place next to the Helmsley Palace." Second level Chinese cuisine at outrageous prices. Both Canton and Shun Lee Palace provide better food for much less.

20 Mott Street (Chinese) L/S
(Moderate)   **964-0380**
20 Mott Street (Pell Street/Bowery)

Dress code: None

All major credit cards accepted

When guests have asked for "someplace in Chinatown," we have not hesitated to send them to 20 Mott Street. In an area that is notorious for grubby restaurants, we could rely on their ambience and the recognized quality of their cuisine. The menu is huge but uneven. Try the Chinese-style roast duck—it's delicious.

"21" Club, The (American/French)
L (Very expensive)   582-7200

21 West 52nd Street (Fifth/Sixth Aves.)
   Dress code: Jacket and tie
   All major credit cards accepted

Despite a much ballyhooed revamping and astronomical prices, something seems to be a little wrong with everything on the menu. Nevertheless, "21" retains a loyal following of well- heeled regulars.

♀ Union Square Cafe (Eclectic) L
🔑   (Expensive)   243-4020

21 East 16th Street (Union Square/Fifth Ave.)
   Dress code: None
   All major credit cards accepted

Danny Meyer shot into the top ranks with his new restaurant. An innovative, Italian-based menu, attentive service and a spacious setting have made this relative newcomer deservedly popular. The risotto, bombolotti in Cognac and cream, and roasted chicken with polenta are excellent choices. The wine list is both extensive and reasonably priced.

Vanessa (Continental) S (Expensive)   243-4225
289 Bleecker Street (East of Seventh Ave. So.)
   Dress code: None
   All major credit cards accepted

While not up to its old standards, Vanessa is still not a place to be overlooked. The pretty, flower-filled room makes for a romantic atmosphere but does not offset the general feeling of ordinariness.

View Lounge & Restaurant, The
L/S (Expensive)   704-8900

The Marriott Marquis Hotel, 1535 Broadway
(45th/46th Sts.)
   Dress code: Jacket
   All major credit cards accepted

A revolving restaurant and lounge on top of a First Class Hotel. You have a choice of Italian, French, or American cuisine in the restaurant, or you may opt for just a snack and drinks in the elegant lounge. Beautiful views of midtown make this one of the most popular places for before and after theater. It's packed when the big conventions are in town.

Water's Edge, The   (American)   S
(Expensive)   1-718-482-0033
44th Drive and East River Drive, Queens
> Dress code: Jacket
> All major credit cards accepted

Alas, the food here doesn't quite measure up to the breath-taking view of Manhattan. For your convenience a free water shuttle departs from the 23rd Street Marina to the Water's Edge every hour on the hour from 6:00 P.M. to 10:00 P.M. and returns on the half-hour between 6:00 P.M. and 11:00 P.M.

Wilkinson's Seafood   (Seafood)   S
(Expensive)   535-5454
1573 York Avenue (83rd/84th Sts.)
> Dress code: None
> All major credit cards accepted

This is one of those places that Michelin would declare "worth a detour." Serving dinner only, it ranks as the best of the Upper East Side seafood restaurants. Staff, decor, and presentation are all first rate.

Windows on the World
(Continental)   S   (Expensive)   938-1111
One World Trade Center (107th Floor)
> Dress code: Jacket and tie
> All major credit cards accepted

The view and the wine list are both spectacular. The continental cuisine is adequate but not great. Since we assume you journeyed to the 107th floor for the view, you probably will have a wonderful time. Most folks do.

World Yacht Cruises   (Continental)
S   (Expensive)   929-7090
Pier 62 (23rd St. & Hudson River)
> Dress code: Proper casual attire on lunch cruises; jacket and tie on dinner and brunch cruises; jeans and sneakers prohibited
> All major credit cards accepted

One of the best ways to appreciate New York has always been to experience it by boat, and what better way than to combine a cruise with dinner and dancing. World Yacht offers dinner, lunch, and Sunday brunch cruises; enormous picture windows give everyone a clear view of the world's most famous skyline. During the summer, it is not unusual for these cruises to sell out a month in advance, so plan way ahead.

Wylie's Ribs & Co.   (Ribs)   L/S
(Moderate)   757-7910
59 West 56th Street (Fifth/Sixth Sts.)
> Dress code: None
> All major credit cards accepted

While the guests at the luxury hotels where we worked never mentioned the name, the habitues of First Class hotels fall all over themselves to take their families to Wylie's. If your clan says "Barbecue," this is the place to take them.

Zarela (Mexican) L/S (Moderate) 644-6740
953 Second Avenue (50th/51st Sts.)
   Dress code: None
   Credit cards: AE & DC
The newest entry for "Best Mexican," it's crowded, noisy and full of the friendly Mexican camaraderie one expects. The upscale Mexican cuisine is fantastico.

RESTAURANTS, BRUNCH

American Festival Cafe	Cafe Des Artistes
Cafe Pierre	Cafe Un Deux Trois
Cameo's	Carlyle Restaurant, The
Empire Diner	Flutie's
Greene St. Cafe	La Gauloise
Landmark Tavern	Le Regence
Le Relais	Petrossian
Mickey Mantle's	Odeon
O'Neal's Balloon	Palm Court, The
P.J. Clarke's	River Cafe, The
Rosa Mexicano	Russian Tea Room, The
Sign of the Dove	Tavern on the Green
View Lounge & Restaurant, The	Water's Edge, The
Windows on the World	World Yacht Cruises

RESTAURANTS BY TYPE OF CUISINE

American

American Festival Cafe	An American Place
Arcadia	Aureole
Coach House, The	Empire Diner
Four Seasons, The	Greene St. Cafe
Odeon	Mickey Mantle's
Red Blazer, Too	Quilted Giraffe, The
Sign of the Dove	River Cafe, The
Tavern on the Green	Spirit of New York

Time and Again   Terrace V

Water's Edge, The   "21" Club, The

Chinese

🔑 Canton   Chin Chin

Dish of Salt   Fu's

Pearl's   🔑 Shun Lee Palace

Tse Yang   20 Mott Street

Continental

Cafe Luxembourg   Cameo's

Carlyle Restaurant, The   🔑 Cellar in the Sky

One if by Land,
     Two if by Sea   🔑 Rainbow Room, The

Sardi's   Vanessa

🔑 Windows On The World   World Yacht Cruises

Delicatessen

🔑 Carnegie Deli   Second Avenue Kosher
     Delicatessen

Stage Deli

French

Aurora   🔑 Bouley

Brasserie   🔑 Cafe Des Artistes

Cafe Pierre   🔑 Chanterelle

Crepes Suzette   China Grill

Le Boite en Boise   Hubert's

🔑 La Grenouille   🔑 La Cote Basque

🔑 Lafayette   🔑 La Reserve

🔑 Le Cygne   🔑 Le Cirque

🔑 Le Regence   🔑 Le Perigord

🔑 Marie-Michelle   🔑 Lutece

Maxim's   Maurice

🔑 Montrachet   Mondrian

Prunelle   🔑 Petrossian

🔑 Terrace, The

French Bistro

Au Tunnel   Cafe Un Deux Trois

🔑 Chez Josephine   Chez Louis

La Gauloise
La Tulipe
Quartorze

La Ripaille
Le Relais
Rene Pujol

Indian

Akbar
♪ Darbar

Bukhara
Raga

Italian

Angelo's of Mulberry
    Street
Bellini
C.J. Blanda
Elaine's
♪ Gotham Bar & Grill
Il Cortile
Il Nido
La Camelia
Lusardi's
Orso
Parioli Romanissimo
Primola
♪ Rosemarie's
San Domenico
Tre Scalini

Barbetta
Bice
♪ Cent'anni
Giordano
Il Cantinori
♪ Il Mulino
Il Valletto
Lattanzi
Mamma Leone's
Palio
♪ Primavera
Roma di Notte
S.P.Q.R.
Sfuzzi

Japanese

Benihana of Tokyo
Inagiku
Seryna

♪ Hatsuhana
Mitsukoshi

Mexican

Rosa Mexicano

♪ Zarela

Pizza

♪ John's Pizzeria

Seafood

Captain's Table, The
♪ Le Bernardin

♪ Oyster Bar, The
Wilkinson's Seafood

♪ John Clancy's
♪ Manhattan Ocean Club,
    The
♪ Sea Grill, The

Steaks

Ben Benson's	Christ Cella
Gallagher's Steakhouse	🔑 Palm, The
🔑 Peter Luger's Steakhouse	Post House, The
🔑 Smith & Wollensky	Spark's Steakhouse

RESTAURANTS BY GEOGRAPHIC LOCATION

Chinatown

🔑 Canton	20 Mott Street

Greenwich Village

Coach House, The	🔑 Cent'anni
Il Cantinori	🔑 Gotham Bar & Grill
Indochine	🔑 Il Mulino
🔑 John's Pizzeria	🔑 John Clancy's
La Ripaille	La Gauloise
One if by Land, Two if by Sea	La Tulipe
Vanessa	Quatorze

Little Italy

Angelo's of Mulberry Street	Il Cortile
S.P.Q.R.	

Theater District

American Festival Cafe	Aquavit
Au Tunnel	Barbetta
Bellini	Ben Benson's
B. Smith's	Cafe Un Deux Trois
🔑 Carnegie Deli	🔑 Chez Josephine
Crepes Suzette	China Grill
Gallagher's Steak House	Dish of Salt
Jezebel	Giordano
La Caravelle	Joe Allen
Landmark Tavern	🔑 La Reserve
Lattanzi	🔑 Le Bernardin
Mamma Leone's	Orso
Palio	Pearl's

Rene Pujol	Sardi's
⚷ Sea Grill, The	Stage Deli
"21" Club, The	View Lounge & Restaurant, The

TriBeCa

⚷ Bouley	⚷ Chanterelle
⚷ Montrachet	Odeon
⚷ Rosemarie's	

SoHo

Greene St. Cafe

Rialto Florists	688-3234
707 Lexington Avenue (57th/58th Sts.)	
Richard Metz Golf Studio, Inc.	759-6940
35 East 50th Street (Madison/Park Aves.)	
Richard Rodgers Theater	221-1211
226 West 46th Street (Eighth Ave./Broadway)	
Ridiculous Theater Co.	691-2271
1 Sheridan Square	
Rihga Royal Hotel	838-7070
150 West 54th Street (Sixth/Seventh Aves.)	
Rissin's Jewelry Clinic, Inc.	575-1098
4 West 47th Street	
Ritz Carlton Hotel, The	757-1900
112 Central Park South (Sixth/Seventh Aves.)	
Ritz Theater	239-6200
225 West 48th Street	
River Cafe, The	1-718-522-5200
1 Water Street, Brooklyn	
River Club	751-0100
447 East 52nd Street	
Riverside Church, The	222-5900
Riverside Drive (West 122nd St.)	
Rizzoli	
31 West 57th Street	759-2424
250 Vesey Street (Battery Park City)	385-1400
Rockefeller Center Skating Rink	757-5731
Rockefeller Center Plaza, Fifth Avenue (49th/50th Sts.)	
Roger Smith Winthrop Hotel	755-1400
501 Lexington Avenue	
Roosevelt Hotel, The	661-9600
Madison Avenue at 45th Street	
Roosevelt–St. Luke's Hospital	554-7000
Ninth Avenue and 59th Street	

Rosa Mexicano	**753-7407**
1063 First Avenue (58th St.)	
Roseland Ballroom	**247-0200**
239 West 52nd Street	
Rosemarie's	**285-2610**
145 Duane Street (West Broadway/Church St.)	
Roundabout Theater Co.	**420-1883**
100 East 17th Street	
Royale Theater	**239-6200**
242 West 45th Street	
Royalton Hotel	**869-4400**
44 West 44th Street	
Rumplemeyer's	**775-5800**
50 Central Park South (Fifth/Sixth Aves.)	
Russian Tea Room, The	**265-0947**
150 West 57th Street (Sixth/Seventh Aves.)	
Rusty Staub's on 5th	**682-1000**
575 Fifth Avenue	

S

S & W	**924-6656**
165 West 26th Street	
S. Beckstein	**475-4653**
130 Orchard Street	
S.P.Q.R.	**925-3120**
133 Mulberry Street (Hester/Grand Sts.)	
Sabena	1-800-955-2000
Saint Laurie, Ltd.	**473-0100**
897 Broadway	
Saks Fifth Avenue	**753-4000**
611 Fifth Avenue (50th St.)	
Salisbury Hotel	**246-1300**
123 West 57th Street (Sixth/Seventh Aves.)	
Sam Goody's	
51 West 51st Street (Sixth Ave.)	**246-8730**
666 Third Avenue (43rd St.)	**986-8480**
Samuel Beckett Theater	**944-9300**
410 West 42nd Street	
San Domenico	**265-5959**
240 Central Park South	
Sands Hotel/Casino	**1-609-441-4000**
Indiana Avenue at Brighton Park (Atlantic City, NJ)	

Sandy Hook Information   1-718-448-3900

Sardi's   221-8440
234 West 44th Street (Broadway/Eighth Ave.)

SAS–Scandinavian Airlines   1-718-657-7700

Saudi Arabia (Consulate of)   752-2740
866 United Nations Plaza

Sea Grill, The   246-9201
19 West 49th Street (Fifth/Sixth Aves.)

Seaport Line, The   669-9400
207 Front Street

Second Avenue Kosher Delicatessen   677-0606
156 Second Avenue (10th St.)

Second Childhood   989-6140
283 Bleecker Street

Second Church of Christ, Scientist   877-6100
Central Park West (68th St.)

Second Stage Theater   873-6103
2161 Broadway (76th St.)

SECRETARIAL SERVICES

American International Executive
        Business Center   308-0049
Inge F. Rothenberg, President
14 East 60th Street, Suite 307
Fax: 1-212-308-2785
    Monday–Friday 9:00 A.M.–7:00 P.M. $35.00 per hour
    Late nights & Saturday $50.00 per hour
    Sunday $65.00 per hour
Inge's secretaries type, transcribe, take dictation, and
are extremely well versed on computers and word
processors. They are the saviors of many a traveling
businessperson.

Dial-a-Secretary
521 Fifth Avenue   348-9575
149 East 81st Street   348-8982
    Although they don't pick up or deliver, Dial-a-Secretary
is open even on holiday weekends.

Park East 56   418-0400
Executive Center, 128 East 56th Street

Sensuous Bean, The   **724-7725**
60 West 70th Street

Serendipity   **838-3531**
225 East 60th Street (Second/Third Aves.)

Seryna   **980-9393**
11 East 53rd Street (Fifth/Madison Aves.)

Sfuzzi   **873-3700**
58 West 65th Street (Columbus Avenue/Central Park
West)   **529-1330**

Shakespeare & Co.
2259 Broadway (81st St.)   **580-7800**
716 Broadway (Washington Place)   **529-1330**

Shea Stadium   **1-718-507-8499**
Flushing, Queens

Sheraton Centre   **581-1000**
Seventh Avenue (51st St.)

Sheraton City Squire   **581-3300**
790 Seventh Avenue (51st St.)

Sheraton Park Avenue   **685-7676**
45 Park Avenue

Sherry Netherland   **355-2800**
781 Fifth Avenue (59th St.)

Sherry-Lehman   **838-7500**
679 Madison Avenue (61st/62nd Sts.)

SHIPS

One of the finest maritime facilities in the country is the new Passenger Ship Terminal which is on the Hudson River between 48th and 52nd Streets in Manhattan. In addition to streamlined baggage handling and customs facilities it has rooftop parking and bus connections to midtown.

For information on ships in port or arriving, call:

Captain of the Port of New York   **668-7936**

Passenger Ship Terminal   **246-5450**

Sandy Hook Information   **1-718-448-3900**

American Cruise Lines   **1-203-345-8501**
1 Marine Park, Haddam, CT   **1-800-243-6755**

Bermuda Star Lines   **1-201-837-0400**
1086 Teaneck Road, Teaneck, NJ   **1-800-237-5361**

Chandris Fantasy Cruises   **223-3003**
900 Third Avenue, New York, NY   **1-800-621-3446**

Cunard Line   **661-7777**
555 Fifth Avenue, New York, NY   **1-800-221-4770**

Epirotiki Lines   **599-1750**
551 Fifth Avenue, New York, NY   **1-800-221-2470**
The Chairman of the Board and his wife were frequently guests of McDowell's at the St. Regis Hotel, and their exotic cruise line is not to be believed. Out-of-this-world trips to exotic places.

Ivaran Lines   **809-1220**
1 Exchange Plaza, New York, NY   **1-800-451-1631**

Sun Line Cruises   **397-6400**
1 Rockefeller Plaza, New York, NY   **1-800-872-6400**

SHOPPING

Descriptions of these famous places to shop can be found under STORES. We list their addresses here for quick reference.

Abercrombie & Fitch   **832-1001**
Trump Tower, 725 Fifth Avenue (56th/57th Sts.)

A La Vieille Russie   **752-1727**
781 Fifth Avenue (59th St.)

A. Sulka   **980-5226**
301 Park Avenue (55th St.)

Ann Taylor   **832-2010**
3 East 57th Street (Fifth/Madison Aves.)

Baccarat   **826-4100**
625 Madison Avenue (58th/59th Sts.)

Bally   **751-2163**
681 Madison Avenue (62nd St.)

Bottega Veneta   **371-5511**
635 Madison Avenue (60th St.)

Brooks Brothers   **682-8800**
346 Madison Avenue (44th St.)

Buccellatti   **308-5533**
Trump Tower, 725 Fifth Avenue (56th/57th Sts.)

Bulgari   315-9000
730 Fifth Avenue (57th St.)

Burberry   371-5010
9 East 57th Street (Fifth/Madison Aves.)

Cartier   753-0111
653 Fifth Avenue (52nd St.)

Chanel   355-5050
5 East 57th Street (Fifth/Madison Aves.)

Charles Jourdan   644-3830
Trump Tower, 725 Fifth Avenue (56th/57th Sts.)

Charivari   787-7272
58 West 72nd Street

Church's English Shoes   755-4313
428 Madison Avenue (49th St.)

Coach Leatherware   594-1581
754 Madison Avenue (65th St.)

Courreges   319-5766
520 Madison Ave.

Crouch & Fitzgerald   755-5888
400 Madison Avenue

David Webb   421-3030
7 East 57th Street

Dean & DeLuca   431-1691
560 Broadway (Prince Street)

Dunhill Tailors   355-0050
65 East 57th Street (Madison/Park Aves.)

Elizabeth Arden   407-7900
691 Fifth Avenue (54th St.)

Fortunoff   343-8787
681 Fifth Avenue

Fred Joillier   832-3733
703 Fifth Avenue (55th St.)

Fred Leighton   288-1872
781 Madison Avenue (66th St.)

Georg Jensen   759-6457
683 Madison Avenue (61st St.)

Giorgio Armani   988-9191
815 Madison Avenue (67th St.)

Givenchy Boutique	772-1040
954 Madison Avenue (75th St.)	
Gucci	826-2600
689 Fifth Avenue (54th St.)	
Hammacher Schlemmer	421-9000
147 East 57th Street	
Harry Winston	245-2000
718 Fifth Avenue (56th St.)	
Hermès	751-3181
11 East 57th Street (Fifth/Madison Aves.)	
H. Stern	688-0300
645 Fifth Avenue (51st St.)	
Hoya Crystal	223-6335
450 Park Avenue (56th/57th Sts.)	
James Robinson	752-6166
15 East 57th Street (Fifth/Madison Aves.)	
Kenzo	737-8640
824 Madison Avenue (69th St.)	
Krizia	628-8180
805 Madison Avenue (67th/68th Sts.)	
Lanvin	838-4330
701 Madison Avenue (62nd St.)	
Laura Ashley	752-7300
21 East 57th Street (Fifth/Madison Aves.)	
Limited, The	838-8787
691 Madison Avenue (62nd St.)	
Louis Vuitton	371-6111
51 East 57th Street (Madison/Park Aves.)	
Manhattan Art & Antiques Center	355-3300
1050 Second Avenue	
Mark Cross	421-3000
645 Fifth Avenue (51st St.)	
Martha	
475 Park Avenue (58th St.)	753-1511
Trump Tower, 725 Fifth Avenue	
(56th/57th Sts.)	826-8855
MCM	688-2133
717 Madison Avenue (63rd/64th Sts.)	
Paul Stuart	682-0320
Madison Avenue at 45th Street	

Ralph Lauren   606-2100
867 Madison Avenue (72nd St.)

H. Stern   688-0300
645 Fifth Avenue (51st St.)

Steuben Glass   752-1441
715 Fifth Avenue (56th St.)

A. Sulka   980-5226
301 Park Avenue (55th St.)

Tiffany & Co.   755-8000
727 Fifth Avenue (57th St.)

Tourneau   758-3265
500 Madison Avenue (52nd St.)

F.R. Tripler   922-1090
300 Madison Avenue (46th St.)

Valentino   772-6969
825 Madison Avenue (68th St.)

Van Cleef & Arpels   644-9500
744 Fifth Avenue (57th St.)

Yves Saint Laurent   988-3821
855 Madison Avenue (71st St.)

Shoreham Hotel   247-6700
33 West 55th Street (Fifth/Sixth Aves.)

Short Line Tours   354-4740
166 West 46th Street

Shubert Theater   239-6200
225 West 44th Street

Shun Lee Palace   371-8844
155 East 55th Street (Lexington/Third Aves.)

Sidney Janis Gallery   586-0110
110 West 57th Street

SIGHTSEEING

See also **MUSEUMS for a complete description including hours and admission fees**

American Museum of Immigration   422-2150
The Statue of Liberty
    Monday–Friday 9:00 A.M.–6:00 P.M.
    Saturday & Sunday 9:00 A.M.–7:00 P.M.
    By subway: #1 train to South Ferry

American Museum of Natural History   769-5000
Central Park West at 79th Street

AT & T Infoquest Center   **605-5555**
550 Madison Avenue (56th St.)
>   Tuesday 10:00 A.M.–9:00 P.M.
>   Wednesday–Saturday 10:00 A.M.–6:00 P.M.
>   Free
>   By subway: E or F train to 53rd Street; #4, #5, or #6
>   train to 59th Street
>   By bus: M1, M2, M3, or M4

Forty permanent interactive exhibits of the technology involved in communications. It includes photonics, microelectronics, computer design, and robotics. This is actually much more interesting than it sounds and lets you learn how to make a microchip and your own videos.

Battery Park
>   By subway: #1 train to South Ferry
>   By bus: M1 or M6

Created by landfill, these 21 acres extending from Bowling Green to the junction of the Hudson and East Rivers offer an unparalleled view of New York Harbor and the Statue of Liberty. That peculiar structure near the statue of Verrazano is an air vent for the Brooklyn Battery Tunnel. This is the departure point for ferries to Staten and Liberty Islands. Should you become enamored of this area and consider moving here, you'll be in good company: Battery Park City's condos house the highest proportion of residents with an annual income over $75,000.

Brooklyn Bridge
An architectural triumph and brilliant feat of engineering, the Brooklyn Bridge was the longest suspension bridge in the world when it was opened on May 24, 1883, and the first link over the East River between Manhattan and Brooklyn. For a truly memorable and dramatic walk, take the IND Eighth Avenue subway to High Street-Brooklyn Bridge in Brooklyn and return to Manhattan on the bridge's wooden pedestrian path. Viewed through the filigree of cables, the Manhattan skyline is spectacular, particularly at sunset. This would be ideal to combine with an excursion to South Street Seaport.

Brooklyn Museum   **1-718-638-5000**
300 Eastern Parkway, Brooklyn

Carnegie Hall   **903-9790**
154 West 57th Street (Seventh Ave.)
>   Object of the classic exchange:
>>   Tourist: "How do I get to Carnegie Hall?"
>>   Taxi Driver: "Practice man, practice."
>   Admission (regular tour):
>   Adults $6.00

Students/Senior citizens $5.00
Children (under 12) $3.00
By subway: N or R train to 57th Street
By bus: M6 or M7

Beautifully restored to its original grandeur, Carnegie Hall is open for tours Tuesday and Thursday at 11:30 A.M., 2:00 P.M. and 3:00 P.M. There is also a special "Tour and Tea" which includes a visit to the famous Russian Tea Room next door. Call 903-9790 for information. The regular tour has become one of New York's most popular entertainments with tourists.

Cathedral Church of St. John the Divine, The   316-7540

Amsterdam Avenue at 112th Street
Open daily 7:00 A.M.–5:00 P.M.
Tours Monday–Saturday at 11:00 A.M. and 2:00 P.M.
By subway: #1 train to 110th Street and Cathedral Parkway
By bus: M4 or M5

The length of two football fields, the Cathedral of St. John the Divine is the world's largest Gothic church. Its magnificent stained glass windows, Biblical garden, Barbarini tapestries and eclectic gift shop reward the adventurous souls who venture into the outskirts of Harlem.

Insiders' Tip: Have lunch across the street at the Green Tree Hungarian Restaurant, a great value, frequented by students of Barnard and Columbia. The mulled wine takes the Cathedral's chill from your bones.

Central Park

By subway: Most Uptown and Downtown trains
By bus: Most buses except those on the far East Side

From 59th to 110th streets, between Fifth Avenue and Central Park West. 840 acres of green in the midst of the urban jungle.

Chelsea

Rich in historical interest, Chelsea (the area between Fifth Ave. and the Hudson River, between 14th and 34th Sts.) is once again becoming fashionable. The Chelsea Hotel, on West 23rd Street (Seventh/Eighth Aves.), has been home to many of our famous artists and writers.

Children's Museum of Manhattan   721-1234

The Tische Building, 212 West 83rd Street (Broadway/Amsterdam Ave.)

Chinatown

By subway: #4, #5, or #6 train to Canal Street, then walk east; N or R train to Canal Street/Chinatown

Everybody knows what a "Chinatown" is—we think ours is special. Don't miss the chance to stroll through its crowded streets and to eat in some of the best Chinese restaurants in the country.

Chrysler Building
405 Lexington Avenue (42nd St.)
>By subway: #4, #5, #6, or #7 train to Grand Central
>By bus: M101, M102, or M104

The world's tallest building for one year, this outstanding example of art deco architecture is our choice for most beautiful skyscraper in the world. With its needle sharp spire piercing the skyline, it puts to shame most of the more recently constructed buildings. As the name Chrysler should tell you, the building has a lot to do with cars. Many of the features are lifted from the automobile grills and radiator caps of the late 1920s.

Circle Lines   563-3200
Pier 83, West 42nd Street at the Hudson River
>Adults $15.00
>Children (under 12) $7.50
>Group rates available for 25 or more adults
>By subway: Any train to 42nd Street. Then take the crosstown bus
>By bus: M16 or M42 crosstown

We joined the crowd again this October and were quickly reminded of how beautiful our city can be when you can stand back far enough to see it. From mid-March until late November, these three-hour boat rides provide an incredible view of the famous skyline. As the boat makes a complete circle around Manhattan Island, your guide gives a running commentary on the various sights you are sailing past. You sail down the Hudson River, past the financial district with all of its new buildings, and out to the Statue of Liberty. This is a wonderful way to see the Statue if you don't want to actually go inside. After a brief pause to allow the cameras to click, you sail on through New York Bay and up the East River. This is one of the very best ways to see New York and its landmark buildings and bridges. Remember, you are on the water and dress accordingly. In the spring and fall it can be chilly. The boats are quite large and have adequate space both inside and out. The bathrooms are clean, and there is a snack bar where we stuffed ourselves with hot dogs and soft drinks. Bon Voyage!

City Hall
>Monday–Friday 10:00 A.M.–3:30 P.M.
>By subway: #4, #5, #6, N, or R train to City Hall

By bus: M1, M6, M101, or M102
A landmark building with special exhibits.

Cloisters, The   923-3700
Ft. Tryon Park

Commodities Exchange Center
Visitor's Gallery   938-2025
Four World Trade Center
  Tours by appointment
  Monday–Friday 9:30 A.M.–3:00 P.M.
    By subway: #1, E, or K train to the World Trade Center
    By bus: M10

COMEX is the country's largest exchange which trades in commodities. The riskiest, and by far the most complex system of trading, it permits a wide range of business people, investors, and speculators to match their wits against the odds as they buy and sell for future delivery. COMEX is the most active metals market, trading not only gold and silver but also aluminum and copper. These tours are of interest primarily to those who invest in commodities or are students of the trading systems.

Cooper–Hewitt Museum   860-6868
2 East 91st Street (Fifth Ave.)

Dakota, The
1 West 72nd Street (Central Park West)
    By subway: B, C, or K train to 72nd Street
    By bus: M10

Yes, *Rosemary's Baby* was filmed here, although Ira Levin actually set it in the Osborne at 57th Street and Seventh Avenue. John Lennon used to live here, and Lauren Bacall, Richard Chamberlain, and other luminaries still call this home.

Ellis Island   363-3200
    By subway to ferry: #1 train to South Ferry

For millions of terrified but hopeful refugees, Ellis Island symbolized the gateway to the freedom and riches they hoped to enjoy in America. A visit here is an emotionally charged event—you follow the same journey as the immigrants did, from the ferry slip to the entry arches, into the baggage rooms, up the staircase into the Registry Room. It was in this great hall that immigrants were processed, and either admitted to the promised land or turned back. No one who passed through here ever forgot the experience. Mayor Fiorello LaGuardia worked here as a young man during one of the busiest periods of immigration and wrote that he never became immune to the heartbreak of denying entry to people. Several permanent exhibits present the history of immigration in America. Among the most interesting is "Treasures from Home," a display of actual objects brought along by those who were leaving their homeland forever. To raise money for this restoration, Lee Iaccoca devised the "Walll of Glory"—for a contribution you could have the name of an ancestor inscribed here—and visitors enjoy searching for names of their relatives. Ellis Island stands as a fitting tribute to the millions who courageously built new lives for themselves and contributed to the greatness of America.

Ferry service runs from Battery Park Monday–Friday from 9:00 A.M.–5:00 P.M., and from 9:00 A.M.–6:00 P.M. on weekends. The one sour note is that high fares ($6.00 for adults, $3.00 for children under 12) make visiting Ellis Island an expensive proposition for families.

Empire State Building   736-3100
350 Fifth Avenue (34th St.)
    Open daily: 9:30 A.M.–Midnight
    Adults $3.25
    Children/Senior citizens $1.75
    By subway: #6 train to 33rd Street
    By bus: M2, M3, M5, or M32

Everybody's favorite skyscraper, even King Kong's. For a while this was the world's tallest building. The views from the 86th floor outdoor observatory and 102nd floor enclosed viewing area are dazzling. It's a great place to start your visit to New York.

Federal Hall National Memorial   264-8711
26 Wall Street
    Monday–Friday 9:00 A.M.–5:00 P.M.
    Admission Free
    By subway: #2, #3, #4, or #5 train to Wall Street
    By bus: M1 or M6

This handsome and well-known building stands on the site of Washington's inauguration as first President of the United States. In addition to permanent exhibitions on George Washington and the Bill of Rights, changing exhibits in the balcony galleries offer a fascinating glimpse of Colonial New York.

Federal Reserve Bank of New York   720-6130
33 Liberty Street
    Tours:
    Monday–Friday 10:00 A.M., 11:00 A.M., 1:00 P.M.,
    & 2:00 P.M.
    Admission: Free
    By subway: #2, #3, #4, or #5 train to Wall Street
    By bus: M1 or M6

Reservations must be made at least seven days in advance. The interesting thing about this building is that it contains 10,000 tons of gold. Guided tours lead visitors through the gold vault, providing an overview of the bank's operations.

Forbes Galleries   206-5548
62 Fifth Avenue (12th St.)
    Hours:
    Tuesday, Wednesday, Friday, and Saturday 10:00 A.M.–
    4:00 P.M.
    Thursday: Groups by advance reservation only
    Admission: Free
    By subway: B, D, L, N, R, #4, #5, or #6 train to
    Union Square
    By bus: M2, M3, or M5
This is where you can see Malcolm Forbes's fabulous collection of Faberge Easter eggs and over 12,000 toy soldiers.

Fraunces Tavern Museum   425-1778
54 Pearl Street (Broad St.)

Frick Collection   288-0700
1 East 70th Street

Gracie Mansion   570-4751
East End Avenue at 88th Street
    Tours:
    Wednesday (March–November) 10:00 A.M.–4:00 P.M.
    Suggested Admission:
    Adults $3.00
    Senior citizens $1.00
    By subway: #4, #5, #6 train to 86th Street
    By bus: M15 up First Avenue or M18 crosstown
    Reservations are required for all tours
The official residence of New York's mayors since 1941.

Grand Central Station   935-3960
42nd Street and Park Avenue
    By subway: #4, #5, #6, #7 train or Shuttle from
    Times Square
    By bus: M1, M2, M3, M4, M5, M101, M102, M104, or
    M42 crosstown
One of New York's most important Beaux Arts buildings, the station offers free weekly tours on Wednesday at 12:30 P.M., sponsored by the Municipal Art Society. Tours meet at Chemical Bank on the main concourse. We've always found the great vaulted ceiling fascinating. It is decorated with the constellations of the zodiac and has tiny lights to indicate stars.

Grant's Tomb   666-1640
122nd Street and Riverside Drive
    Wednesday–Sunday 9:00 A.M.–5:00 P.M.
    Admission: Free

By bus: M5 or M104

Learn the answer to the eternal question,"Who's buried in Grant's tomb?"

Greenwich Village

By subway: #1 train to Christopher Street; also A, C, E, F, N, R, or #6 train, depending upon what part of the Village you want

By bus: M1, M2, M3, M5, M6, M10, M101, M102, or M15

The name "Greenwich Village" brings to mind images of starving artists, beatniks reciting poetry in coffee houses, and political radicals talking revolution. The low rents which once attracted the not-yet-famous to this area have long disappeared, but the particular essence of "The Village" has remained. Its narrow streets, lined with houses rather than gigantic apartment buildings, maintain as close as New York gets to a "small town" atmosphere. Restaurants abound, serving everything from Haute Cuisine to the latest ethnic craze, and you can still "discover" new talent in the many comedy clubs.

Guggenheim Museum	360-3500

1071 Fifth Avenue (89th St.)

Hayden Planetarium (American Museum of Natural History)	769-5920

Central Park West (81st St.)

Adults $4.00

Students/Senior citizens $3.00

Museum Members $3.00

Children (under 12) $2.00

By subway: B, C, or K train to 81st Street

By bus: M10 to 79th Street

Sky Show

A series of shows based on the position of the heavenly bodies at various times. Shows such as *The Seven Wonders of the Universe, The Star of Christmas*, and a look at the cutting edge of astronomy called *Frontiers*. Times of performance can vary so be sure to call for the schedule. Cost is included in the price of admission to the planetarium.

Laser Rock Show

One of the most popular shows at the planetarium. A combination of visual and sound elements that make for a wonderful experience. Purchase tickets at the box office for Friday or Saturday performances. Cost is $6.00.

International Center for Photography	860-1777

1130 Fifth Avenue (94th St.)

Intrepid Sea–Air–Space Museum	489-6900

Pier 86 (46th Street and Hudson River)

Jewish Museum   **860-1888**
1109 Fifth Avenue (92nd St.)

Lincoln Center for the Performing Arts   **877-1800**
Broadway between 63rd–66th Streets
    Guided tours daily 10:00 A.M.–5:00 P.M.
    Admission:
    Adults $6.25
    Senior citizens $5.25
    Children (under 12) $3.50
    By subway: #1 train to 66th Street
    By bus: M5, M7, or M104
Lincoln Center is one of the city's major landmarks. It is comprised of several notable buildings, the most important of which are the Metropolitan Opera House, the New York State Theater, and Avery Fisher Hall, home to the New York Philharmonic. The Juilliard School of Music is across 65th Street to the north of the main plaza complex. The Revlon Fountain is a major attraction in the center of the plaza and was the focus of a wonderful scene between Zero Mostel and Gene Wilder in the film *The Producers*. Cafes in front of Avery Fisher Hall provide a great place for lunch or a light dinner while people-watching.

Little Italy
    By subway: Take any train to Canal Street and walk east to Mulberry Street. Little Italy is on the north side of Canal Street. We recommend a taxi.
One of New York's oldest enclaves, Little Italy extends from Houston to Canal Streets. It's particularly bustling during the Feast of San Gennaro, held for 10 days in September. It would be criminal to wander through this area without stopping at Ferrara's for a sample of their luscious pastries. Other favorites along Mulberry Street include S.P.Q.R., Il Cortile, and Umberto's Clam House, where Joey Gallo was rubbed out.

Loeb Boathouse in Central Park   **288-7281**
Near 72nd Street
    Rowboat rental $6.00 per hour
    Gondola rides $20.00 per half hour
There is free trolley service nightly from East 72nd Street to the boathouse, 6:30 P.M.–11:00 P.M.

Lower East Side
This area still retains some of the character of the thousands of refugees from Eastern Europe who settled here at the end of the 19th century. Restaurants such as Sammy's Famous Rumanian, Bernstein-on-Essex Street (Kosher Chinese), Veseleka, and Christine's Polish Kitchen continue to draw crowds for their home cooking and reasonable prices. On Sunday, shopping for bargains at the discount stores on

Orchard, Delancey, and Grand Streets is a popular pastime for New Yorkers and visitors alike.

Metropolitan Museum of Art	879-5500

Fifth Avenue & 82nd Street

Mormon Visitor's Center	595-1825

2 Lincoln Square
   Daily 10:00 A.M.–8:00 P.M.
   Admission Free
   By subway: #1 train to 66th Street
   By bus: M5, M7, or M104

The Church of Jesus Christ of the Latter-Day Saints had its beginnings right here in New York State. Multimedia displays and movies depict the church's origins.

Morgan Library, The Pierpont	685-0008

29 East 36th Street (Madison Ave.)
   Tuesday–Saturday 10:30 A.M.–5:00 P.M.
   Sunday 1:00 P.M.–5:00 P.M.
   Closed Monday and holidays
   Suggested admission:
   Adults $3.00
   Students and Senior citizens $1.50
   By subway: Lexington Avenue #6 train to 33rd Street
   By bus: M1, M2, M3, M4, or M32

Built by financier J. Pierpont Morgan in 1906, this opulent museum/research library houses Morgan's exceptional collection of art, rare manuscripts, and rare books. The collection includes such diverse items as medieval jeweled book bindings, Mary Shelly's own copy of *Frankenstein*, Napoleon's love letters to Josephine, and three Gutenberg Bibles. The library regularly presents special exhibits of particular interest and is a must for book lovers.

Morris–Jumel Mansion	923-8008

Edgecomb Avenue at West 160th Street
   Tuesday–Saturday 10:00 A.M.–4:00 P.M.
   Admission $2.00
   By subway: #1 train to 157th Street
   By bus: M2, M3, M100, or M101

Washington's headquarters in 1776, Manhattan's oldest residence is now a museum.

Museum of American Folk Art	977-7298

2 Lincoln Square
Broadway (65th/66th Sts.)

Museum of the American Indian	283-2420

Broadway and 155th Street

Museum of Broadcasting	752-7684

23 West 52nd Street

| **Museum of the City of New York** | 534-1672 |

Fifth Avenue at 103rd Street

| **Museum of Modern Art** | 708-9400 |

11 West 53rd Street

| **NBC Tours** | 664-4000 |

30 Rockefeller Plaza
   Monday–Saturday 9:30 A.M.–4:30 P.M.
   Admission $7.00
   By subway: B, D, or F to Rockefeller Center
   By bus: M1, M2, M3, M4, M5, M7, or M32

This fascinating 55 minute tour takes you behind the scenes at NBC's studios. Includes "Saturday Night Live" and "The Today Show" sets.

| **New York City Fire Museum** | 691-1303 |

278 Spring Street

| **New York Historical Society** | 873-3400 |

170 Central Park West
   Tuesday–Saturday 10:00 A.M.–5:00 P.M.
   Sunday 1:00 P.M.–5:00 P.M
   Closed Monday
   Admission:
   Adults $2.00
   Children $2.00
   By subway: B or C train to 81st Street
   By bus: M10

A neglected jewel of a museum, The Historical Society contains a comprehensive display of Tiffany lamps and the definitive collection of works by John James Audubon.

| **New York Public Library** | 930-0501 |

Fifth Avenue at 42nd Street
   Tours: Monday–Saturday 11:00 A.M. & 2:00 P.M.
   Admission: Free
   By subway: #4, #5, #6, or #7 train to Grand Central
   By bus: M1, M2, M3, M4, M5, M32, M42 crosstown,
      or M104

The Public Library is high on the list of places most valued by New Yorkers and contains books ranging from a Gutenberg Bible to Sherlock Holmes in Yiddish. While tourists may not be interested in the scholarly quality of items available, they might wish to take one of the free tours through this remarkable landmark building. They are extremely interesting and draw a large crowd. Patience and Fortitude, the literary lions, guard the entrance.

| **New York Stock Exchange** | 656-5167 |

20 Broad Street (Wall St.)
   Tours: Monday–Friday 9:30 A.M.–3:30 P.M.
   Admission: Free

By subway: #2, #3, #4, or #5 train to Wall Street
By bus: M1 or M6

The world's largest securities marketplace, setting for the popular motion picture "Wall Street," the Stock Exchange's true stories are livelier than any fiction. Unescorted tours depart every half hour.

Radio City Music Hall Productions
50th Street and Avenue of the Americas   246-4600
Backstage tours $6.00
By subway: B, D F, or S train to Rockefeller Center
By bus: M1, M2, M3, M4, M5, M6, or M7

An hour-long tour of the back-stage area showing all of the wonderful mechanisms that have made spectacular production possible. The stage is supposedly the largest theater stage in the world. Tours meet in the lobby.

Riverside Church   222-5900
Riverside Drive at 122nd Street
Monday–Saturday 11:00 A.M.–3:00 P.M.
Sunday Noon–4:00 P.M.
By subway: #1 train to 125th Street
By bus: M5 or M104

A Baptist church serving the Columbia University area, the main attraction for tourists is the view from the bell tower. Rising 392 feet above Riverside Drive, it affords magnificent views of both Manhattan and the Hudson River.

Rockefeller Center
Fifth and Sixth Avenues (47th/52nd Sts.)
By subway: B, D, or F train
By bus: M1, M2, M3, M4, M5, M6, or M7

Recently purchased by the Japanese, this symbol of New York was the world's first real estate project to encompass offices, stores, restaurants, and an entertainment complex. This "city within a city" contains such New York landmarks as the Rainbow Room, NBC Studios, Radio City Music Hall, and the world's most famous skating rink. You can explore this fabulous 24-acre underground complex on your own with a walking map from the visitors center in the lobby of the GE Building (formerly the RCA Building). Our favorite event here is the December gathering of 400 (Yes, 400!) tuba players to perform Christmas carols.

St. Patrick's Cathedral   753-2261
Fifth Avenue at 50th Street
Daily: 7:00 A.M.–8:00 P.M.
By subway: #6 train to 51st Street
By bus: M1, M2, M3, or M4

Seat of the Archdiocese of New York, St. Patrick's is one of the finest Gothic-style structures in America.

St. Peter's Church   935-2200
Citicorp Center, Lexington Avenue at 54th Street
  Jazz vespers, Wednesday 12:30 P.M.
  Suggested donation $2.00
  By subway: E or F train to 53rd Street; #6 train to
  51st Street
  By bus: M101 or M102

Short Line Tours   354-4740
166 West 46th Street
  By subway: #1 train to 42nd or 50th Street
  By bus: M101 or M104
Offers a wide spectrum of bus tours ranging from two
and a half hours to all day. Very popular with tourists and
we've never had a complaint.

SoHo
  By subway: N or R train to Prince Street; #6 train to
  Spring Street; #1 train to Houston or Canal Streets
  By bus: M1, M5, M6, or M10
Once a deserted warehouse area, SoHo (an acronym for
SOuth of HOuston—pronounced HOWston) has developed into a thriving center of art galleries, trendy clothing
boutiques, and restaurants. At the time we went to press,
this area of approximately 30 square blocks contained more
than 25 antique stores, some 40 restaurants, 75 art galleries,
and almost 100 boutiques. A living museum of cast-iron architecture, SoHo was declared a historic district in 1973.

South Street Seaport   Phone: SEA-PORT
Fulton Street at the East River
  By subway: #2, #3, #4, or #5 train to Fulton Street
  By bus: M15
This restored landmark area, recreating 19th century
New York, with its charming shops, restaurants and inter-
national food court, attracts tourists and New Yorkers alike.
Big on charm, the redevelopment is aimed specifically at
tourist dollars and the area is sadly lacking in real quality.
Be warned that the restaurants currently in operation offer
dreadful food at high prices. Stick to the hot dog stands.

South Street Seaport Museum   669-9400
207 Front Street

Staten Island Ferry
  By subway: #1 train to South Ferry
Still New York's biggest bargain. One-way fare $.50, pay-
able on leaving Manhattan. No charge for the return trip.

Statue of Liberty   363-3200
  By subway to the ferry: #1 train to South Ferry
A universal symbol of freedom and opportunity, "Lady
Liberty" has welcomed visitors for over 100 years. Largely

ignored by New Yorkers, this is our #1 tourist attraction. Ferries depart from Battery Park directly to Liberty Island. You can also get a wonderful view of the Statue from the Circle Line boats or the Staten Island Ferry.

Temple Emanu-el   744-1400
Fifth Avenue at 65th Street
    Daily 10:00 A.M.–5:00 P.M.
    Friday 10:00 A.M.–4:00 P.M.
    By subway: #6 train to 68th Street
    By bus: M1, M2, M3, or M4
Built in 1929, this is the home of the city's oldest Reformed congregation. The building is Romanesque in style, with obvious Eastern (Byzantine) influence. The main hall is huge and seats 2,500 worshippers.

Trinity Church   602-0800
Broadway and Wall Street
    Museum Hours:
    Monday–Friday 9:00 A.M.–11:45 A.M., and 1:00 P.M.–3:45 P.M.
    Saturday 10:00 A.M.–3:45 P.M.
    Sunday 1:00 P.M.–3:45 P.M.
    By subway: #2, #3, #4, #5 train to Wall Street
    By bus: M1 or M6
    Tours of the church weekdays: 2:00 P.M.
This financial district landmark still holds its own against the skyscrapers of lower Manhattan. The tranquil church and graveyard offer solace to tourists, job-hunters, and world-weary Wall Streeters. George Washington worshipped at nearby St. Paul's Chapel.

United Nations   963-7713
First Avenue between 45th and 46th Streets
    Tours in English daily 9:15 A.M.–4:45 P.M.
    Tours in other languages, call   963-7539
    Adults $4.50
    Students $2.50
    Senior citizens $4.00
    Children under 5 not admitted
    By subway: Any train to 42nd Street then the M42 bus
    By bus: M42 crosstown bus or the M104
All New Yorkers know that their city is the center of the universe, and having the United Nations here reinforces this belief. More than 30 million visitors have taken the tour which allows them to see the meeting place of the world's leaders. Free tickets for General Assembly and Council meetings are sometimes available on a first-come, first-served basis. Check at the information desk in the General Assembly lobby.

Whitney Museum of American Art   **570-3600**
945 Madison Avenue (75th St.)

**Whitney Museum at the Equitable
    Center**   **544-1000**
787 Seventh Avenue (52nd St.)

World Financial Center   **945-0505**
The Hudson River (Vesey/Liberty Sts.)
    Monday–Saturday 10:00 A.M.–7:00 P.M.
    Sunday Noon–5:00 P.M.
    By subway: #1, E, or K train to the World Trade Center
    By bus: M10

One of the largest and newest places to visit in the financial district. Made up of four towers of granite and reflective glass, it was designed by Cesar Pelli, the noted architect. It includes many shops such as Barney's, Bally of Switzerland, and Rizzoli Bookstore, as well as Godiva Chocolates. The Hudson River Club promises to be a premier restaurant. It also is home of the much touted Winter Garden (a majestic space with beautiful palm trees, not to be confused with the Winter Garden Theater at 50th Street and Broadway). A good place to take a break if you are sightseeing in the Wall Street area. The best news for tourists, of course, is that there are bathrooms near the West Street entrance.

World Trade Center   **466-4170**
Church and Liberty Streets
    Observation deck open daily: 9:30 A.M.–9:30 P.M.
    Adults $2.95
    Children $1.50
    By subway: #1, E, K, N, or R train to Cortlandt Street/World Trade Center (W.T.C.)
    By bus: M10

Another spot to visit downtown. Again, it has shops, restaurants, and all of the usual things. It also contains the highest observation platform and a bar on the 107th floor. You may wish to stop in at the Commodities Exchange Center on the ninth floor.

Sign of the Dove   **861-8080**
1110 Third Avenue (65th St.)

SINGLES BARS

Amsterdam's on Amsterdam   **874-1377**
428 Amsterdam Avenue (80th/81st Sts.)
Rub shoulder-pads with the upscale.

Arizona 206   838-0440
206 East 60th Street (Second/Third Aves.)
Delicious southwestern food and a great-looking crowd.

Jim McMullen's   861-4700
1341 Third Avenue (76th St.)
A young professional's haven.

P.J. Clarke's   759-1650
915 Third Avenue (55th St.)
Dwarfed by the towering corporate headquarters built
over it, Clarke's boasts one of the city's most elaborate mahog-
any and cut-glass bars, and one of the best jukeboxes in town.

T.G.I. Friday's   832-8512
1152 First Avenue (63rd St.)
One of the best singles spots on the Upper East Side.
Open until 1:00 A.M. during the week and until 3:00 A.M. on
Friday and Saturday.

60th Street Heliport   880-1234
East 60th Street (East River)

Sky Rink   695-6556
450 West 33rd Street (Ninth/Tenth Aves.)

Skyward The Select Club   704-5262
165 Water Street

Sloane Hospital for Women   694-2500
622 West 168th Street

Smith & Wollensky   753-1530
797 Third Avenue (49th St.)

Smith Limo   247-0711

SOHO

SoHo is one of the magic words that conjures up, for
most tourists and New Yorkers, a vision of elegant art galleries and high fashion designer goods. But the price for
this has been high. Lost to this area are the hundreds of artists who originally clustered there for the cheap rent for
large work spaces. The ambience of SoHo is altered forever.

But the good news is that the vision is still true. There really are wonderful galleries to browse through and shops
that will boggle your mind. SoHo is now one of the busiest
tourist attractions in town. Go about 11:00 A.M. and walk
around for a while to get a feeling for the neighborhood.
Pay particular attention to the cast iron construction of the
buildings which has qualified it as a historic preservation
area. There are several good restaurants for lunch and then
some serious shopping and visits to galleries.

South Street Seaport   **Phone: SEA-PORT**
Fulton Street (East River)

    Children's Center   **669-9400**
    165 John Street

    Museum   **669-9400**
    207 Front Street

**South Street Seaport Museum Book
    and Chart Store**   **669-9455**
209 Water Street

South Street Theater   **279-4200**
424 West 42nd Street

Sotheby's   **606-7000**
1334 York Avenue (72nd St.)

Spain (Consulate of)   **355-4080**
150 East 58th Street

Spark's Steakhouse   **687-4855**
210 East 46th Street (Second/Third Aves.)

Spirit of New York   **279-1890**
Pier 9 (foot of Wall St.)

SPORTING GOODS

    Al Lieber's World of Golf   **242-2895**
    147 East 47th Street (Lexington/Third Aves.)

    Athlete's Foot   **586-1936**
    16 West 57th Street (Fifth/Sixth Aves.)
        Monday–Friday 10:00 A.M.–7:00 P.M.
        Saturday–Sunday Noon–6:00 P.M.

Gone are the days when one pair of Keds sufficed for all sports. Whether you need running, aerobic, tennis, golf, or walking shoes, Athlete's Foot will have a style and size to suit you.

    Herman's Sporting Goods   **730-7400**
    135 West 42nd Street (Broadway/Avenue of the
    Americas)
        Monday–Friday 9:30 A.M.–7:00 P.M.
        Saturday 9:30 A.M.–6:00 P.M.

Shop here for reasonable prices on name brands (Adidas, New Balance, Nike, and Reebok) and golf, tennis, and exercise equipment.

    Horizontal   **826-2922**

Located next to the Vertical Club, the Horizontal offers New York's largest selection of bodywear—all top quality and at top prices.

Monday–Friday 10:00 A.M.–9:00 P.M.
Saturday 11:00 A.M.–7:00 P.M.
Sunday 11:00 A.M.–6:00 P.M.
Closed Sunday in the summer

Hudson's   473-0981
97 Third Avenue (12th/13th Sts.)
Monday–Thursday 9:30 A.M.–8:00 P.M.
Friday–Saturday 9:30 A.M.–7:00 P.M.
Sunday Noon–6:00 P.M.

New York's answer to L.L. Bean, Hudson's outfits both the true sportsmen and those who want the outdoors "look." Takes up the entire city block, so there are lots of choices.

Paragon Athletics   255-8036
867 Broadway (17th/18th St.)
Monday–Friday 10:00 A.M.–8:00 P.M.
Saturday 10:00 A.M.–7:00 P.M.
Sunday 11:00 A.M.–6:00 P.M.

The best. A well-versed staff and enormous selection distinguish Paragon from its competitors.

Richard Metz Golf Studio, Inc.   759-6940
35 East 50th Street

SPORTS BARS

Meeting friends for dinner but can't stand to miss the Big Game? You'll be able to enjoy both at:

Mickey Mantle's   688-7777
42 Central Park South

New York's premier sports bar. Ten television screens plus a sports video library. Stick to simple selections (hamburgers, chicken pot pie, hickory smoked ribs) or the surprisingly good pasta.

Rusty Staub's on 5th   682-1000
575 Fifth Avenue (47th St.)
Baby back ribs are a good bet here.

Sports Phone   976-1313

Spring Lake Golf Club   1-516-924-5115
Route 25 and Bartlett Road, Middle Island, NY

St. Bartholomew's Church   751-1616
109 East 50th Street

St. Clare's Hospital   586-1500
415 West 51st Street

St. James Theater   398-0280
246 West 44th Street

St. Luke's Hospital	**870-6000**
Amsterdam Avenue and 114th Street	
St. Malachy's Church	**489-1340**
239 West 49th Street	
St. Marks Bookshop	**260-7853**
13 St. Marks Place (Second/Third Aves.)	
St. Moritz on the Park	**755-5800**
50 Central Park South (Sixth Ave.)	
St. Patrick's Cathedral	**753-2261**
Fifth Avenue (50th St.)	
St. Peter's Lutheran Church	**935-2200**
Lexington Avenue (54th St.)	
St. Regis Hotel, The (Opening Spring 1991)	
2 East 55th Street (Fifth Ave.)	
St. Thomas Church	**757-7013**
1 West 53rd Street	
St. Vincent's Hospital	**790-7000**
Seventh Avenue and 11th Street	

STADIUMS

Meadowlands, The   **1-201-935-8222**
East Rutherford, NJ
> Special bus service is available for each event. Call for exact times and gate numbers.

Shea Stadium   **1-718-507-8499**
Flushing, Queens
> By subway: #7 train from Times Square or Grand Central Station directly to Shea Stadium
> Train service also available from the Long Island Railroad

Yankee Stadium   **293-6000**
161st Street, The Bronx
> By subway: On the West Side, take the IND D train uptown; on the East Side, take the Lexington Avenue IRT #4 "Jerome Avenue" train uptown

Stage Deli	**245-7850**
834 Seventh Avenue (53rd/54th Sts.)	
Stair & Company	**517-4400**
942 Madison Avenue	
Stand-Up New York	**595-0850**
236 West 78th Street (Broadway/Amsterdam Ave.)	

Stanhope Hotel, The	**288-5800**
995 Fifth Avenue (81st St.)	
Stanrose Dress Company	**736-3358**
141 West 36th Street	
Star Sapphire	**688-4711**
400 East 59th Street (First Ave.)	
Staten Island Ferry	**806-6940**
Battery Park	
Statue of Liberty	**363-3200**
Steuben Glass	**752-1441**
715 Fifth Avenue (56th St.)	
Steven Corn Furs, Inc.	**695-3914**
141 West 28th Street	

STORES

See also **DEPARTMENT STORES**

New York is a shopper's paradise. Listed below are the stores we have found to be of most interest to visitors (not including department stores).

Abercrombie & Fitch 832-1001
Trump Tower, 725 Fifth Avenue (56th/57th Sts.)
Founded in 1892, Abercrombie & Fitch is famous for its gadgets (such as the renowned 60-second razor), active and classic sportswear, and exclusive gifts.

A La Vieille Russie 752-1727
781 Fifth Avenue (59th St.)
When you enter through the small revolving door into the quiet of this shop you are greeted by Ms. Rose Casella, who immediately makes you feel as though all of the wonderful pieces of jewelry have been brought together just for you. The name, which means "In old Russia," is an indication of what's in store for you. They specialize in antique Russian jewelry, including Faberge, and decorative art objects made of precious metals and stones. Don't be surprised if you find imperial seals or initials on these unique treasures.

Ann Taylor 832-2010
3 East 57th Street (Fifth/Madison Aves.)
Classic American women's clothing.

Baccarat 826-4100
625 Madison Avenue (58th/59th Sts.)
Our favorite crystal! A goblet McDowell bought there 30 years ago for $50.00 is now practically priceless. Elegant

simplicity is the hallmark of their design. Beautiful vases, carafes, stemware, and art objects delight the eye. They also carry Ceralene Limoges china and Cristofle silver flatware.

Bally   751-2163
681 Madison Avenue (62nd St.)
While known principally for shoes made of super-fine leathers, they also carry a selection of elegant clothing.

Bottega Veneta   371-5511
635 Madison Avenue (60th St.)
Quality leatherware "when your own initials are enough."

Brooks Brothers   682-8800
346 Madison Avenue (44th St.)
This is the flagship store of that most famous of all American chains. Once known exclusively for its high-quality conservative men's clothing, there is now a floor for women. Their service is unbeatable.

Buccellatti   308-5533
Trump Tower, 725 Fifth Avenue (56th/57th Sts.)

Bulgari   315-9000
730 Fifth Avenue (57th St.)
With the opening of their new Fifth Avenue store, the Bulgaris marked their 100th anniversary as world class jewelers. Their twelve shops, in the world's most exotic cities, enable them to provide the kind of service their clientele demands and we would all like to receive. Bring lots of money!

Burberry   371-5010
9 East 57th Street (Fifth/Madison Aves.)
Distinctive British clothing including their signature raincoats have established Burberry's reputation.

Cartier   753-0111
653 Fifth Avenue (52nd St.)
This once respected establishment needs a visit from top management. When we visited recently, sales people were popping gum and the security guards were lounging in the hallways, making it difficult to pass from room to room. Hardly the environment to attract the upper crust clientele who can afford those wonderful jewels. We also thought the austere, white display cases rather tacky choices for the presentation of Cartier's best.

Chanel   355-5050
5 East 57th Street (Fifth/Madison Aves.)
Classic French clothing, purses, and accessories.

Charles Jourdan   **644-3830**
Trump Tower, 725 Fifth Avenue (56th/57th Sts.)

Charivari   **333-4040**
18 West 57th Street

Church's English Shoes   **755-4313**
428 Madison Avenue (49th St.)
In an atmosphere as relaxing as a fine English library, Church's attentive staff guarantees the perfect fit in an enormous variety of shoe styles. They have sales several times a year—watch for them.

Coach Leatherware   **594-1581**
754 Madison Avenue (63rd St.)
Good, solid craftsmanship has established Coach as the place to shop for leather goods. Their style is conservative and very much their own. Women love their handbags.

Cole-Haan   **421-8440**
61st Street and Madison Avenue
Handmade Italian leather goods. Luggage, briefcases, and handbags are but a few of the many beautifully crafted items available.

Crouch & Fitzgerald   **755-5888**
400 Madison Avenue (48th St.)
For over 150 years, discriminating shoppers have headed here for high-quality leather briefcases, luggage, and desk accessories.

David Webb   **421-3030**
7 East 57th Street (Fifth/Madison Aves.)
Jackie O. shopped here every chance she got, if memory serves us right. While not to everyone's taste, their jewelry is distinctive and will be immediately identified by the knowledgeable.

Fendi   **767-0100**
720 Fifth Avenue (56th St.)
Famous for its handbags, Karl Lagerfeld designed furs, and women's ready-to-wear clothing. Suits are in the $1,200–1,800 range. One of the newest major stores in the city, it is owned by the Fendi family of Rome and is operated by five sisters.

Fortunoff   **758-6660**
681 Fifth Avenue (54th St.)
"The Source" for silver flatware, hollowware, and jewelry.

Fred Leighton   **288-1872**
781 Madison Avenue (66th St.)

A nice place to look for some of the more recent "antiques." Beautiful pieces by Faberge and Cartier, as well as art deco. They also have a lot of loose gems in case you like to design your own jewelry.

Georg Jensen   759-6457
683 Madison Avenue (61st St.)
Contemporary crystal, Royal Copenhagen porcelain, and their distinctive patterns in both silver flatware and jewelry.

Giorgio Armani   988-9191
815 Madison Avenue (67th St.)

Givenchy Boutique   772-1040
954 Madison Avenue (75th St.)
Timeless fashions for women of impeccable taste and considerable wealth.

Gucci   826-2600
689 Fifth Avenue (54th St.)

Hammacher Schlemmer   421-9000
147 East 57th Street
This is probably the most difficult of all stores to describe. They specialize in the unusual, not to say bizarre. Our favorite was a battery powered swan, large enough for two, made to use in your private pond. Try to get their catalog.

Harry Winston   245-2000
718 Fifth Avenue (56th St.)
One of the most renowned jewelers in the country. Their interest is in the highest quality gemstones and the conservatively designed settings required to display them. Everything is of investment quality and, needless to say, service is impeccable.

Henri Bendel   247-1100
10 West 57th Street (Fifth/Sixth Aves.)
Primarily thought of as a women's clothing store, they also carry all of the various accessories and cosmetics one associates with a small department store. They do have a selection of clothing for men and all of their designs are of fine quality

Hermès   751-3181
11 East 57th Street (Fifth/Madison Aves.)
The equestrian patterns on their famous silk scarves pay homage to Hermès' beginnings as makers of leather harnesses and saddles. While you can still buy a saddle here, most shoppers prefer to take home ties, scarves, gloves, handbags or other exquisite leather goods.

STORES

James Robinson, Inc.   752-6166
15 East 57th Street (Fifth/Madison Aves.)
No list of the best shops is complete without James Robinson and its upstairs companion, James II. The friendly and helpful staff, under the direction of Edward Munves, Jr., cater to the wide spectrum of customers and browsers who frequent the shop. His daughter, Joan Boening, is the fourth generation to continue the family traditions of service and connoiseurship. Collectors have long been familiar with the wonderful antique jewelry and silver that span centuries of fine craftsmanship. As a family enterprise dedicated to excellence, they operate their own centuries-old workshops in England in order to ensure the quality of their wonderful handmade sterling silver flatware and coffee sets.

Kenzo   737-8640
824 Madison Avenue (69th St.)

Krizia   628-8180
805 Madison Avenue (67th St.)
The home base of high-fashion designer Mariucca Mandella.

Lanvin   838-4330
701 Madison Avenue (62nd St.)

Laura Ashley   752-7300
21 East 57th Street (Fifth/Madison Aves.)
Laura Ashley's floral patterns, dainty dresses, and distinctive housewares have won her a large following.

Limited, The   838-8787
691 Madison Avenue (62nd St.)

Louis Vuitton   371-6111
51 East 57th Street (Madison/Park Aves.)
Everybody recognizes these initials. Vuitton products are not just status symbols, they are beautifully made and meant to last a lifetime.

Manhattan Art & Antiques Center   355-4400
1050 Second Avenue (56th St.)
Antique lovers will be delighted to find 104 stores (under one roof) that are open seven days a week. They offer great diversity in quality, selection, and price.

Mark Cross   421-3000
645 Fifth Avenue (51st St.)
Everybody knows Mark Cross's leather goods, long the standard by which such products are measured.

Martha   826-8855
Trump Tower, 725 Fifth Avenue (56th/57th Sts.)
Exquisite evening clothes by all of the best designers.

MCM   688-2133
717 Madison Avenue
Luggage, handbags, shoes, ties, apparel, and perfume
make up their stock in trade. Everything is handcrafted and
of superior workmanship.

Mikimoto   586-7153
608 Fifth Avenue (49th St.)
Pearls are a classic accessory, and Mikimoto's necklaces
are among the finest available in this country.

Nat Sherman–Tobacconist   751-9100
711 Fifth Avenue (55th St.)   1-800-221-1690
Nat Sherman modestly advertises his shop as "the
most prestigious tobacco emporium in the world." What
can we say? When McDowell was a concierge at The St.
Regis, it was certainly handy to have his store right
across the street and to feel confident about the service
and quality of merchandise he provided to his guests.
They only disappointed him once, by being closed when
Jimmy Breslin (on his wedding day) needed a stogie in a
hurry. Nat Sherman has everything you might want in
the way of tobacco products, humidors, and special gift
items for the smoker.

Paul Stuart   682-0320
Madison Avenue at 45th Street
Opulent men's clothing at opulent prices. Crowded, but
friendly service and high-quality merchandise are redeem-
ing graces.

Ralph Lauren   606-2100
867 Madison Avenue (72nd St.)
Ralph Lauren's classic designs displayed in the timeless
elegance of the converted Rhinelander Mansion.

H. Stern   688-0300
645 Fifth Avenue (51st St.)
Famous for its classic designs in rubies and emeralds,
H. Stern also carries a full line in semiprecious gems such as
tourmaline, citrine, and amethyst.

Steuben Glass   752-1441
715 Fifth Avenue (56th St.)
Showrooms that resemble some of the better museums
display the artistry, in crystal, of Steuben craftsmen. And
it's all for sale! The objects range from functional pieces

such as vases, bowls, candlesticks, and decanters to the purely ornamental items so sought after by collectors. Beautiful engraving is used as counterpoint to the lustrous, luminous crystal, and is a hallmark of Steuben. Alone among American companies, Steuben competes with the world's best for dominance in the highly competitive field of lead crystal, where production quantities are low and prices are high.

A. Sulka   **980-5226**
301 Park Avenue (55th St.)
Sulka's 90-year-old tradition of uncompromising standards has men flocking here for custom shirts, silk underwear, and elegant haberdashery.

Tiffany & Co.   **755-8000**
727 Fifth Avenue (57th St.)
In our experience as concierges, this was one of the most sought-after stores. Everybody wants to take home one of the distinctive Tiffany shopping bags with a goody in it. Known worldwide for the quality of its offerings, its scope encompasses everything from china through those exquisite jewels we all dream about.

Timberland   **754-0434**
709 Madison Avenue (63rd St.)
Rugged shoes handcrafted from full-grain leathers. Be sure you *really* like the style—these shoes never wear out.

Tourneau   **758-3265**
500 Madison Avenue (52nd St.)
New York's largest and finest selection of watches. Patek Philippe, Baume & Mercier, Piaget, Rolex, and others beckon enticingly from their glittering windows, and trade-ins are welcomed.

Treasures of the Orient
The Sheraton Center   **581-4620**
811 Seventh Avenue (53rd St.)
The St. Regis
2 East 55th Street (Fifth Ave.)
Temporarily relocated during renovation, Treasures of the Orient has been a standby at the St. Regis for over 50 years. Joe Harris traditionally carries a fine stock of elegant Oriental *objets d'art*, including jade bowls and carvings, precious snuff bottles, and jewelry. His VIP clientele currently phone him at the Sheraton Center for their special needs and look forward to seeing him back at the luxurious St. Regis in 1991.

F.R. Tripler   **922-1090**
366 Madison Avenue (46th St.)

Four floors of traditionally styled, classic men's clothing plus old-fashioned, friendly, knowledgeable, and attentive service make Tripler a haven. The small women's department also pleases.

Valentino   772-6969
825 Madison Avenue (68th St.)

Van Cleef & Arpels   644-9500
744 Fifth Avenue (57th St.)

Waterford Wedgwood   759-0500
713 Madison Avenue (63rd St.)

Their 1986 merger brought together these legendary names in hand-cut Irish crystal and fine English bone china. You can find anything from an ashtray to museum-quality presentation pieces here.

Yves Saint Laurent   988-3821
855 Madison Avenue (71st St.)

Storyland   517-6951
1369 Third Avenue (78th st.)

Strand Bookstore   473-1452
828 Broadway (12th St.)

Stringfellow's   254-2444
35 East 21st Street (Park Ave./Broadway)

STROLLERS

See **RENTALS, STROLLERS**

Stuyvesant Bicycle   254-5200
349 West 14th Street (Eighth/Ninth Aves.)

SUBWAYS

The only way to travel for millions of New Yorkers was physically upgraded during the Koch administration and is constantly undergoing repair. However, due to the politicians' and voters' unwillingness to deal with the social problems of the legitimately homeless, the beggars, and the (often) talentless musicians who inhabit the system, it is basically a slum on wheels. It is also the fastest way to get from one place to another and is relatively safe during daytime and evening hours. The fare is $1.15 and if you are a group of four (or even less) it may not cost much more to take a taxi. Subway maps are available for the asking at token booths and one is provided in the front of this book. We recommend the #1 train from midtown to South Ferry for tourists who want both the subway experience and the Statue of Liberty.

Suga	421-4400
115 East 57th Street	
Sullivan Street Playhouse	674-3838
181 Sullivan Street	
Sun Line Cruises	397-6400
1 Rockefeller Plaza	
Superior Weaving & Mending	
Company, The	929-7208
41 Union Square West (17th St.)	
Surrey Hotel	288-3700
20 West 76th Street (Madison Ave.)	
Sussex Clothes, Ltd.	279-4610
302 Fifth Avenue	
Sutton East Tennis	751-3452
488 East 60th Street (York Ave.)	
Swann Galleries	254-4710
104 East 25th Street	
Sweden (Consulate of)	751-5900
825 Third Avenue	
Sweet Basil	242-1785
88 Seventh Avenue South (Bleecker St.)	
Sweetwater's	873-4100
170 Amsterdam Avenue (68th St.)	
Swissair	1-718-995-8400
Switzerland (Consulate of)	758-2560
444 Madison Avenue	
Syndeham Family Care Hospital	686-7500
Manhattan Avenue and 123rd Street	

T

T.G.I. Friday's	832-8512
1152 First Avenue (63rd St.)	
Taj Mahal	1-609-449-1000
1000 Boardwalk at Virginia Avenue	
Atlantic City, NJ	

TAPES/RECORDS
See **RECORDS/TAPES**

Tavern on the Green   **873-3200**
Central Park West at 67th Street

Taxi Commission Lost and Found   **869-4513**
Call the above number if you have left something in a taxi. But don't expect to get it back. The next person to get in the cab probably took it . . . particularly if it was valuable. Your best defense is an offense. From now on pay attention to the name and number of the cab driver—they're posted next to the meter. And the best way to avoid problems is to keep your hands on your possessions.

TAXIS

The New York City Taxi Commission regulates the 11,787 yellow taxis that you see operating in the boroughs of New York. They are metered for in-city destinations. Out-of-town fares should be established with the driver before you start. These metered taxis are the only vehicles authorized to pick-up passengers on the streets. Fares start at $1.50 and increase by $.10 every few minutes or every few blocks. An additional $.50 is added to the tab from 8:00 P.M. until 6:00 A.M.

TEA/COFFEE

See **COFFEE/TEA**

TEA ROOMS/SERVICE

Barclay Terrace, The   **755-5900**
Hotel Intercontinental, 111 East 48th Street
   Monday–Friday 3:00 P.M.–5:30 P.M.
Red leather banquettes, paintings by John Singer Sargent, and a sedate atmosphere barely compensate for the soggy finger sandwiches and mediocre pastries served here. Of the eight varieties available, the Barclay blend is the best tea.

Carlyle, The   **744-1600**
35 East 76th Street
High tea is served in the Gallery, a small area between the bar and the restaurant, daily from 3:00 P.M. to 5:30 P.M.

Helmsley Palace, The   **888-7000**
455 Madison Avenue (50th/51st Sts.)
   Daily 2:00 P.M.–5:00 P.M.
Be entertained by a harpist while enjoying a royal high tea in the former music room of the Villard House. Fortnum

& Mason teas accompany an endless procession of sandwiches, scones, and cakes.

Mayfair Regent, The   288-0800
Park Avenue at 65th Street
   Daily 3:00 P.M.–5:30 P.M.
Full tea, served in the elegant Lounge, includes finger sandwiches and scones. You may also order a la carte.

Palm Court, The   759-3000
The Plaza, Fifth Avenue and 59th Street
   Monday–Saturday 3:45 P.M.–6:00 P.M.
   Sunday 4:00 P.M.–6:00 P.M.
As you enter the Palm Court, the day's choices of pastries are displayed before you. A violinist and pianist entertain while both tourists and even the most jaded New Yorkers enjoy the passing scene.

Pembroke Room   838-1400
The Lowell, 28 East 63rd Street
   Daily 3:30 P.M.–6:30 P.M.
What a perfect place for a clandestine rendezvous! Tucked away on the second floor, the Pembroke Room is like someone's very elegant private salon. High tea includes a selection of sandwiches, scones, tea breads, and pastries.

Terrace Five   371-5030
Trump Tower, 725 Fifth Avenue (56th/57th Sts.)
   Monday–Saturday 3:15 P.M.–5:00 P.M.
Take a break from shopping and enjoy a choice of classic tea (sandwiches, scones, and sweets), or a heartier array of pate, cheese, and smoked chicken breast. Wines and champagnes by the glass are also available.

Ted's Fine Clothing   966-2029
83 Orchard Street

Telecharge   239-6200

TELEGRAMS

Western Union (for information)   1-800-325-6000
All Western Union offices and their affiliates are listed in the NYNEX White Pages. They all can provide complete service including sending and receiving money. Our experience has been with the following offices which are conveniently located in the midtown and Wall Street areas. If you have problems call the information number.

For Telex, Mailgram, or Cablegram by telephone:

Western World Telex Service	**732-2252**
116 Nassau Street	

To send or receive money, plus all other services:

Western Union	**354-9750**
1440 Broadway	
Western Union	**509-1852**
1 Western Union Plaza	

TELEPHONE NUMBERS

The following is a list of the most requested telephone numbers in the city. Keep in mind that there is a small extra charge for numbers starting with the 976 exchange. Also be aware that there is a sizable charge added to your hotel bill for calls made from your hotel room. These can add up very quickly.

AAA Road Service	**757-3356**
Ambulance	**911**
Atlantic City, NJ	
Central Reservations	**1-800-833-7070**
Bus and Subway Information	**1-718-330-1234**
Coast Guard	**668-7000**
Con Ed Emergency	**683-8830**
Crime Victims Hotline	**577-7777**
Dow Jones Report	**976-4141**
FBI	**335-2700**
Fire	**911**
Folk Music Line	**666-9605**
Jazz Line	**1-718-465-7500**
Lotto Results	**976-2020**
Madison Square Garden	**563-8300**
New York Public Library Telephone Reference	**340-0849**
OTB (Off-Track Betting) Results	**976-2121**
Park Events	**360-1333**
Parking Violations Bureau	**477-4430**
Poison Control	**340-4494**
Police Emergency	**911**

Racing Results	976-2121
Rape Helpline	267-7273
Sports Phone	976-1313
Taxi Commission Lost and Found	869-4513
Time	976-1616
Towed Cars Pier 76, Twelfth Avenue and 38th Street	971-0770
Traffic Department (New York City)	830-7500
Traffic Information	1-518-449-1293
Travelers' Aid	944-0013
U.S. Customs	466-5550
U.S. Passport Office	541-7700
Visitors Bureau	397-8222
Weather	976-1212
Western Union	962-7111
Zip Code Information	967-8585

TELEX

If your hotel does not offer telex service, you will find reliable and efficient service at:

HQ-Headquarters Companies

237 Park Avenue	**949-0722**
730 Fifth Avenue	**333-8700**
53 Wall Street	**558-6400**

MCI International 40 Broad Street	**607-6680**

Our list of telex services was originally much more extensive, but as we double-checked just before going to press, we found that many places had gone out of business because everyone is using fax machines these days.

Temple Emanu-el Fifth Avenue (65th St.)	**744-1400**
1018 515 West 18th Street (Tenth Ave.)	**645-5157**

TENNIS

Tennis is a big deal in the city. Maybe it is because any form of game or exercise is so much trouble to take part in.

Whether it is a game in the park or the championship matches, there is always a line.

Armory Tennis Corp.   **686-2525**
8 Lexington Avenue (25th/26th Sts.)

Columbus Racquet Club   **663-6900**
795 Columbus Avenue (97th/100th Sts.)
Nine outdoor courts. Open only from April through October.

Crosstown Tennis   **947-5780**
14 West 31st Street (Fifth Ave.)
Four courts offering only the minimum comforts. This may explain why it is frequented by some of the top stars when they are here for the tournaments.

Midtown Tennis Club   **989-8572**
341 Eighth Avenue (27th St.)
Eight courts and the services of a fine group of pros keep this one of the busiest places in town.

Sutton East Tennis   **751-3452**
488 East 60th Street (York Ave.)

Tennis Club–Grand Central Terminal   **687-3841**
15 Vanderbilt Avenue
Two courts inside Grand Central Station. Also boasts an exercise room.

Village Courts   **989-2300**
110 University Place (12th St.)

Tennis Club–Grand Central Terminal   **687-3841**
15 Vanderbilt Avenue

Terrace V   **371-5030**
Trump Tower, Level Five, 725 Fifth Avenue
(56th/57th Sts.)

Terrace, The   **666-9490**
400 West 119th Street (Amsterdam Ave./Morningside Dr.)

Teuscher Chocolate
620 Fifth Avenue (49th/50th Sts.)   **246-4416**
25 East 61st Street   **751-8482**

THEATERS

Tickets for most Broadway plays are available by phone through the Ticketron and Telecharge systems (*see* TICKETS). Tickets may be charged to American Express,

MasterCard, or Visa. Unfortunately, the exact seating locations will not be given out by phone.

Actors Playhouse   691-6226
100 Seventh Avenue South (Christopher/Grove Sts.)

Ambassador   239-6200
215 West 49th Street (Eighth Ave./Broadway)

Astor Place Theater   254-3760
434 Lafayette Street (Astor Place)

Barrymore   239-6200
243 West 47th Street (Eighth Ave./Broadway)

Belasco   239-6200
111 West 44th Street (Sixth/Seventh Aves.)

Biltmore   582-5340
261 West 47th Street (Eighth Ave./Broadway)

Booth   239-6200
222 West 45th Street (Eighth Ave./Broadway)

Broadhurst   239-6200
235 West 44th Street (Seventh/Eighth Aves.)

Broadway   239-6200
1681 Broadway (53rd St.)

Brooks Atkinson   719-4099
256 West 47th Street (Eighth Ave./Broadway)

Cherry Lane   989-2020
38 Commerce Street

Circle in the Square   581-0720
1633 Broadway (50th St.)

Circle in the Square (Downtown)   254-6330
159 Bleecker Street (Sullivan St.)

City Center   246-8989
131 West 55th Street

Cort   239-6200
138 West 48th Street (Sixth/Seventh Aves.)

Double Image Rep. Co.   245-2489
304 West 47th Street

Douglas Fairbanks   239-4321
432 West 42nd Street

Eugene O'Neill   246-0220
230 West 49th Street (Eighth Ave./Broadway)

Gershwin   586-5100
222 West 51st Street (Eighth Ave./Broadway)

Golden   239-6200
252 West 45th Street (Eighth Ave./Broadway)

Harold Clurman 594-2370
412 West 42nd Street

Hecksher 534-2804
1230 Fifth Avenue (104th St.)

Helen Hayes 944-9450
240 West 44th Street (Seventh/Eighth Aves.)

Hudson Guild 760-9810
441 West 26th Street

Imperial 239-6200
249 West 45th Street (Eighth Ave./Broadway)

Intar 239-0827
420 West 42nd Street

Jack Lawrence 307-5452
359 West 48th Street (Eighth/Ninth Aves.)

John Houseman 967-9077
450 West 42nd Street

Joyce 242-0800
175 Eighth Avenue (17th St.)

Judith Anderson 736-7930
422 West 42nd Street

La MaMa Annex 475-7710
66 East 4th Street

Lambs 997-1780
130 West 44th Street (Ave. of the Americas/Broadway)

Longacre 239-6200
220 West 48th Street (Eighth Ave./Broadway)

Lucille Lortel 924-8782
121 Christopher Street (Bleecker/Hudson Sts.)

Lunt-Fontanne 575-9200
205 West 46th Street (Eighth Ave./Broadway)

Lyceum 239-6200
149 West 45th Street (Ave. of the Americas/Seventh Ave.)

Madison Square Garden 564-4400
Seventh Avenue and 32nd Street

Majestic 239-6200
245 West 44th Street (Seventh/Eighth Aves.)

Manhattan Theater Club 645-5848
131 West 55th Street

Mark Hellinger 757-7064
247 West 51st Street (Eighth Ave./Broadway)

Martin Beck   246-6363
302 West 45th Street (Eighth/Ninth Aves.)

Minetta Lane   420-8000
18-22 Minetta Lane (MacDougal St./Ave. of the
Americas)

Minskoff   869-0550
200 West 45th Street (Eighth Ave./Broadway)

Mitzi Newhouse   787-6868
Lincoln Center

Music Box   239-6200
239 West 45th Street (Eighth Ave./Broadway)

Neil Simon   757-8646
250 West 52nd Street (Eighth Ave./Broadway)

Orpheum   477-2477
126 Second Avenue (8th St.)

Palsson's Supper Club   595-7400
158 West 72nd Street

Pearl Theater Company, The   645-7708
125 West 22nd Street

Plymouth   239-6200
237 West 45th Street (Eighth Ave./Broadway)

Promenade   580-1313
2152 Broadway (76th St.)

Provincetown Playhouse   477-5048
133 MacDougal Street (West 3rd/West 4th Sts.)

Public Theater   598-7150
425 Lafayette Street (Astor Place)

Raft Theater   947-8389
432 West 42nd Street

Ridiculous Theater Co.   691-2271
1 Sheridan Square

Richard Rodgers Theater   221-1211
226 West 46th Street (Eighth Ave./Broadway)

Ritz   239-6200
225 West 48th Street (Eighth Ave./Broadway)

Roundabout Theater Co.   420-1883
100 East 17th Street

Royale   239-6200
242 West 45th Street (Eighth Ave./Broadway)

St. James   398-0280
246 West 44th Street (Seventh/Eighth Aves.)

Samuel Beckett 410 West 42nd Street	**944-9300**
Second Stage 2161 Broadway (76th St.)	**873-6103**
Shubert 225 West 44th Street (Seventh/Eighth Ave.)	**239-6200**
South Street 424 West 42nd Street	**279-4200**
Sullivan Street Playhouse 181 Sullivan Street (Bleecker/W. Houston Sts.)	**674-3838**
Theater Four 424 West 55th Street	**246-8545**
Top of the Gate 160 Bleecker Street (Sullivan/Thompson Sts.)	**475-5120**
Virginia 425 West 52nd Street (Eighth Ave./Broadway)	**977-9370**
Vivian Beaumont Lincoln Center	**239-6200**
Westside Arts Center 407 West 43rd Street	**541-8394**
Winter Garden 1634 Broadway (50th St.)	**239-6200**
Theater Four 424 West 55th Street	**246-8545**
Thomas Schwenke, Inc. 956 Madison Avenue	**772-7222**
Three Lives & Company, Ltd. 154 West 10th Street (at Waverly Pl.)	**741-2069**
Throgs Neck Bridge Throgs Neck Expressway, Bronx	
Ticketron	**246-0102**

TICKETS, SPORTING EVENTS

Telecharge	**239-6200**
Ticketron	**246-0102**

Baseball

New York Mets Shea Stadium, Flushing, Queens	**1-718-507-8499**
New York Yankees Yankee Stadium, The Bronx	**293-6000**

Basketball

New York Knicks   **563-8300**
Madison Square Garden, 4 Penn Plaza

Football

New York Giants   **1-201-935-8222**
Giants Stadium, Meadowlands, East Rutherford, NJ

New York Jets   **421-6000**
Giants Stadium, Meadowlands, East Rutherford, NJ

Hockey

New York Rangers   **563-8300**
Madison Square Garden, 4 Penn Plaza

Tennis

Tournament of Champions   **1-718-268-2300**
West Side Tennis Club, Tennis Place, Forest Hills,
Queens

U.S. Open Tennis Championships   **1-718-271-5100**
USTA National Tennis Center, Flushing Meadows-
Corona Park, Queens

TICKETS, TELEVISION SHOWS

ABC (Channel 7)
Write to:
    ABC Guest Relations
    36 A West 66th Street
    New York, NY 10023

CBS (Channel 2)   **975-2476**
For tickets to "The Morning Program," write to:
    CBS Ticket Bureau
    524 West 57th Street
    New York, NY 10019
CBS needs one and a half to two months lead time. You
may also call.

NBC (Channel 4)
For tickets to, "The Cosby Show," "Late Night with
David Letterman," "Donahue," or "Saturday Night Live,"
send a postcard to:
    NBC Tickets
    30 Rockefeller Plaza
    New York, NY 10112
There is a limit of two tickets per request, and children
under 16 years of age are not admitted. It's necessary to

write many months in advance of your planned visit—
"Late Night with David Letterman" has an 18-month waiting list.

TICKETS, THEATERS

Tickets for Broadway and off-Broadway shows, concerts,
ballet and other musical events may be ordered by phone
and charged to a major credit card. The major services are:

Carnegie Charge	**247-7800**
Telecharge	**239-6200**
Ticketron	**246-0102**

With the soaring price of tickets to Broadway and off-
Broadway shows ($50.00 is the average these days), visitors
as well as native New Yorkers take advantage of the same-
day, half-price tickets available at the following locations.
Leave your MasterCard at home; only cash or travelers'
cheques are accepted. There is a $1.50 service charge per
ticket.

TKTS Booth
Duffy Square (47th St. & Broadway)
> Open Daily 3:00 P.M.–8:00 P.M.
> Matinee tickets 10:00 A.M.–Curtain time

Lower Manhattan Theater Center
Two World Trade Center, Mezzanine Level
> Monday–Saturday 11:00 A.M.–5:30 P.M.
> Off-Broadway tickets sold 11:00 A.M.–1:00 P.M.

Despite the inconvenience of traveling far downtown,
savvy theater-goers frequent this location. Shorter lines
and the luxury of waiting indoors in inclement weather
make it worth the trip. A limited number of matinee and
Sunday tickets are available one day ahead of performance
date.

Music & Dance Booth
Bryant Park (42nd St. & Sixth Ave.)
> Tuesday, Thursday, Friday Noon–2:00 P.M., 3:00 P.M.–
> 7:00 P.M.
> Wednesday, Saturday 11:00 A.M.–2:00 P.M., 3:00 P.M.–
> 7:00 P.M.
> Sunday Noon–6:00 P.M.

Tickets for Monday performances are available the Sunday before performance date.

Tiffany & Co.   **755-8000**
727 Fifth Avenue (57th St.)

Timberland	**754-0436**
709 Madison Avenue	
Time	**976-1616**
Time & Again	**685-8887**
The Doral Tuscany Hotel, 116 East 39th Street	
(Park/Lexington Aves.)	

TIPPING

Nothing smooths your way quite as much as the judiciously placed tip. Remember that people in the service industries in New York are not well paid. Since tips make the difference between living well and just surviving, they will work hard to get them. It is important to understand how to use tips to get the best service. While there are some areas in which guidelines may be given, the old adage that it is gauche to overtip is a myth. You will always find people who do their jobs well regardless, but if you like excellent service you must pay for it—particularly in the restaurant and hotel business.

There are no rules for tipping a concierge. In general these are the people who will consistently give you the most and best regardless. A favorite guest was a judge from Texas who gave $1.00. On the other hand, there are guests who think nothing of giving $500 tips. It's up to you. The following is a list of people whose tips have become reasonably well established by custom. The amounts mentioned are the minimums and you should feel free to increase the tip based on the amount of satisfaction you have received.

Taxi drivers 15%–20% of the fare
Bellmen $1.50 per bag
Restaurant Captain 5%–10% of the check
Waiters 15%–20% of the check
Airport porters $1.00–1.50 per bag

In New York you will frequently meet the owners of restaurants, it is not correct to tip them. Many people bring gifts to owners (and to others they frequently encounter) as a way to express their gratitude for fine service. Another of the guests McDowell was particularly fond of (a permanent resident) used to bring him little desserts every day. He looked forward to it as an expression of her appreciation.

So you can see that tipping is not as cut and dried as most advisors would have you believe. Just remember, if you are happy with service and tip what you think the extra effort was worth, it is probably right.

TKTS BOOTH
See **TICKETS, THEATER**

TOBACCO

Alfred Dunhill	**489-5580**

620 Fifth Avenue

One of the world's most exclusive tobacconists, Dunhill offers a wide range of cigars, custom-blended tobaccos and unusual gift items for the hard-to-please man.

Davidoff of Geneva	**489-5580**

535 Madison Avenue

J & R Tobacco Corp.	**869-8777**

11 East 45th Street

Weekdays 8:00 A.M.–6:00 P.M.

Saturday 9:00 A.M.–4:00 P.M.

World's largest discount cigar store, handling all popular brands.

Nat Sherman–Tobacconist	**751-9100**
711 Fifth Avenue (55th St.)	**1-800-221-1690**

Nat Sherman modestly advertises his shop as "the most prestigious tobacco emporium in the world." When McDowell was a concierge at The St. Regis, it certainly was handy to have this store right across the street.

Pipeworks & Wilke	**956-4820**

16 West 55th Street

Established in 1862, Pipeworks & Wilke carries a complete range of handmade and antique pipes. Its custom-blended tobaccos are legendary.

Top of the Gate	**475-5120**

160 Bleecker Street

Top of the Sixes	**757-6662**

666 Fifth Avenue

Top of the Tower	**355-7300**

The Beekman Tower Hotel, 3 Mitchell Place

TOPS OF BUILDINGS

New York is a wonderful place to see from the top of a building. From the vantage point of a bar or observation deck on a high floor, you can see the city laid out your feet in all of its miniaturized beauty. Nighttime turns the city into a fairyland of tiny lights as the buildings are lit up and cars turn on their headlights. Here are a few of our favorite places.

City Lights Bar   938-1111
One World Trade Center (107th Floor)
The very highest place in town. It's so far from the ground that the view is unreal, more akin to being in an airplane. A great experience.

Top of the Sixes   757-6662
666 Fifth Avenue
A large restaurant and piano bar stretching the length of the Fifth Avenue side of the block wide building. Great views up Fifth Avenue to Harlem. A favorite time is twilight. You'll enjoy seeing the transition as day fades into night.

Top of the Tower   355-7300
The Beekman Tower Hotel, 3 Mitchell Place
On top of a small hotel, this bar provides a wrap around terrace which has views of the entire city. The most interesting part may well be its proximity to the United Nations and the East River. Many is the time we've gone there to unwind after a hard day at the office.

View, The   704-8900
The Marriott Marquis Hotel, 1535 Broadway (45th St.)
A romantic revolving bar atop the giant, First Class Marriott Marquis hotel in midtown. With both a bar and a restaurant which boasts three different cuisines this is a very popular spot for both the theater crowd and conventioneers. Live entertainment and dancing are extra attractions which compete with the beauty of city lights. Our favorite is, of course, the lights of the Chrysler Building.

Tourneau   758-3265
500 Madison Avenue (52nd St.)

TOURS

American Sightseeing International/Short Line Tours   354-4740
166 West 46th Street

Backstage on Broadway   575-8065
228 West 47th Street

Campus Coach Line   682-1050
545 Fifth Avenue

Circle Line Sightseeing Yachts, Inc.   563-3200
Pier 83, 42nd Street at the Hudson River
March to November only

Even New Yorkers enjoy this informative three-hour ride. The Manhattan skyline is breathtaking from the water.

Gray Line of New York, The   397-2600
900 Eighth Avenue (53rd/54th Sts.)
    Tour days and times vary so call for information
    Credit cards accepted: AE, V, & MC

If you've been in New York for more than a few hours you are familiar with the big Gray Lines tour buses. With 23 different tours to offer, they are constantly shuttling to and fro with their loads of tourists. It's probably the best way to see the city for the first time. Particularly if you're not sure what you really want to see and do. There are tours of every part of the city with knowledgeable guides to point out all of the attractions. Foreign language tours are available.

Harlem Spirituals, Inc.   302-2594
1457 Broadway

Island Helicopter Sightseeing   683-4575
34th Street Heliport at the East River

Manhattan Helicopter Tours   247-8687
Heliport at West 30th Street at the Hudson River

The Metropolitan Museum of Art   570-3711
Fifth Avenue at 82nd Street

The Met can provide multilingual tour guides and special interest tours. Their Travel Services Division is there to help you. Tours can be as brief as one hour if you are pressed for time. Breakfast or lunch can be arranged if required.

The NBC Studio Tour   371-7174
GE Building, 30 Rockefeller Plaza
    Monday through Saturday 10:00 A.M.–4:00 P.M.
    Reservations are required

Seaport Line   669-9400
207 Front Street

**Short Line Tours/American
    Sightseeing International**   354-4740
166 West 46th Street

TOWED CARS

Both of the addresses listed below perform the same function. If your car has been impounded by the city for a traffic violation, it will be taken to one of them. The cost of retrieving your car is $150. Checks may be accepted but if you have outstanding summonses, parking violations, or registration irregulations (for example, car not registered in your name) you will probably need cash or a certified check.

Pier 60	**924-1068**
Eleventh Avenue and 19th Street	
Pier 76	**971-0770**
Twelfth Avenue and 38th Street	

Tower Airlines	**1-718-917-4368**

Tower Records	
692 Broadway (4th St.)	**505-1500**
1967 Broadway (66th St.)	**496-2500**
4th and Lafayette Streets	**505-1505**

Town Hall	**840-2824**
123 West 43rd Street	

TOYS

One of the most important ingredients in our city is the childlike quality of the natives who will normally walk all over you. If you don't believe us try to get into F.A.O. Schwartz just before Christmas. Stop in at some of these stores for the toys of your dreams.

Childcraft	**753-3196**

150 East 58th Street (Lexington & Third Aves.)
   Monday–Friday 10:00 A.M.–5:45 P.M.
   Saturday 10:00 A.M.–4:45 P.M.

A huge selection of wooden blocks, crafts, games, musical instruments, and educational toys put Childcraft at the head of the class.

Darrow's Fun Antiques	**838-0730**

309 East 61st Street (First/Second Aves.)
   Monday–Friday 11:00 A.M.–7:00 P.M.
   Saturday 11:00 A.M.–4:00 P.M.

Toys to make grown-up children recall their own childhoods.

F.A.O. Schwartz	**644-9400**

767 Fifth Avenue (58th St.)
   Monday–Saturday 10:00 A.M.–6:00 P.M.
   Thursday 10:00 A.M.–8:00 P.M.
   Sunday Noon–5:00 P.M.

Although parents vainly suggest visiting the Museum of Natural History, or at least the Empire State Building, relentless children insist that F.A.O. Schwartz be their first stop. A doorman dressed as a toy soldier welcomes you to two floors of pure delight. Be aware that it is mobbed the month before Christmas.

Go Fly a Kite   472-2623
153 East 53rd Street (Citicorp Center)
    Monday–Friday 10:30 A.M.–7:30 P.M.
    Saturday 10:30 A.M.–5:45 P.M.
    Sunday Noon–5:45 P.M.
Everything from paper kites for a dollar to custom-made models for over a thousand.

Lionel Madison Trains   777-1110
105 East 23rd Street (Lexington/Park Aves.)
    Monday–Friday 7:45 A.M.–5:00 P.M.
    Saturday 8:00 A.M.–4:00 P.M.
    Closed Saturday during July and August
A must for the serious collector, with a wonderful display of antique trains, as well as new electric sets by LGB, Lionel, and Marklin.

Second Childhood   989-6140
283 Bleecker Street
    Monday–Saturday 11:00 A.M.–6:00 P.M.

Traffic Department (New York City)   830-7500

Traffic Information   1-518-449-1293

Trailways Bus Lines   730-7460

Travelers' Aid   944-0013

Travellers Bookstore, The   664-0995
22 West 52nd Street (75 Rockefeller Plaza)

Tre Scalini   688-6888
230 East 58th Street (Second/Third Aves.)

Triboro Bridge
125th Street at Second Avenue

Trinity Church   602-0800
74 Trinity Place (Wall St.)

Trix Bar   265-9240
234 West 50th Street (Broadway/Eighth Ave.)

Tropica   867-6767
Pan Am Building Concourse, 200 Park Avenue

Tropicana   1-609-340-4000
Iowa Avenue at the Boardwalk (Atlantic City, NJ)

Trump Air   972-4444
30th Street Heliport   1-201-865-6900
30th Street and the Hudson River

Trump Castle   1-609-441-2000
Brighton Boulevard and Huron Avenue (Atlantic City, NJ)

Trump Plaza Hotel/Casino	**1-609-441-6000**
Mississippi Avenue at the Boardwalk (Atlantic City, NJ)	
Trump Shuttle	**1-800-247-8786**
Trump Tower	
725 Fifth Avenue (56th/57th Sts.)	
Tse Yang	688-5447
34 East 51st Street (Madison/Park Ave.)	
Tudor Hotel	986-8800
304 East 42nd Street (Second Ave.)	
Tunnel, The	244-6444
220 Twelfth Avenue (27th St.)	
Turkey (Consulate of)	247-5309
821 United Nations Plaza	

TUXEDOS

See **RENTALS, FORMAL WEAR, MEN**

TWA	290-2121
20 Mott Street	964-0380
20 Mott Street	
"21" Club, The	582-7200
21 West 52nd Street (Fifth/Sixth Aves.)	

TWENTY-FOUR HOUR SERVICES

See also MONEY MACHINES

AAA Road Service	695-8311
Airline Delivery Services	687-5145
60 East 42nd Street	
Ambulance	**911**
Amoco	
153 Seventh Avenue (20th St.)	255-9611
1855 First Avenue (96th St.)	289-8832
Animal Medical Center	838-8100
510 East 62nd Street (York Ave.)	
Brasserie, The	751-4840
100 East 53rd Street (Lexington/Park Aves.)	
Bullit Courier	
42 Broadway (Wall St.)	952-4343
405 Lexington Avenue (Chrysler Bldg.)	983-7400
203 West 38th Street (Broadway)	221-7900
Coast Guard	668-7936

Con Edison	**683-8830**
Crime Victims Hotline	**577-7777**
Executive Telex Service, Ltd.	**732-2252**
116 Nassau Street	**1-800-4 A TELEX**
TELEX: 2260000 ETLX UR	**FAX: 212-619-1545**
12041 XAS NYK	**CABLE: TELEXCOM**
Fire	**911**
FBI	**553-2700**
Jet Air International	**233-2282**
	1-516-752-8985
	1-800-622-2205
Kaufman Pharmacy	**755-2266**
Lexington Avenue and 50th Street	
La Guardia Aircraft Charter Service	**1-718-476-5366**
(Division of East Coast Airways)	**1-800-732-9001**
New Jersey Transit	**1-201-460-8555**
New York Delicatessen	**541-8320**
104 West 57th Street (Sixth Ave.)	
PC Express Rentals	**807-8234**
Poison Control Center	**764-7667**
Police	**911**
Post Office, Main	**967-8585**
33rd Street (Eighth Ave.)	
Rape Hotline	**267-7273**
Rialto Florists	**688-3234**
707 Lexington Avenue (57th/58th Sts.)	
Staten Island Ferry	**806-6940**
St. George Ferry Terminal, Battery Park	
Telex and Fax	**949-0722**
237 Park Avenue	

24-hour Newsstands
Broadway at 72nd, 79th, 94th, 96th, & 104th Streets
First Avenue at 65th & 86th Streets
Second Avenue at St. Mark's Place
Second Avenue at 50th Street
Second Avenue at 53rd Street
Third Avenue at St. Mark's Place & 54th Street
Lexington Avenue at 64th & 89th Streets
Sixth Avenue at 8th, 48th, & 57th Streets
Eighth Avenue at 23rd, 42nd, & 46th Streets

U.S. Secret Service	**466-4400**

Western Union (for information)	**1-800-325-6000**

Ty's   **741-9641**
114 Christopher Street (Bleecker/Bedford Sts.)

U

U.S. Customs	**466-5550**
U.S. Open Tennis	**1-800-922-2030**
U.S. Passport Office	**541-7700**

Uncle Charlie's   **255-8787**
56 Greenwich Avenue (east of Seventh Ave.)

Union Club   **734-5400**
101 East 69th Street

Union League   **685-3800**
38 East 37th Street

Union Square Cafe   **243-4020**
21 East 16th Street (Union Square/Fifth Ave.)

United Air Fleet   **262-2200**
823 Eleventh Avenue   **1-800-262-2209**

United Airlines   **1-800-241-6522**

United Kingdom (Consulate of)   **752-5747**
845 Third Avenue

United Nations   **963-7713**
First Avenue (45th/46th Sts.)

United Nations Plaza Hotel   **355-3400**
1 United Nations Plaza (44th St.)

United Parcel Service   **695-7500**
643 West 43rd Street

Universal Costumes Co.   **239-3222**
535 Eighth Avenue

University Club   **247-2100**
1 West 54th Street

Urban Center Books   **935-3592**
457 Madison Avenue (51st St.)

US AIR   **1-800-428-4322**

USO (United Services Organization)

Gen. Douglas MacArthur Memorial
Center   719-2364
587 Seventh Avenue (41st/42nd Sts.)
Monday–Saturday 10:00 A.M.–9:00 P.M.
Sunday 9:00 A.M.–7:00 P.M.
Open every day of the year.

The New York branch of the USO is available to all members of the armed forces who are on active duty, their dependents and guests. Services available include tickets to TV shows, movies, clubs, athletic and sports events, and Broadway and off-Broadway shows. These tickets are normally available on the day of performance and are at discount prices. Discounts are also available for hotels, sightseeing tours, and some restaurants.

The facilities at the USO include a comfortable lounge area, snack bar, TV lounge, and locker room for storing luggage.

V

Valentino   772-6969
825 Madison Avenue (68th St.)

Van Cleef & Arpels   644-9500
744 Fifth Avenue (57th St.)

Vanessa   243-4225
289 Bleecker Street (Seventh Ave. So.)

Vanguard Tours, Inc.   931-9250

Varig Airlines   682-3100

Venezuela (Consulate of)   826-1660
7 East 51st Street

Ventura Yacht Services, Inc.   1-516-944-8415
15 Orchard Beach Boulevard,
Port Washington, NY   1-800-645-6308

Verrazano Narrows Bridge
Ft. Hamilton, Brooklyn

Veterans' Administration Hospital   686-7500
First Avenue and 24th Street

VETERINARIANS

Animal Medical Center   838-8100
510 East 62nd Street (York Ave.)

This is the world's largest, most sophisticated hospital for animals. It has eight floors, 200 cages and is open 24 hours a day, every day of the year. There is no better place for your sick friend.

Animal Emergency Clinic   988-1000
240 East 80th Street (Second/Third Aves.)
    Open every day 9:00 A.M.–1:00 A.M.

Viasa Airlines   486-4360

Vidal Sassoon   535-9200
767 Fifth Avenue (58th St.)

Video Shack   581-6260
1608 Broadway (49th St.)

Vieth, Renate (Masseuse)   521-9292

View Lounge & Restaurant, The   704-8900
The Marriott Marquis Hotel, 1535 Broadway
(45th/46th Sts.)

Village Courts   989-2300
110 University Place (12th St.)

Village Gate   475-5120
160 Bleecker Street (Thompson St.)

Village Vanguard   255-4037
178 Seventh Avenue South (11th St.)

Virgin Atlantic Airlines   1-800-862-8621

Virginia Theater   977-9370
425 West 52nd Street

Visitors Bureau   397-8222

Vista International Hotel   938-9100
Three World Trade Center

Vivian Beaumont Theater   787-6868
Lincoln Center

Vogel's Eurocars, Inc.   1-914-968-8200

W

Waldenbooks
57 Broadway (Rector/Exchange Sts.)	269-1139
931 Lexington Avenue	249-1327
270 Park Avenue (48th St.)	370-3758

Waldorf Astoria Hotel   355-3000
301 Park Avenue (49th/50th Sts.)

Waldorf Towers   355-3100
100 East 50th Street (Park Ave.)

Wales Hotel   876-6000
1295 Madison Avenue (92nd St.)

Warwick Hotel   246-2700
65 West 54th Street (Avenue of the Americas)

Washington Square Park
Fifth Avenue and Waverly Place

Water's Edge   1-718-482-0033
44th and East River Drive, Queens

Waterford Wedgwood   759-0500
713 Madison Avenue (63rd St.)

Weather   976-1212

Wellington Hotel   247-3900
Seventh Avenue (55th St.)

Wentworth Hotel   719-2300
59 West 46th Street (Fifth/Sixth Aves.)

West 30th Street Heliport   563-4442
West 30th Street and the Hudson River

West Side Bicycle Store   663-7531
231 West 96th Street (Broadway)

Westbury Hotel   535-2000
15 East 69th Street (Madison Ave.)

Western Union   962-7111

Westside Arts Center   541-8394
407 West 43rd Street

Whitehead & Mangan   242-7815
375 Bleecker Street

Whitestone Bridge
Hutchinson River Parkway, Bronx

Whitney Museum at the Equitable Center   544-1000
787 Seventh Avenue (52nd St.)

Whitney Museum of American Art   570-3600
945 Madison Avenue (75th St.)

Wilkinson's Seafood   535-5454
1573 York Avenue (83rd/84th Sts.)

William Doyle Galleries   427-2730
175 East 87th Street

Williamsburg Bridge
Delancy Street at Clinton Street

Willoughby's Camera Store	**564-1600**
110 West 32nd Street (Sixth/Seventh Aves.)	
Windows On The World	**938-1111**
One World Trade Center (107th Floor)	
Wine & Liquor Outlet	**308-1650**
1114 First Avenue (61st St.)	
Winter Garden Theater	**239-6200**
1634 Broadway (50th St.)	
Wittenborn Art Books	**288-1558**
1018 Madison Avenue	
1634 Broadway (50th St.)	
Wollman Memorial Ice Skating Rink	**517-4800**
Central Park	
Women's–Roosevelt Hospital	**870-6000**
1111 Amsterdam Avenue	
Works, The	**799-7365**
428 Columbus Avenue (81st St.)	
World Financial Center	**945-0505**
Battery Park City, Vesey/Liberty Sts. at the Hudson River	
World Trade Center	**466-4170**
Church and Liberty Sts.	
World Yacht Cruises	**929-7090**
Pier 62 (23rd St. & the Hudson River)	
Wylie's Ribs & Co.	**757-7910**
59 West 56th Street (Fifth/Sixth Aves.)	
Wyndham Hotel, The	**753-3500**
42 West 58th Street (Fifth/Sixth Aves.)	

Y

Yacht Owners Association of New	
York	**736-6526**
225 West 34th Street	

YACHTS

In celebration of the renovation of the Statue of Liberty, many yacht companies offered special sailings around Liberty Island, and we concierges were invited on promotional cruises to become acquainted with their services. Adele arrived at the appointed pier just as her ship was pulling out and hopped on board. She was rather surprised that no representative of the company approached her for the expected sales talk, so she started introducing herself to her co-sailors. To her chagrin, she discovered that she was not among her fellow concierges, but had joined top executives of an insurance company on a private charter. Jolly, extremely gracious, and relieved at having found someone with whom they did not have to discuss business, they seemed to take special glee in introducing her as "Adele, the stow-away. Her business is giving people directions."

Our biggest challenge so far was chartering a yacht on four hours notice for a disgruntled banker who couldn't get space on a scheduled cruise. With ample notice, these companies can plan something quite splendid—anything from a cocktail party to an elaborate dinner with dancing.

Enticer Motor Yacht Corporation   354-8844
500 Fifth Avenue
Operates from May through November. Can handle up to 60 people for cruises.

Entrepreneur Yacht Charters Corp.   722-2386
The Raconteur, a 70-foot yacht is available for groups up to 40 and the Entrepreneur II, a 130-foot yacht, can handle up to 149 people for real luxury cruising. Executive chef on board to ensure quality cuisine.

Manhattan Yacht Charters   772-9430
233 East 81st Street (Second/Third Aves.)

Ventura Yacht Services, Inc.   1-516-944-8415
15 Orchard Beach Boulevard   1-800-645-6308
Port Washington, NY
Yachts in all sizes for all occasions. Fully staffed and catered.

World Yacht Cruises   627-2775
Pier 62, West 23rd Street at the Hudson River
A fleet of luxury restaurant-yachts to cater to your every need. We have used them successfully for groups as small as four people who said they were treated like royalty on their own yacht with their own chef and staff. A wonderful way to entertain business associates.

Yacht Owners Association of New York   736-6526
225 West 34th Street
Acting as a broker for over 400 licensed captains, this association matches you up with the ship of your dreams.

Yara's Yachting, Inc. 864-0654
PO Box 1825, NY 10150
Yara arranges everything from daily rentals of motor yachts to dinner parties for several hundred.

Yale Club 661-2070
50 Vanderbilt Avenue (45th St.)

Yankee Stadium 293-6000
161st Street, Bronx

Yara's Yachting, Inc. 864-0654
PO Box 1825, NY 10150

Yonkers Racetrack 1-914-968-4200

Yugoslavia (Consulate of) 838-2300
767 Third Avenue

Yves Saint Laurent 988-3821
855 Madison Avenue (71st St.)

Yves Saint Laurent Men's Boutique 371-7912
859 Madison Avenue (71st St.)

Z

Zabar's 787-2000
2245 Broadway (80th St.)

Zarela 644-6740
953 Second Avenue (50th/51st Sts.)

Zeller Tuxedos 355-0707
201 East 56th Street (Second/Third Aves.)

Zinno 924-5182
126 West 13th Street (Sixth/Seventh Aves.)

Zip Code Information 967-8585

ZOOS

Bronx Zoo 220-5100
Bronx Park 367-1010
185th Street and Southern Boulevard, Bronx
  Open every day of the year
  Monday–Saturday 10:00 A.M.–5:00 P.M.
  Sunday–Holidays 10:00 A.M.–5:30 P.M.
  Admission:
  Tuesday–Thursday Donation Suggested
  Friday–Monday

Adults $3.75
Children $1.50
By subway: #5 Lexington Avenue Line to 180th Street
By bus: M11 express bus stops on Madison Avenue at
26th, 32nd, 39th, 47th, 53rd, 63rd, 69th, 84th, & 99th
Streets.
To return: Zoo visitors are picked up at Bronxdale
Gate. The bus stops at Fifth Avenue at 98th, 85th, 59th,
51st, 43rd, 36th, & 23rd Streets.
Fare $3.50 each way
Exact fare required

One of the largest zoos in the world, and the largest in the
U.S. It has an enormous variety of animals in 42 exhibits.
They are shown in habitats that are as similar as possible to
the real thing. Take the Monorail through "Wild Asia," and
if you have the kids with you, let them pet the animals in the
Children's Zoo.

Central Park Zoo   **439-6500**
Fifth Avenue (64th St.)
Admission:
Adults $1.00
Senior citizens $.50
Children $.25
By subway: N train to Fifth Avenue; #4, #5, or #6 train
Lexington Avenue Line; or the B, N, or R train to
59th Street.
By bus: Fifth or Madison Avenue buses M1, M2, M3,
or M4.

Five and a half acres of delight! After six years and a $35
million renovation, the Central Park Zoo reopened in August 1988. It will be operated by the New York Zoological
Society, instead of the Parks Department. But the biggest
change (aside from the fact that there is now an admission
charge) is the replacement of most of those great big animals which used to live here with much smaller ones. The
lions and tigers and camels have been sent to better homes
in larger zoos. They have been replaced with penguins,
puffins, lizards, small deer, and many other fascinating crit-
ters which will live comfortably in the new habitats. Needless to say, those sea lions still steal the show! And now you
can watch their underwater antics through large plate glass
windows! This is a sightseeing attraction that you must not
miss, and it's one of the few where you'll have to compete
with native New Yorkers, who are already in love with it.